Highlights Among the Hudson River Artists

BOOKS BY *Clara Endicott Sears*

BRONSON ALCOTT'S FRUITLANDS

GLEANINGS FROM OLD SHAKER JOURNALS

THE BELL RINGER

FIDDLER'S GREEN

DAYS OF DELUSION

THE GREAT POWWOW

SOME AMERICAN PRIMITIVES

HIGHLIGHTS AMONG THE HUDSON RIVER
ARTISTS

A VIEW OF THE HUDSON FROM WEST POINT

Robert W. Weir (1803–1889)
Signed and dated: 1869
Size 35 × 61

HIGHLIGHTS
AMONG
The Hudson River Artists

CLARA ENDICOTT SEARS

With Illustrations

HOUGHTON MIFFLIN COMPANY BOSTON

The Riverside Press Cambridge

1947

The Riverside Press

CAMBRIDGE · MASSACHUSETTS

PRINTED IN THE U.S.A.

Acknowledgments

THIS IS TO acknowledge with thanks the kind co-operation of Mr. Howard N. Doughty, of Ipswich, Massachusetts, who allowed me to quote freely from his unpublished manuscript of the life of his great-great uncle, Thomas Doughty, the noted landscape painter.

I am also indebted to Mr. John H. Baur, of the Brooklyn Museum, Brooklyn, New York, who permitted me to quote from his copy of the autobiography of Worthington Whittredge.

To Mr. Robert C. Vose, Boston, Massachusetts, and Mr. Charles D. Childs, Boston, Massachusetts.

To Miss Ethelwyn Manning, Librarian, Frick Art Reference Library, New York, and to Miss Bartlett Cowdrey, for her article "William Henry Bartlett and the American Scene," in the *New York History*, vol. 22, October, 1941.

Foreword

THIS BOOK on the Hudson River artists, with illustrations, makes no attempt to compete with the learned writings by art experts in the past. It is written in the simplest manner possible — as though I were sitting in the midst of a small circle of friends, describing the lives and successes and various experiences of those talented men to whom we owe so much, and who added greatly in a picturesque way to the early part of the nineteenth century.

I have been given the opportunity to quote from unpublished manuscripts and family records which throw revealing light on some of the more personal lives, now famous in the art history of our country. These illustrations of their paintings start a collection which will be placed in a new ell of the Picture Gallery, one of the group of buildings at Fruitlands and the Wayside Museums, Inc., situated on Prospect Hill, in the old town of Harvard, Massachusetts. I am the founder of these old and historic Wayside Museums.

They are open to the public during the summer months.

CLARA ENDICOTT SEARS

HARVARD, MASSACHUSETTS, 1947

Contents

Illustrations

PRIMITIVES

THE NEXT STEP

THE HUDSON RIVER SCHOOL OF PAINTING

Introduction

IT WAS KEATS who wrote these immortal and penetrating words:

> "Beauty is truth, truth beauty" — that is all
> Ye know on earth, and all ye need to know.

These lines typify the convictions held by the artists of the Hudson River School of Painting in 1828.

Difficult as it is to realize it now, our Republic was only fifty-two years old at that date, when these young men with hearts afire started out to show the Old World, from which their parents and grandparents had come, the transcendent beauty of the New World of which they were citizens. It was an all-American venture, shot through with a patriotism of the sincerest kind. They were more or less like young crusaders out in search of some holy grail.

Up to this time, after the Colonists had won their freedom, the days had been taken up by the rank and file building homesteads to house themselves and their families, hoping their children and grandchildren would keep them for generations. The clan feeling was very prevalent. The zest and enthusiasm of this New World as it grew into being, and the patriotism it engendered, burned in the blood of every man, woman, and child. It was the land of opportunity for which their forebears had yearned, which they had bought with their blood, and the time had now come when Youth took a new step forward towards cultural and artistic issues and a group of young men, imbued with the spirit of idealistic adventure, felt the urge to show the rest of the world the marvelous beauty of the scenery of the far-flung land in which they lived. Things, and thoughts, and aspirations move quickly in these United States. Soon their influence began to be felt. They unconsciously revealed the spirit of romance, the lofty ideals and spiritual values inherent in the American mind, and its capacity for immortalizing and showing forth beauty.

When this particular group of artists started out on their venture, they were the pioneers of landscape painting in this country on a substantial basis. There had been portrait painters — Stuart, Copley, and others, to say nothing of the itinerant portrait painters who traveled the countryside, but landscape painting had not as yet held any definite position in the development of art. Therefore, these young men felt a new world within a new world opening out before them.

They were not ignorant of art in starting out, for it so happened that almost all of them had been full-fledged engravers, or had been thoroughly trained in that profession; therefore drawing came easily and spontaneously to them, with a minute observance of detail. This appreciation of detail was prevalent all over the world at that time, and the engraver was held in high esteem. England, Germany, Italy, France, Holland were all famed for their engravers. Accuracy of detail permeated all branches of art, and influenced the technique and methods of painting in oils. It was a period when demonstrating the truth was one of the essential aims to strive for, and was one of the first things demanded by critics of paintings or any other specimens of art. An exact reproduction of Nature was required. The minutest detail could not be ignored.

Now, art is fundamentally influenced by, and therefore expresses, the desires and ideals held at a given period of development. These are largely the outcome of the public mind, with its beliefs, its requirements, its aspirations, and reveals its mental attitude, which unconsciously influences the imaginations of artists who are sensitive to such vibrations. The prevailing desire of the public in those days was for peaceful scenes, and pastoral scenes with glimpses of quietly flowing rivers winding through fertile meadows, and cows drinking from the banks or seeking the shade of broad spreading trees, or sunsets gilding the sedges in the marshes. It may be that these desires came as a result of the strain of developing and establishing a new country, which made peace and the assurance of security seem conditions to be greatly valued and sought for. But that was evidently not the only reason for it. England through her art was expressing the same desire, as well as Holland, and Italy, still under the influence of her Salvator Rosa, and France, still impressed by the genius of her Claude Lorrain.

But still another surge was stimulating the visions of the Hudson River artists. It was like a call from the wilds. There were the great waterfalls of America, the awe-inspiring peaks of the Rocky Mountains, the great mysterious canyons of the West, the majestic power of Niagara, the glories of the White Mountain range, and the strange beauty of the Palisades rising from the banks of the Hudson River, with their mysterious legends. All these stirring scenes wrought by Nature kindled the imagination and ambition of the young artists. They had but one thought and one aim and they set forth assiduously to make them realities.

What one misses in the various accounts heretofore given of these Hudson River artists is a more living picture of their lives and experiences. Their pictures have been fully described through many sources, and the main features of their lives have been touched on, but many things have been left out that might make life seem to glow in their veins once more. They all had different characteristics and different temperaments. Some were gay and others were serious, but all were young (excepting Asher B. Durand) and all good friends, and had memorable times together. They had a surprising amount of common sense as well, and were broad-minded enough to realize the necessity of study. Nearly all of them went to Europe as soon as they could collect money enough to do so, and made a point of carefully studying the pictures of the old masters in Italy. They went to the exhibitions of paintings in Paris, and to the Royal Academy and the National Gallery in London, and they went to Düsseldorf to analyze the technique of that famous school of art. They learned much and absorbed much, and when they began to exhibit their own paintings, their work aroused the greatest amount of curiosity and admiration. To these foreigners it was something new and to be considered.

Of course, what we call American art did not come up from nowhere — things do not happen that way. The men who emigrated to this country from foreign lands naturally and perhaps unconsciously brought with them the standards of art that they had inherited from their own nation, and these revealed themselves more or less in the awakening art of this young republic. The English, French, Italian, German, Spanish all gave a certain color to the work of our own artists when they started out to reproduce on canvas what they saw in nature. But out of the combination of all these inherited methods and theories of art arose something that expressed the feeling of the new country with unmistakable clarity — an almost intangible something, yet vitally real, which was recognized all over the world as unquestionably American.

When our artists returned to America, well versed in the art of painting, strangely enough a spirit purely American was still revealed in the pictures they painted. It seemed so deeply ingrained in them that nothing could change it. It belonged, as they did, to the young republic. "They boasted themselves to be the first really native school [which was true — according to Samuel Isham]." These young men were not Colonials. Their parents in most cases had come to this country to make it their home, and their sons had become a part of the land, and were proud of it. They were the first Americans to place the stamp of Americanism on landscape painting in this country which was only fifty-two years old and still in the making. That is a record not to be forgotten. That is one reason, apart from the intrinsic beauty of their work, that art lovers in these United States are turning to it with a new appreciation of its value. They were, so to speak, the pioneers. Their work therefore has become historic.

The following list is composed of the most prominent artists of the Hudson River School of Painting, whose lives are described in this book as far as it is possible to do so with the meager material that has been found to draw upon. And the illustrations are of their pictures, to be seen in this collection:

Thomas Doughty	Frederick Edwin Church
Asher Brown Durand	George Inness
Thomas Cole	Alvan Fisher
Albert Bierstadt	Thomas Birch
John Frederick Kensett	William Louis Sonntag
Jasper F. Cropsey	John William Casilaer
Robert Walter Weir	Alexander Helwig Wyant
William M. Hart	T. Worthington Whittredge
Thomas Hewes Hinckley	Charles Codman
Thomas Hill	François Régis Gignoux
Victor De Grailly	George L. Brown

In addition to these will be a small collection of examples of early primitive landscapes, and after them a small collection of examples of the next stage that followed — unsigned paintings by artists of definite talent whose names have become lost in the hurry of the years. Artists were very careless about signing their pictures in those days. These lead up to the examples of the beautiful pictures of the Hudson River School. The whole forms an unbroken line of the early landscape painting of the country during the nineteenth century. The process of development is always interesting, and in this case reveals true art struggling to the surface, and finally succeeding.

Highlights Among the Hudson River Artists

CHAPTER I

Victor De Grailly and William H. Bartlett

No COLLECTION OF THE Hudson River paintings is entirely complete without showing some examples of that elusive artist named Victor De Grailly. He was a Frenchman who came to this country about 1840 and returned to France in 1870. His paintings were very popular. He was a prolific copyist of Bartlett's drawings, making oil paintings of them.

William H. Bartlett made practically a whole tour of the American continent, making very beautiful drawings finished in water color, about six inches square, to be used ultimately in making engraved illustrations. There has been so much controversy and misunderstanding regarding De Grailly's paintings and Bartlett's drawings that a great effort has been made herewith to unravel the mystery. Many people have considered Bartlett as a painter in oils. This is not true, nor is it true that he was an engraver. What he did was to paint water colors in minute detail for the use of engravers. De Grailly, in coming to this country, was evidently very much impressed by Bartlett's drawings, and being blessed with a keen artistic sense, got permission to paint from these copies in oil. His paintings, usually two to two and a half feet square, were largely of the Hudson River with the Palisades rising on either side of the picture, and innumerable sailboats drifting on the river. The views were usually taken from West Point.

The following quotations are from able critics who have made a study of the subject:

1

It is known that William H. Bartlett made a series of such water-color sketches for the engravings in a book called *American Scenery*, by N. P. Willis, Esq., Publishers, J. S. Virtue, 26 Ivy Lane, London. It is also known that many oil paintings copied from the engravings in this book were painted almost as soon as the book appeared, and the popularity of this work created the demand for copies of many of the views that continued for years.

Many others besides De Grailly copied these drawings in oil.

It appears that in recent years many oils identical in subject with the engraved views in Bartlett's book have appeared on the market with the signature of Bartlett on them. Some of these were obviously poor efforts of faking. Others are excellent pieces of painting contemporary with Bartlett.

Because of the number of these so-called Bartlett paintings, a serious effort to establish their validity, or lack of it, has been made by several people. The result of their work shows no positive proof that Bartlett painted in oils. It does show ample positive proof that he was accustomed to work in water color. These sketches were approximately the size of the engravings which appeared in the book *American Scenery*. One of the original sketches by Bartlett is in this collection.

Until some definite proof can be given that any oil painting signed by Bartlett is actually from the hand of that artist, the assumption must be made that the oil paintings bearing his name are copies by other men who traded on Bartlett's popularity to assist in the sale of their own works.

I have put all this in detail in an attempt to straighten out the confusion, which is so prevalent, that exists regarding Bartlett's work and De Grailly's paintings. In the collection at Fruitlands and the Wayside Museums, Inc., at Harvard, Massachusetts, there are several examples of the De Grailly paintings taken from Bartlett's water color drawings.

Plates 14-20 will show these.

CHAPTER 2

Thomas Doughty
(1795–1856)

Thomas Doughty was born in Philadelphia on the nineteenth of July, 1793. He was one of a large family, and began to show artistic ability very early in his young life, but as so often happens when there are many mouths to feed, he was not allowed to develop that side of his nature. In fact, his family deplored the dreamy poetic quality which led him to love the woods, the streams, the hills and valleys, and to seek their company whenever he could get a chance to escape from the home duties of doing chores, running errands, chopping wood, which the male members of large families are supposed to do. He was hardly old enough to hold a gun when he began roaming the beautiful region that lies along the shores of the Delaware, the Schuylkill, and the Brandywine. His father noticed this, and took the matter in hand. The moment the boy was old enough he made arrangements with a firm in the leather business to take him as an apprentice and hold him to his job in order to eradicate these tendencies which he believed threatened his whole future. But while he could control the physical and material side of the boy's life, he had no power to subdue the inner longings of his heart to follow a career that would satisfy his love of the beautiful in nature. To Thomas every shadow that fell from passing clouds on the slope of a green hillside was enough to fill his heart with joy. While working conscientiously at the leather business, in which his father hoped to transform him into a successful business man, he was all the while dreaming of a different fate. Yet at sixteen years of age he was still working at this trade.

Now it so happened that the already renowned artist, Charles

Willson Peale, was at that time painting in Philadelphia, as well as Thomas Sully, both of them painting portraits of some of the notables of the city. The very fact of their being there was enough to stir into action all young Doughty's longings to pursue an artistic career to which he felt himself drawn. He became restless and rebellious in his heart over the restrictions of the leather business which seemed to hang upon his shoulders like a dead weight. He looked about him for an avenue of escape, but the meager pay he was receiving was not enough to enable him to act independently, and he realized that he must bide his time until he could pay his own way towards freedom. From the outside world he kept hearing the names Peale and Sully spoken of as great portrait painters, and it fanned the flames of his overwhelming desire to earn a living by palette and brush.

Doughty's nature was a persistent one. Every available hour apart from his regular business he devoted to painting, relying upon this great gift which he believed he possessed. Whenever he got the chance, he sought his old haunts along the shores of the Delaware, the Schuylkill, and the Brandywine, and the fervor of his awakening talent increased more and more as he worked, and the vision of a glowing future took shape within his brain and spurred him on.

Now, in 1822 the Pennsylvania Academy of Fine Arts in Philadelphia was putting on its eleventh exhibition of American paintings, and young Doughty decided to break loose from the shackles of the leather business and experience his first real encounter with the public. He entered eight of his landscapes. It was on this occasion that his name was listed for the first time as an exhibiting artist with pictures in the show. It was a crucial moment in his life. It seemed to him that his whole future hung in the balance. If the critics approved of his landscapes and his method of painting, then he could see the outlines of success appearing on his horizon; he could not bring himself to contemplate the other alternative, he did not dare allow such thoughts to take shape in his brain.

Just then another young artist turned up, a portrait painter named Alvan Fisher whose portraits were already attracting a good deal of attention. He was entering some of them in this exhibition, and he and Doughty met frequently while waiting for the opening day. He was a year older than Doughty, and had had more experience in the world, but he had many of the same idealistic ambitions that the latter had in regard to his art, and a bond of sympathy and understanding grew strong between them. They became friends from then on.

In the meantime the exhibition was in preparation. Anyone who has to do with such affairs knows that there are always moments of seeming chaos to work against, when pictures are arriving by every express, when agitated artists are hovering in the offing, making suggestions, some good, some bad, but above all, pleading that their particular paintings be given the right kind of treatment and a good light that will show them off to their best advantage. In spite of his added year and wider experience, Fisher was still in the process of making his way as an artist such as he hoped to become, and it can be imagined that it was with some trepidation that our two young men looked forward to the day when the doors of the exhibition would be thrown open and the public allowed to pour in.

At last the day came, and Philadelphia turned out for it in great style. The work of both our artists was well received; in fact, among the landscapes, Doughty's made a decided hit. It settled his career for him. Under the spur of exhilaration he promptly fell in love. It sometimes happens just that way.

Now the regrettable part of this is that most of the family papers and notes regarding the home life of Thomas Doughty, which his great-great nephew, Mr. Howard Doughty, had inherited from his father, were burned in a great pier fire in New York in 1870, so that nothing remains to give any idea of what Doughty's young wife was like. There are no records to tell what sort of temperament she had, nor what her tastes were. All that is known about her is that her name was Sarah, that a little son was born to them, who died in 1827, and that some claim they had several children, a daughter Rosamond and another son. In this account of Doughty as an artist, therefore, an impenetrable veil obscures his home life, which is to be deplored.

At that time Philadelphia held a very distinctive place as an art center, and drew many prominent artists to her doors. Various exhibitions of greater or less importance were held there, and, emboldened by his first attempt, Doughty very frequently had paintings on view.

It was at one of these exhibitions that another artist named Thomas Birch appeared on the scene and entered some of his pictures. They were seascapes, and the public was taking note of them. The old saying that "birds of a feather flock together" was true in this case, for still another artist turned up, named Thomas Cole, who was later to be recognized as one of the outstanding painters of the Hudson River group, with an extraordinarily imaginative mind. Cole was nine years younger than Doughty and of a very sensitive make-up. It is said of him that when he went into this exhibition "his heart sank as he felt his deficiency in Art when standing before the paintings of Birch and Doughty." (Dunlap.)

Now, at that time it became the fashion to paint some of the beautiful estates belonging to Philadelphia notables, and one of the leading merchants of that city — a Mr. Robert Gilmore — became very much impressed by Doughty's landscapes, and some years afterwards he wrote as follows: "Thomas Doughty was then a landscape painter of Philadelphia. I bought several of his pictures, especially his studies from nature on the spot, which are his best performances. He painted two views of my country seat." [Doughty MSS.]

By the time he was twenty-seven it was evident which way his destiny was leading him. Boston also held out opportunities for a young artist, and he made up his mind that there was where he should go, so he packed up his belongings and set out for new fields.

Here is something by his own pen written in later life regarding those early years:

> I may as well say that the only instruction I ever received was almost in my childhood, at a most excellent school. Our master used to allow the boys who evinced any talent for drawing, one afternoon a week to practice, but without an instructor. He would inspect the drawing himself, but the time is so far back that I have no recollection as to the results of my studies. I merely remember the fact that I did draw at that time.

Again he wrote:

> In 1818 I attempted three or four paintings in oil, but they were mere daubs inasmuch as I had never received any instruction in oils. The other and only opportunity that ever occurred was in the latter part of my apprenticeship, when I received one quarter's tuition at a night school in drawing in India ink. [Doughty MSS.]

This is a valuable glimpse of the beginning of Doughty's career as an artist. It verifies the statement that he was practically self-taught in this his chosen profession, which may account more or less for the fact that afterwards, when he became famous, he never lost the individual touch that characterizes his work and gives his landscapes the ineffable and poetical charm that pervades them.

He never seemed to be drawn towards portrait painting, although that was the lucrative branch of the profession at that period. It was the beauty of Nature that enthralled Doughty. He saw in her an endless variety of charms, and to capture on canvas her whimsical moods seemed worth his most serious efforts.

Mr. Howard Doughty writes on this subject:

> There is nothing to indicate that my great-granduncle ever attempted portrait painting. He apparently launched himself into a career that was without precedent in the United States, for although there had been many paintings that were straight landscapes, no painter in the country before Doughty had ventured to attempt a career by the painting of landscapes only.

Thomas Doughty had one outstanding gift that gave him an advantage over many young men who choose a career — he was absolutely what one might call "one pointed" in his work. His whole mind, and all his ambition, was to reveal to others what he himself saw in Nature. Her beauty appealed to him even more than the human face, and he made the study of her the mainspring of his life.

So in leaving Philadelphia he challenged a new adventure and started out on his chosen career.

He had never been to Boston before and so knew nothing about the place, and had no idea where to go for lodgings or how to provide for himself. He was fortunate enough to find inexpensive rooms, where it was possible for him to work without being molested. Moreover, he found to his great satisfaction that his friend Alvan Fisher, who had been to Europe to study, had returned and taken up his residence in Boston, so the two young artists worked side by side.

In 1831 the Boston Athenaeum was ready to give a notable exhibition of the works of American artists. The Athenaeum stood very high as regards its art exhibits, and only paintings of real note were eligible. Nothing daunted, Doughty entered some of his paintings and they were at once accepted. It was his second step up the ladder of fame. The following write-up of the exhibition was written by I. R. Butts in one of the leading newspapers:

> We have a crowd of artists around us, whose reputations belong to the country and are identified with it, such as Allston, Harding, Cole, Alexander, Pratt, Doughty, Fisher, Goodrich, Badger, Johnston, Salmon, Miss Hall, Grain, Osgood, the three Sullys, Birch, Peale, Leslie, Newton, Frothingham, Weir, Miss Scholly, Codman, and others whose names are household words.

About Doughty he writes:

> Every person is ready to acknowledge the beauty and truth of Doughty's landscapes. He must have been a nice and enthusiastic observer of the great processes of Nature, and have wandered among her sylvan places with an eye ever open to behold her beauty, and a spirit poetically touched with her wonderful harmony and simplicity.

This was a tremendous send-off for him and the results were immediately noticeable. He was definitely in the public eye from now on.

But the applause of the public is one thing and the gathering in of pennies is another, and after some serious thinking on his part he decided upon the plan of giving lessons in painting. It proved to be a good one. That was a time when it was the fashion for young people — young ladies especially — to learn how to paint, just as they learned how to sing a little, and play the harp a little, and dance a little, and so acquire what were called "accomplishments"; therefore it created quite a stir among them when the following advertisement appeared in the *Boston Transcript* on June 5, 1832:

Mr. Doughty respectfully informs the ladies and gentlemen of Boston that he has located himself in Mr. Harding's new building on School St., where painting in oils, drawing, and water colors, will be taught in all their branches. Early application is particularly requested, as Mr. Doughty wishes to form his classes. Terms made known at his rooms.

Now, it is evident that this advertisement caught the eye and appealed to Miss Elizabeth Peabody of Peabody, Massachusetts, whose sister Sophia (later the wife of Nathaniel Hawthorne) happened to be an invalid at the time and was much afflicted by headaches. It occurred to the sister that learning to paint might divert Sophia's thoughts from her ailment, so she at once wrote to Doughty, asking him if it would be possible for him to come to Peabody to give lessons to her sister who, she explained to him, was too much of an invalid to leave her room. Doughty agreed to do this, and the two young women awaited his appearance with much curiosity.

The physical appearance of this artist is not often mentioned in contemporary comments, but John Neal, an *American Magazine* writer, described Doughty in this way: "He was a man of average size, with a generous, warm-hearted, healthy look and manner, which if not absolutely genial, was something better — sincere, and hearty."

But Doughty was a man of somewhat uneven temperament. Like most real artists he had his moments of great exhilaration, followed by depths of despondency. It shows in his paintings. Some are all sunlight, and are warm and mellow. In others there are traces of great seriousness, as though clouds were drifting across his blue skies.

This was the artist who was coming to teach the art of painting to Miss Sophia Peabody. The latter wrote of Doughty as a teacher in the following way:

> This morning Mary came in and threw a beautiful bouquet of flowers at me, which I crowed over for a time. Then I rose from my couch. I worked a little at my painting, and then Mary Channing came gliding in upon me like a dream, with more flowers — the Scotch rose, and many more things among them.
>
> Mr. Doughty came in as bright as possible. The cool breezes, the flowers and so forth put him into an excellent humor. He said it was luxury to

sit and paint here, and so [she added] he created a glowing bank in broad sunshine.

Mr. Russell called, and came up to my studio. He thought such a studio and such an occupation must cure my headaches. [Doughty MSS.]

Doughty's method of teaching was to make his pupils watch him while he painted, and in his absence imitate what they had seen him do. Then he would come for the next lesson and paint some more on his picture.

Apparently he made a point of never explaining anything, or of answering any questions. He believed in training the sight to unerring accuracy through complete concentration. The rest, he claimed, would follow through the individual talent and creative ability of the pupil, untouched by suggestion.

Probably few of the artist's pupils were as charming as Sophia Peabody, but he evidently succeeded as a teacher, for he continued his classes up to 1833, when he changed his dwelling to 202 Tremont Street, near Court Street.

In July of this year 1833, an article came out in the *Knickerbocker Magazine* entitled "The Fine Arts in America," one of the earliest articles to claim a distinctively American type of painting by the artists whose landscapes were attracting great attention at that time.

The following paragraph quoted from it is significant of the approval and pride the general public was showing in regard to the work of these so-called Hudson River artists: "To every landscape painting for which our country has such eminent advantages, we have artists competent to represent our scenes. The pictures of Doughty and Cole have a character decidedly American. The former infuses into his pictures all that is quiet and lovely, romantic and beautiful in Nature."

Up to this time Doughty and Cole had had little opportunity to meet each other in anything but a most transient way, but their names were frequently cited together. Both of them were sending specimens of their work to the same exhibitions, so the public had a good chance to pass judgment on them.

Having been successful in selling many of his landscapes, Doughty became more ambitious and moved again, this time to 220 Washington Street. This shows that he was already rising in the scale of living, for this was then an exclusive and residential part of Boston. The houses were mostly dignified mansions, with gardens enclosing them, or with well-kept plots of grass surrounded by flowering shrubs.

The classes in painting now met here, and these were especially arranged for the convenience of men pupils. The Doughty manuscript wisely remarks that "the hours of teaching would not fit in very well with the schedule of the men of Boston today," for an advertisement that appeared at this time in many of the newspapers of the day ran thus: "A class for gentlemen can be accommodated from 5:30 A.M. to 7:30 A.M."

But Doughty was evidently more or less of a restless temperament. When 1837 came he again wanted a change of address. Whether this restlessness came from himself, or from his family, or from the discovery that the rents were too high for him to indulge in, we have no way of knowing. It may be that his family found fault with the location. It was true that at that time the street was beginning to lose its residential character, though there were still many dwellings belonging to private families. These dwellings were on or near the present site of Filene's store. (Doughty MSS.)

Inspired by the success of its former exhibition the Boston Athenaeum held another, to which Doughty contributed twelve more of his landscapes. Four of them were owned by J. P. Cushing. The others were for sale.

Now, in certain quarters it was stated that while the public enjoyed going to exhibitions of paintings at this time, there was little inclination shown towards purchasing them. However, there was certainly no such attitude shown in Boston or New York or any of the principal art centers. On the contrary, the sales ran very high, and the attendance at the exhibitions was surprisingly great. The Athenaeum could boast of having received nearly ten thousand dollars in admission fees and catalogues, indicating that more than ten thousand visitors had been admitted to them, and many of these were purchasers. (Doughty MSS.)

It must be remembered that the population in those days was meager in comparison with that of the present, nor was art considered or understood as generally by the rank and file of the public. The majority of those who attended art exhibitions were lovers of art, which makes these figures all the more impressive.

Doughty first found lodgings in the Harding building, erected and owned by Thomas Harding, a portrait painter (to be distinguished from Chester Harding), and started giving exhibitions there, with admissions at twenty-five cents and season tickets at fifty cents. These exhibits aroused a good deal of competition, for up to that time the Boston Athenaeum had had things all its own way. But as it turned out it was evident that there was ample material for both, for both were successful.

A catalogue of this particular exhibition in the Harding building is preserved in the files of the Boston Athenaeum. In it are listed one hundred and sixty-nine paintings exclusively the production of Boston artists. There were twenty-three portraits by Chester Harding, forty-three paintings by Alvan Fisher (these comprised figure pieces, portraits, and a few landscapes), forty-three landscapes by Thomas Doughty, four portraits by Foster, one portrait by Healy, three figure pieces by Hawes, landscapes by Hubbard, two portraits by Pratt, a copy of Titian by Russell, and a miniature by Trott.

Of the forty-three landscapes that Doughty had in this exhibition fifteen were loaned by Bostonians, the others being all marked "for sale." The subjects were all of New England scenery.

The comments of the press in regard to these landscapes reveal the way Doughty's varying temperament entered into his work. The Boston *Galaxy* printed a sketch by a correspondent of *The Atlas* on the style of Doughty, the artist. Here are some quotations from it:

> Doughty's paintings are subdued, quiet, and almost uniformly sad. . . . In all his pictures, however, we see the manner of the artist, or we should say, perhaps, the mind of the poet, softening the tints, the grouping, the incidents of the scene to the same love and spirit of sadness. . . . We are never tired of contemplating the paintings of Doughty. Their beauty does not weary us. We can gaze upon them till we are familiar with

every minute that slumbers in their soothing repose. The artist is an ornament to his profession, and an honor to our city.

On the other hand, the *New England Magazine* in reviewing the exhibition said this:

> The next side contains the pictures of Mr. Doughty, and on a bright day one can look a great way into his sunny landscapes. They are peculiar and charming — they are in his own style, and after the manner of no one else. He paints not only a picture but an atmosphere.

It may have been this trait that he had of throwing his mood, his temperament, his thoughts into his pictures which gave them the peculiarly appealing quality and which helped to make them such a success with the public.

About this time, as things seemed to be progressing well with him, Doughty thought he would enlarge his sphere of action and decided that a few exhibitions in the South would be to his advantage. Accordingly he gathered some of his pictures together, choosing those that he thought would make the most appeal to a new audience, and made arrangements to ship them aboard a packet which would sail at a near date, while he would arrive there by land in time to get an exhibition hall in readiness in which to open his exhibit to the public. But many artists are impossible when it comes to dealing with the practical things of life. He was most certainly one of them. He let his precious paintings sail away without insuring them, and a bad storm arose when the ship was halfway to its destination and it was wrecked. All Doughty's paintings went to the bottom of the sea — a complete and total loss. (Doughty MSS.)

Needless to say it made a deep impression on him and he became almost despondent in consequence. More or less crippled financially as well as in body and mind, he retired to his studio to reflect on the best course for him to follow after such a blow. But he was made of good American stuff which cannot be cast down for long. Following the example of Harding, he made a venture to use his own studio as a showroom, and on May 8, 1835, the following notice appeared in the *Boston Evening Transcript*: "Doughty is exhibiting at his room, 220 Washington Street, to which there is free access, a number of landscapes which he has just finished, and intends to sell on Monday. Some of them are surpassingly beautiful."

The venture turned out to be a great success. Henry Harrington of the Boston *Galaxy,* who later went to New York and worked on the *Mirror,* was so moved by one of the paintings called "Indian Summer," which was later exhibited at the Boston Athenaeum in 1836, that he burst into poetry and dedicated a poem of thirty-six lines to it, beginning:

> Pause! Holy quietness pervades the scene.

Moreover, one of the paintings was sent to England where it was greatly admired, and English visitors to the country began to show a great interest in Doughty's landscapes. The British Minister to the United States is said to have paid him twenty-five hundred dollars for one of his paintings, which was a very high price for a landscape in those days. (Doughty MSS.)

This encouragement put Doughty on his feet again, and made him long for more worlds to conquer, so he planned to go to London in the fall of 1837. He set sail for England with all the curiosity and enthusiasm of a man who had lived more or less of a restricted life — first in the leather business, then as a teacher of art, but now as a widely known and successful landscape painter.

On his way over he, so to speak, took account of stock, promising himself not to be disappointed if his paintings were not understood or liked. He realized that he had his own method of painting which probably would be very different from the English style. In showing his pictures he wanted to emphasize his belief that each artist should copy nature as he himself saw it. Being well aware that no two people saw things exactly alike, he therefore held to the fact that the only safe and honest path to follow was to paint according to one's own vision, regardless of criticism.

He arrived in London as a total stranger, though his works had gone before him, and sought out rooms in Fitzroy Square, where he was told that the American artists who had preceded him were wont to take lodgings. Then he got his pictures together for exhibition purposes.

In the spring his paintings appeared on the walls of the Pall Mall Exhibition. It is interesting to see what the London papers had to say about Doughty.

In its issue of June 23, 1838, the London *Athenaeum,* one of the leading English weeklies, remarked on the number of American artists who were coming over to London, Osgood being one of them and Healy another, and the latest one, Thomas Doughty, whose landscapes were to be seen at the Pall Mall Exhibition, "and who stands, we believe, in the foremost rank in that department at home." And this same reporter recalled the earlier artists who had been there, namely, West, Allston, Leslie, Trumbull, Newton, and others who were none of them distinguished when they came, but afterwards "occupied distinguished stations in their art."

When this Pall Mall Exhibition came off in the spring of 1838, it was near the opening of the London season. Presumably the English Court had been in mourning up to that time, for William IV had died just the year before, on June 20, 1837, but on June 28, 1838, the Coronation of Queen Victoria was to take place, and London was all agog with the prospects of this in view. While waiting for the historic day people sought diversion, crowds from every walk in life frequenting theaters and exhibitions of all kinds, one of the latter being the Pall Mall Exhibition where the paintings of our American artists were to be seen.

One can imagine a bevy of London fashionables entering the doors of the exhibition hall and gazing at the works of these artists from across the Atlantic. Of course the American newspapers were full of it, as well as those in London. Doughty came off with flying colors. One comment was copied from the *Knickerbocker Magazine* in New York. It ran thus in speaking of the crowd at the Pall Mall Exhibition: "The cognoscenti first stared, then wondered, and finally admired. All agree that the style of the American painter, Thomas Doughty, was unique, and all heartily concurred that it was 'magnificent, though odd.'"

Another issue of the *Knickerbocker Magazine* spoke again of the success of the American artists in London, and contained the following comment by the art critic Hoffman:

> Indeed at the present time, the works of Cole, Doughty, Fisher and others may vie with the most eminent of their European contemporaries. The American School of Landscape Painting is decidedly and peculiarly original, fresh, bold, brilliant and grand. Without wishing to institute comparisons, we may mention Doughty of Boston as eminently combining these qualities in his various works. He must undoubtedly be considered the master and founder of a new school. No small honor in this imitative age. We allude chiefly to his pictures of the American autumnal scenery. They are conceived and executed in the spirit of free untrammeled genius. We cannot think that any European artist could produce such pictures.

As to the Coronation of Queen Victoria, the accounts given of it say that the pomp and ceremony of the procession as it wound through the streets of London were most impressive. Our American artists must surely have been on hand to see it, and what a memory to take home with them!

Doughty painted many pictures in England. Being now forty-five years old, and having made a success of his stay there, he decided to return to America, this time making up his mind to settle in New York. He was given a most friendly welcome by the New York newspapers. The New York *Daily Express* wrote:

> We learn this gentleman has lately returned from Europe, and has taken rooms in Water Street near St. John's Park, and he intends becoming a permanent resident of our city. If a man like Doughty cannot command a handsome income among us by his works such as are now exhibited at the "Apollo," it will be because we have no taste for the beautiful, and no wish to encourage genius of the most lofty order.

By this time Doughty had made friends, and lasting friends, with the New York artists of the Hudson River School of painting — or those especially associated with New York as having studios there — which made his setting very harmonious. As has been said before, these artists constituted more or less of a guild, because, although such an organization had never actually been formed, the unity of spirit that bound one to the other through sympathy of interests and work was very striking. Each one seemed to rejoice genuinely in the success of another. There was no such situation as one not getting along with another, on the contrary, their intercourse was like that of a large family. Doughty, already intimate with Alvan Fisher, now became fast friends with Asher B. Durand, whose pupil Casilaer was coming very much to the fore; Hubbard, Rossiter, who was what they then called "a figure painter," but who was very intimate with them all and was associated with the group, and one of the leading younger men — John F. Kensett, also a number of others. It should have been a very happy time with him. His paintings, as we have seen, were taking a great hold on the public, and they were bringing large prices. But here another trouble came to him because of his disagreements with an association called the "Apollo Association" which later became the "Art Union." This Union was a very successful enterprise, and was supposed to be a great help to artists, as it undertook to sell their pictures for them at their own prices, the Union keeping a percentage. It also bought some of their pictures.

All went well for a time until Doughty discovered that some of his pictures were being sold at prices considerably less than what he asked for them, which was a distinct loss to him, one he could not agree to without a strong protest. This led to a situation which caused much unpleasantness between him and the Art Union. His artist's nature could not bear controversy, therefore, although he was so delightfully placed in New York, with a pleasant studio, and in circumstances conducive to furthering a continuance of his ever-growing success, he picked up his things again and moved to Albany. Not finding quite what he wanted there, went to Washington in 1842.

When the spring of 1845 came, Doughty started on a trip to England again, with plans to extend his horizon further by going to the continent. This time he gave his address in London as 3 Park Place, Regent Park.

He arrived there just in time to enter two of his paintings in an exhibition at the Royal Academy. He chose one that he especially liked — "A Summer Shower in New Hampshire," and another called "A View on the Hudson River."

That same spring the British Institution held an exhibition to which he sent a painting of "Windsor Castle," and an American scene called "Early Winter among the Mountains of New Hampshire."

There were numerous most enthusiastic accounts of his work in the newspapers of the time, with every evidence of his selling many landscapes to the British public.

In 1846 he was still working in London at his rooms at 3 Park Place, taking a number of trips to Ireland where he painted some beautiful pictures of Irish landscape.

In the spring of 1846, again exhibiting in the British Institution, he chose to show his painting called "Black Water in Ireland." It is noticeable that he always selected an American landscape to offset a foreign one, and on this occasion he entered "A Peep of the Hudson, Early Autumn."

In spite of his absence from home, however, some of his paintings were hung in the principal exhibitions in New York and Philadelphia, and several of his landscapes that he had painted in England and Ireland were purchased and distributed by the Art Union in New York. (Doughty MSS.)

Having satisfied himself that the English public appreciated his work, as evidenced by the sales he was making there, and in spite of the fact that France was on the verge of a revolution, while King Louis Philippe endeavored to hold fast to the reins of government, Doughty decided to go to Paris and see what kind of a reception his paintings would receive there.

He was in Paris in the spring, just when the horse-chestnut trees were in full bloom, and in spite of the impending revolt against the king, the Champs Elysées and the "Bois" were alive with gay equipages. Barouches filled with beautiful ladies dressed in all the sumptuous attires of the French Court could be seen being driven by coachmen resplendent in handsome liveries, with powdered wigs on their heads and footmen by their sides, as they directed their prancing horses through the Avenue des Acacias, returning from their drive by emerging onto the Champs Elysées down which they rolled, stared at by the public, to the Place de la Concorde. All this must have been a never-to-be-forgotten sight to Thomas Doughty, reared as he had been in the stricter atmosphere of the Quaker city of Philadelphia.

It will be noticed that Doughty always managed to take lodgings in good quarters wherever he went. In Paris he took them at 108 Champs Élysées where the whole of the gay life of the city and the array of royal equipages would pass on any spring afternoon.

Earlier in the season he had forwarded some of his pictures to the Salon and they had been accepted. He was curious to find out what sort of appeal they would make to the French, whose technique in painting was quite different from that of the English.

The opening day of the Salon was March 16. Because of the alarming condition of the political situation, the newspapers, taken up with more vital questions, made fewer comments than usual, which, while unsatisfactory for the artists who were exhibiting, showed that the mind of Paris was not on art at that time — the future of King Louis Philippe was trembling in the balance — sinister grumblings of the populace were heard on all sides — an atmosphere of unrest pervaded the city with ever-increasing volume as each day passed. So about the success of Doughty's paintings there one can say little.

Ever anxious to study art in all its phases in the different cities that he visited, he made the most of his stay in Paris, studying the French technique in the famous gallery of the Louvre and elsewhere. The French methods, however, did not appeal to him as the English did; and the worsening political situation, together with the feeling of being a stranger in the place, after a few months led him to set sail for home and establish himself once more in New York, richer for the experiences that had come his way. These experiences provided him with much food for thought, especially when the following February, 1848, the news came from across the water that Paris had finally and definitely turned against their king, and that he and his queen had been obliged to escape by a back entrance of the Tuileries and travel in disguise, unprovided with anything but the clothes they wore on their backs until they reached England, under the name of Mr. and Mrs. Smith.

In this year of 1848 Doughty became fifty-five years old, according to the Doughty MSS. It was a notable year for him. His landscapes were in great demand and selling at excellent prices. Newspapers and magazines praised him with enthusiasm. When his landscape called "Solitude" appeared in the Exhibition of the National Academy that year, one critic wrote of it enthusiastically, "Doughty's distances are superb."

But also in this same year came a great blow to the artists of the Hudson River School of painting. Thomas Cole, the genius with intense spiritual appreciation of life in its various phases, died.

It came as a great shock to all who knew him. Doughty amongst others must have mourned his decease, for though he had never been thrown with him as an intimate friend, "all the artists of the Hudson River School were deeply affiliated in spirit, if not in actual communication." (Doughty MSS.)

It is interesting to note what the *Knickerbocker Magazine* wrote on this occasion, comparing Doughty's work with Cole's:

> It is of our great Landscape painter Doughty we would now discourse; with due respect for others equal to him perhaps in effort and in inspiration. We say — "our great landscape painter — Cole the gifted and great is dead — he has run his course of Time. At present we must deal with the misty, the atmospheric, the Nature student Doughty. . . . Cole is epochal — Doughty is epilogical. Cole in his later studies is the painter of poetry, Doughty in study perpetual is the painter of Nature."
>
> Let us honor both — the dead renowned, and the living beautiful.

And now Doughty moved his studio to White Street, New York, where he was sought not only by artists but by writers as well, his studio becoming the rendezvous of many interesting people. This year of 1849 to all outward appearances seemed to hit the high mark of Thomas Doughty's career. The demand for his pictures was as great as ever, and the prices as good. In fact, the record as listed in the Art Union shows that he received an income from his works that would have seemed affluence to hundreds of his fellow citizens, yet his serenity was destroyed more or less by his incapacity to retain any money which he received. He was always in arrears, not knowing himself how such sums passed through his hands. One of those artists whose temperaments overmastered them, he thought only of his work and the beauty of nature that he painted; he took no care of the ordinary indebtedness of life, spending money when he had it, and growing despondent when he did not have it. (Doughty MSS.)

From all accounts he was strict in his habits and in his course of life. In one sense only was he somewhat of a bohemian, in his passionate love of the woods and of mountains, which he climbed with delight. However, this certainly would not involve careless spending.

Wrote John Neal in the *American Magazine*:

> I knew him well and I must say I never knew a worthier man or a truer artist. He had his ups and downs, as most artists have, whether poets, painters or musicians, and with a wife and family he sometimes found himself hard up for money. Again and again, after he had gone under he would reappear on the surface, full of courage and strong purpose, swimming for his life and striking out like a hero.

His friends seemed as puzzled as we of today in regard to the heavy load which he seemed always to be carrying, and which shadowed his life. Apparently one and all attributed it to his family, not knowing to what else to attribute it.

N. P. Willis wrote of him as "an artist supporting a large family."

That seemed to be the only plausible reason for the way his money disappeared almost as soon as he acquired it, and the ensuing depression of spirits, which was now showing itself in his face and bearing. He wore a full beard and mustache, and let his hair grow long, which gave him a look suggestive of the poet Longfellow, without the serenity that characterized that poet. It was evident that his health was beginning to fail.

This particular year he passed with his family in Huntington, Long Island (Doughty MSS.), and this is the first reference given to family life. He does not seem to have been equal to painting, as was his inveterate habit; he was evidently weaker in body. He took pleasure in reading the flattering commentaries that the newspapers gave of his work, because that comprised the whole of his life, and it certainly must have made him happy when in writing about him the *Knickerbocker Magazine* called him "Doughty, the all-American Claude Lorrain."

Then came a time when he fell seriously ill, but rallied again, recovering enough to go to Sullivan County, New York, among the foothills of the Catskill Mountains. It was here that he pulled himself together enough to paint some of his most beautiful landscapes.

In 1854 several articles appeared in *Graham's Magazine* on the work of American artists. One of them spoke of Doughty as follows: "Doughty stands in the first rank of American Landscapists. His reputation grew up with the reputations of Cole and Durand, and Dunlap has placed him on a platform with these two great artists." And the article goes on to tell how his pictures found permanent niches in the castles of Europe and in the halls of our own country, and how, when he went to Europe, he made the acquaintance of Sully from whom he received much valuable advice, which, with important tributaries from other notable sources, "wafted him to honor and fame."

Once again Doughty rallied and returned to New York City, taking lodgings at the corner of Greene and Broome Streets, with a studio at 335 Broadway. He was determined to fight all feelings of ill health, and to start work again in the city, but in spite of this determination he grew worse. His friends, looking into the matter, found to their dismay that he had come to the end of his resources, and the question was what to do about it. Daniel Huntington, a well-known sculptor with whom Doughty had been friendly, started an appeal for help. The editor of an art magazine called *The Crayon,* a son of Asher B. Durand, proposed an exhibition of Doughty's works for the latter's benefit. "Doughty is one of the pioneers of our landscape art," he wrote, "and we are sure that a collection of his paintings would be very interesting."

The plan seemed a sensible one, but it came too late. Before any arrangement could be made to get it into shape Doughty, the worshiper and lover of Nature, died on July 22, 1856.

A reporter on the *Boston Evening Transcript,* on hearing of his death, wrote the following: "He was a careful observer of Nature, not forming his style on any favorite model, so that his manner, though intensely peculiar, was decidedly characteristic. He struggled with poverty all his life, and his last days were embittered by want."

Thomas Doughty was an idealist and a dreamer, and a revealer of Nature at its best, but "his judgment was faulty upon mundane things like money." (Doughty MSS.)

He once said to a friend that his ambition was "to appeal to the eye and heart through the medium of canvas and color, by presenting to his fellow countrymen those beautiful scenes with which our country abounds."

In this he most certainly succeeded.

Author's Note: We have included the landscape by Walter M. S. Bayne in the group of paintings by Thomas Doughty because of its similarity to the work of the latter. Those who have seen it question as to whether he was not a pupil of that noted artist. No account of his life can be given, as no information has as yet been found.

CHAPTER 3

Thomas Birch
(1779–1851)

THE MAJORITY OF THE Hudson River artists devoted their energies to painting scenes of beauty among the Catskill Mountains, the Hudson River, the mountains of the West, and all the wild secluded inland regions as yet undiscovered by the public, but a few were drawn by the mysteries of jagged coast lines with surf breaking on peaked rocks, ships sailing into the teeth of a storm, with fog enveloping the horizons, and wrecks on perilous reefs or in mid-ocean with no help near.

Perhaps the most noted of the artists who chose such subjects on which to demonstrate their skill was Thomas Birch, who came with his parents from Warwickshire, England, to this country in 1793, at the age of fifteen.

It was within comparatively few years after arriving here, when he was twenty-three years old, that, having a desire to take up art as a profession but not having made up his mind as to how to begin, he started making what were then called "profile likenesses," because there was a demand for them, and because those he did gave satisfaction.

But he was too ambitious to keep to so restricting a phase of art, and one day in 1807 he happened to board a pilot boat bound for the capes of the Delaware. This visit revealed to him the picturesqueness of ships sailing out of harbors with all sails set, and the moods of a mysterious ocean that could be calm and undisturbed at one time of the day, and lashing itself into a fury within the very next hour.

It started a train of thought in his mind that gradually possessed him. He began to make a study of this temperamental element of nature, and found himself loving it.

When the war with England came in 1812, it brought dramatic opportunities for his historical paintings which he eagerly seized upon. These proved to be his most notable works.

The first completed painting of this kind was an order he received from Mr. James Webster, a publisher in Philadelphia. The subject was "The Engagement of the *Constitution* and the *Guerrière*." Mr. Nicholas Biddle, at one time president of the United States Bank, being impressed by the verve and power of this painting, followed by giving Birch an order for his next effort, which was of "The *Wasp* and the *Frolic*."

Then came a series of pictures as events took place: "The Battles of the Frigate *United States* with the *Macedonian*," "Perry's Victory on Lake Erie," and "MacDonough's Victory on Lake Champlain," and various others which "furnished employment to his pencil in the path he had chosen and in which he stands unrivalled in our country." (Dunlap.)

The rugged shores of the New England coast also made their appeal to him, resulting in at least one beautiful seascape from off the Maine coast.

But Thomas Birch had another string to his bow in the way of subjects to show his talents. His snow scenes are typical of our country districts and were very much prized, as well as many charming landscapes — all painted in the manner of the Hudson River School of painting. It was one of these that he entered in the first exhibition in Philadelphia in which Doughty's landscapes appeared, and it was before the works of these two artists that the young Thomas Cole stood in admiration and reverence. The following quotation shows the impression these paintings made on the public at that time: "His views of Philadelphia are excellent and will perpetuate his fame as long as one of these remains preserved." (Mantle Fielding.)

Thomas Birch died in Philadelphia, January 14, 1851, leaving the well-grounded reputation of being one of the notable artists of his day.

CHAPTER 4

Alvan Fisher

(1792–1863)

THOMAS DOUGHTY's friend, Alvan Fisher, was as complete a contrast to himself as could possibly be found. Perhaps that was why they took to each other. In the first place, Fisher was a thorough New Englander, and more than that, he came from Massachusetts stock, having been born in August, 1792, in Needham.

He was a two-sided man, for apart from his acknowledged talent as an artist, he had a very noticeable capacity for making the two ends meet, and though his head was often in the clouds he was surefooted, and was pretty certain to keep his feet upon the ground — a combination much to be envied in a workaday world. Perhaps it was because he began at the early age of eighteen as a clerk in a country store, which would sharpen the wits of anybody. His friends were more ambitious for him and wanted him to go into a mercantile counting room in the town, but while sitting behind the counter in the aforesaid country store he had had time to think, and when he thought he invariably dwelt upon a secret desire to become an artist. From childhood up he had held this in the back of his mind, and the time had come when he could not be persuaded to renounce this ambition.

His family was evidently in comfortable circumstances, for finding that his mind was made up and that he had chosen his future profession himself, they seem to have made no attempt to alter it.

The question was how to get started. There being at hand no other outlet of an artistic nature, he took up the profession of a "Sign and Ornamental Painter," studying under John R. Penniman, a well-known artist in his day, in good standing, but who, as he got older, became rather careless in his methods, willing to teach painting of any kind to anybody in order to keep himself going. However, since he was really a competent artist, having produced many pieces of work of a descriptive kind, it was greatly to young Fisher's advantage to come under his tuition. It taught him to paint with a strong and decided touch, combined with a sureness of detail that stood him in good stead when he finally developed into an artist of decided ability and became one of the successful members of the Hudson River group.

In writing to William Dunlap about his early life, Fisher states: "I was placed with a Mr. Penniman, who was an excellent ornamental painter. With him I remained upward of two years."

Of this Mr. Penniman Dunlap says:

> He had more talent and skill than many who aspire to higher branches of the art. If he had had that education, or those feelings, which would have led him to aspire to the character and conduct of a gentleman, he would have been a good artist and a respectable citizen; but he became a drunkard, and died despised or lamented, according to those who were acquainted with his talents and his conduct. He had the honor of being the first teacher of Alvan Fisher.

Penniman was one of those picturesque and happy-go-lucky artists who take life lightly; he sang through happy hours and loudly lamented through unhappy ones, so that all his friends might learn of his ill luck. His forte was painting large mural pictures with Rome, Paestum, and other Italian motives for a background. One of his mural paintings hangs on the wall of the Tea Room at Fruitlands and the Wayside Museums, Inc., at Harvard, Massachusetts. It originally belonged to the Honorable Edward Everett of anti-slavery fame and was acquired from his family. A letter from Penniman hangs with it, written while in prison.

In spite of the advantages acquired by Fisher from this colorful gentleman, the former found that he had absorbed from him a method of painting which hampered his style. It had too much of the mechanical ornamental quality which, as he expressed it, "required years to shake off." However, he found also that he had gained much in accuracy of touch and knowledge of composition. Of this period he writes to William Dunlap:

> In 1814 I commenced being an artist by painting portraits at a cheap rate. This I pursued until 1815. I then began painting a species of pictures which had not been practiced much, if any, in this country — with scenes belonging to rural life, winter pieces, portraits of animals, etc. This species of paintings, being novel in this part of the country, I found it to be a more lucrative, pleasant, and distinguishing branch of the art than portrait painting which I had been pursuing.

But this type of work, in spite of its remunerative advantages, failed to satisfy him, though he continued it until 1819-20. Then he resumed portrait painting in all seriousness, intending to make it his principal profession.

He was painting portraits when he went to Philadelphia, and entered some of them in that notable exhibition when he and Thomas Doughty, Thomas Birch, and the then youthful Thomas Cole became known to each other as comrades in the profession of artists while their paintings were displayed on its walls.

On that occasion, Doughty's landscapes won immediate recognition from the public, and one cannot help wondering whether this fact, and his friend's continued success in that branch of the work, could have influenced Fisher's decision to enter into it himself. He did so, however, and with great success, but as has been said before, he was from New England, and shrewd in his ways. He did not give up his portrait painting, but combined the two sources of income, so that if one dropped off for awhile, the other held good.

In his Family Records (*Fisher Family Records*) the following proud assertion is made that "he was a man of decided talents for art, and withal possessed the extraordinary ability to make it pay."

But he was not wholly satisfied with searching around for lucrative methods of indulging his love for art. He felt that he should visit other art centers, especially those on the other side of the Atlantic, in order to gain the inspiration to reach the goal which he had placed before him in his imagination. With this thought in mind he boarded a sailing vessel in 1825, and went first to England, then to France, where he gained practice from copying some of the pictures of the old masters in the famous gallery of the Louvre. He also went as far as Italy, and took a walking tour through Switzerland.

Before going on this trip he had traveled over many parts of his own country, painting landscapes as he went, so by the time he returned from Europe he was well acquainted with innumerable aspects of nature, and was ready to show work that would bring him the immediate recognition of the public.

And now, in spite of the all-absorbing interest in his profession, like his friend Doughty he felt the lack of a home of his own and the joys of home life. On June 2, 1827, he married Lydia, daughter of Abner and Martha (May) Ellis in Dedham, Massachusetts. They had one son.

He was now settled in Boston, opening a studio and gallery of his own on Washington Street, near Summer Street, "and was the first landscape painter to hang out a professional sign in Boston" (*Fisher Family Records*). Thomas Doughty, according to the Doughty MSS., "became associated with him," whatever that means.

And now came a period when both of them were exhibiting their paintings, not only at the frequent Athenaeum showings, but at all the art exhibits of note in the country. It was a busy life and an absorbing one. Doughty's exhibits were all straight landscapes, while Fisher kept to his various branches, and even added another to those, in the way of genre pictures. About these he wrote to Dunlap as follows (*History of the Arts of Design*):

> I believe, sir, you have not seen a class of my paintings, such, for example, as "The Escape of Sergeant Champ," "Mr. Dustin Saving Children from the Savages," "The Freshet," "Lost Boy," etc. As these paintings and many of the like were painted to order for gentlemen of this city, it is this class of pictures that have been as advantageous as any other to my reputation as an artist.

But it is Alvan Fisher as a landscape painter that we are dealing with, and the three illustrations shown in this account will reveal the charm and delicacy of his portrayal of New England scenery.

By the time he was forty-three years old he had "by industry in landscape and portrait painting accumulated the sum of thirteen thousand dollars." (*Fisher Family Records.*) This clouded his cautious nature a little and unexpectedly went to his head, and in a moment of impulse to double that amount if he could, he invested in Eastern lands, and as a result lost the whole of it. "Nothing daunted he again sought success and won it in the accumulation of a few thousand dollars, which by fortunate, or shrewd speculation he greatly increased until possessed of a small fortune." (*Fisher Family Records.*)

Another striking proof of the business capacity that went hand in hand with his very decided artistic talents was his manner of disposing of the paintings which he had failed to sell, which remained piled against the walls of his studio, accumulating dust and cobwebs. Every few years he gathered all these together and held an auction. It is stated that he was known to have held six of these in all, and that each one of them netted him in cash about fifty dollars a picture. This may seem a small sum, but as in each auction he sold just short of one hundred pictures, it came to quite a sum when added up, as well as clearing his studio of his more unimportant work, with the added compensation of nothing having gone to waste.

But there were delightful experiences mingled with these business transactions. In those days there was a famous tavern well known to artists, tucked in among the mountains around North Conway, which was conducted by a man named Thompson. In fact, it was named Thompson's Tavern. The artists of the Hudson River group were wont to meet there, and made it their headquarters while painting the glories of the White Mountains. Alvan Fisher, Thomas Doughty, Thomas Harding and others were habituées of it, and many a visit these made there together, enjoying the delights of comradeship among those delectable hills — painting during the daytime, or wandering about in search of subject, returning towards nightfall to enjoy a good old New England supper, and afterwards an uninterrupted interchange of amusing experiences and gossip of the studios, in the simple rustic eating room of the tavern — lighting their pipes

and seeing visions of success in the smoke that came from them —
pipe dreams of a future worth working for, and more than likely a
"nightcap" before going to their beds. (*Fisher Family Records*.)

Fisher did not approach the art of painting in the way Thomas
Doughty did. The latter worked almost entirely in the open air. The
work he did *al fresco* satisfied him the most. He copied nature as
he saw it. Fisher did not always do that. He would take notes and
make sketches as fully as possible of the scenes that appealed to him,
taking them back to his studio to perfect and amplify. His claim
was that in seeing a bit of landscape the impression of it on an artist's
brain should be so clear-cut and definite that there should be no need
of sitting and looking at this view in nature — a method which runs
the risk of tiring the eyes and even the brain. To fasten the memory
on the impression received would achieve as good results and sometimes even better.

There were those among these artists who held both points of
view, each keeping tenaciously to his own convictions.

It is rather amazing that having become associated with Fisher
and known and admired him as an artist and a friend, Thomas
Doughty did not gain from him some points as regards keeping the
wolf from the door while still remaining a true and sincere artist.
But Doughty was a dreamer, whereas Fisher had his dreams but held
the reins of them well in hand; he was not troubled with fits of
despondency, he kept his composure, and he evidently had the gift
of standing outside of himself and watching results, and adjusting
his life accordingly.

Fisher has left to New England some lovely paintings of her rural
and peaceful scenery. The last part of his life was spent in his home
in Dedham, Massachusetts. From there he went about painting a
scene here and a scene there, revealing that side of his nature that
depicted the true artist in every sense of the word, as will be seen in
the illustrations herewith.

He died in his home on February 14, 1863. Dunlap sums up his
character thus: "Mr. Fisher's uniform conduct through life has
evinced an amiable disposition, and perfect moral worth." (*History
of the Arts of Design*.) Could one say more of an honest man?

CHAPTER 5

Asher B. Durand
(1796–1886)

Another of Thomas Doughty's friends was Asher B. Durand, of Huguenot descent, a man of stalwart character, and only a year younger than himself.

Durand's grandfather, Jean Durand, was a Huguenot refugee from Toulouse in the south of France. The religious disturbances were at their height in that country, and he fled to England where he became naturalized and lived for awhile. But hearing of the great opportunities held forth in America to any man of vigor and determination to succeed, he emigrated to this country, bought land at Milford, Connecticut, and settled down to bring up a family.

It was here that Asher's father was born in 1745. "As a family, inheriting French temperaments, they lived like most genial people, content to take life as it comes." (*Life and Times of Asher B. Durand.*) They were also by nature very firm in their religious beliefs. The sufferings borne by the Huguenots made a deep impression on the generation that followed. It may be said of them that "they were the fine flower of an accomplished people, men of active minds, austere morals, heroic courage, and often of refined manners." (*Life of Asher Durand.*)

Durand's biographer goes on to say: "I lay stress on the fact that the Durand family was of French origin. Certain qualities, talents, and works which distinguish a man are more readily appreciated when one knows from what nationality he has sprung."

His environment also is of importance, and the environment in which Asher Durand was born was that of Jefferson Village, New

Jersey, on a road at the base of the southern end of Orange Mountain.

There were a few scattered houses along that road. The place could hardly be called even a village, it was so small in size. Situated in a valley formed on the west by Orange Mountain, and on the east by a ridge of high ground declining towards Newark, it afforded a nature lover a center of quiet, rural landscape. The woods reached to the top of the mountain, which was covered by an almost unbroken forest, a truly primitive forest full of game of all kinds. It had the charm of wild solitude, the perfect repose of Nature undisturbed by the voice of man. Wandering over this mountain as a boy had much to do with forming young Durand's character and stimulating his love for art.

This was the school in which Nature was his only teacher. One wonders where a boy thus brought up can experience the sort of natural pleasures that youth requires. To be sure, living in the houses along that road that ran at the foot of Orange Mountain were young people — members of large families, at work all day, but at sundown ready to forget that work and give themselves over to enjoying themselves.

Durand's biographer writes:

> Riding behind a fast horse in a gig or wagon was one of their pastimes — not to take anybody's dust, especially if they were accompanied by a sweetheart. This was their great pride. There were Prayer Meetings, revivals and so on. When an outside preacher came to this little settlement, the young men came to these, not only for their spiritual welfare, but also to escort the girls home when the Meetings were over. Then music, generally sacred, brought together the young people of both sexes for singing-school practice in the Meeting House. In the winter, when sleighing was good, there were occasional "straw rides" in wagon bodies set on runners, bound for some remote tavern. Sometimes as many as twenty sleighs, holding as many couples, went gliding through the frozen landscape by moonlight, with the silvery ringing of a thousand bells, and shouts of merry laughter, ending with a supper and dance, and home again before the day breaks.

Such was the character of the remote community in which Asher B. Durand passed the early years of his life. But he took no definite part in it. Not being what one might call a rugged boy, and the youngest of the family, besides being made much of by his mother, he was never made to work on the farm, and was never urged to join in the village amusements, for he was very diffident and serious-minded, and the rough-and-tumble hilarious jollity of the farmers' sons and daughters made no great appeal to him. What gave him keen joy was to watch the mechanical pursuits of his father, who was a maker of clocks and watches. Out of doors he got his pleasure in wandering in the woods and up the mountainside. He knew the habits of the trees and wild flowers. He could tell all the varieties of ferns and lichens to be found there. In their companionship he felt perfectly at home, mentally and physically. He never ceased to marvel at the beauty of all created things when untouched by man. But with all this a desire to make his own way in the world when he grew up and to uphold the traditions of his family was ever present. To be sure, this was continually suggested to him by his family, but it also came spontaneously into his own views regarding his future. In speaking of his childhood he said of himself that he "would hide behind a tree or bush at the approach of a person or vehicle." That he should have so completely overcome this handicap in later life shows the force of his character.

Now, watching his father work upon the intricate mechanism of watches developed a love of detail in Durand's nature, and he began to wonder what sort of profession he could choose in which this love of detail would stand uppermost. It so happened that engraving was becoming a very special art in those days and he decided to try his hand at it. He managed, by great good fortune, to enter the office of the eminent engraver, Peter Maverick, who took an interest in him, and from whom he learned the art with surprising success. *The Life and Times of Asher B. Durand,* by his son John Durand, shows his vignettes engraved for bank notes, and one realizes that here were bits of art that placed him among the most finished engravers of his time. What qualified him for this recognition of his talents

was not only the technical skill he revealed, but the grace and charm
of the compositions, which were wholly his own. They were exquisite specimens of art — precursors of the greater works that were
to follow.

Like most men with French blood in their veins, Durand was versatile. He could turn his hand to almost anything. It happened that
he was the one selected as orator for the great Fourth of July celebration to be held in the Springfield Presbyterian Church in 1817. It
was to be a great occasion for the little New Jersey village, and as
the villagers had seen him grow up from childhood, and remembered
his extreme diffidence, one would have supposed a more seasoned
orator would have been chosen. But this occasion proved that those
days of diffidence had been left far behind him, as will be shown by
a quotation drawn from his speech, which demonstrates the fashion
in those days for bellicose oratory accompanied by somewhat violent
gesticulations. When he rose to make his speech there must have
been many in the audience who wondered what he was going to say.
They soon learned.

> America is the last hope of human greatness [he declared], and warned
> by the red beacon blazing over the wide plains of tyrannic desolation,
> let us shun the fatal path that leads to waste dominion. An eventful era
> is before us! The convulsions of Europe portend some uncommon epoch,
> and the potent hand of Revolution, now evidently lifting over Britain,
> may raise from the ashes of a sinking monarchy, the phoenix of a Re-
> public. . . . In vain the tempest of ambition shall thunder; in vain the
> indignant billows of convulsing anarchy shall dash against its founda-
> tions; it [America] is the last asylum for the rights of man — the hand
> of the Eternal guards it from destruction. . . .
>
> Soldiers in the cause of freedom, I turn to you [undoubtedly the Spring-
> field militia], let not the fire of your patriotism dwindle in your bosoms,
> etc., etc. . . .

This was listened to with rapt attention, vociferously cheered,
and honored especially by the plaudits of the fair sex, as verified by
a lady who was present on that occasion and who in her old age

stated to the writer — "we were astonished that one so young could know so much!"

Anyone who knows anything about art in America is well aware of the great success of Asher B. Durand as an engraver. His first great success was his engraving of Trumbull's large painting of "The Declaration of Independence." It took Durand three years to complete it, and when done, his reputation was firmly established. In fact, when Trumbull saw the engraving he was so delighted and so impressed by it that he wrote to the Marquis of Lafayette as follows:

> I have sent to you a small case containing a proof impression of a print which has been engraved here from my painting of the "Declaration of Independence" by a young engraver, born in this vicinity, and now only twenty-six years old. This work is wholly American, even to the paper and printing — a circumstance which renders it popular here, and will make it a curiosity to you, who knew America when she had neither painters nor engravers, nor arts of any kind, except those of stern utility.

The engraving was published in 1823.

Durand was now in business by himself, and orders came in thick and fast. He was able to expand, and he had the great good fortune to come into possession of the famous painting "Ariadne" by one of the noted painters, Vanderlyn, who had spent much time studying art in Paris, and who had brought this specimen of his art back with him to his own country. The picture was of the nude figure of a woman, very beautiful, and marvelously executed. Having made quite a long stay in Paris, the artist, John Vanderlyn, however, did not realize that paintings of nude figures were not acceptable to the home public at that time. He had hoped to get a large price for it, and exhibited it in New York, but the public turned the other way, and no purchaser appeared, though it was universally admitted by art lovers to be a great piece of work. He therefore became much pressed for money, and finding it a white elephant on his hands, he sold it to Durand for the sum of six hundred dollars. The latter made a most exquisite engraving of it, which later, when the public had grown somewhat hardened to such subjects, brought him a

fame and honor such as he never dreamed of. As regards the painting, it became one of the most noted of its time. Durand kept it for
years in the Historical Society building, and finally sold it by auction
for five thousand dollars, after more than thirty years' possession.
The purchaser at the auction was Joseph Harrison of Philadelphia,
and after his death his widow presented it to the Philadelphia Academy of Fine Arts, where we understand it remains to this day.

In the meantime, Durand was happily married, and having made
a success of his business of engraving, he moved to New York to take
advantage of a broader field to work in.

Park Goodwin, in the *Life of William Cullen Bryant,* gives a description of the New York of those days, as follows:

> Within, the city streets were narrow. . . . They were frequented by loose
> pigs; were badly lighted by rusty oil lamps; and poorly watched by con-
> stables in huge capes and leathern caps. . . . More compact than now, the
> inhabitants were generally more intimately acquainted with one another.
> Everybody took part in what was going on. The resources of enjoyment
> — theatres, operas, concerts, balls and excursions were limited; but they
> were open to all. Family visiting was common, so it was easy to get into
> "society," and the taverns were not so much frequented by wayfarers as
> by residents, to whom they answered the purpose of clubs and restaurants.
> Each of them in fact had its special circle of gossips and clever men. All
> the celebrities of the professions — the stage or of literature, were there
> to be met with, and seated at the little tables on the well-sanded floor,
> with pipes in their mouths, and jugs of punch at their elbows, they dis-
> cussed politics, books, playactors, and the events of social life.

Durand's son John writes of this time:

> Neither prosperity nor social privileges diverted my father from his
> professional pursuits. His leisure hours were devoted to drawing or to
> painting from nature, for after having become convinced that the art of
> engraving was narrowing in its effect, he had taken up paint and brush,
> and was now absorbed in this new experience.

Indefatigable in his determination to absorb art in all its phases,
he wandered through Hoboken carrying his palette and brushes with
him in case he saw something that struck his fancy. He attended

classes at the Academy of Fine Arts, and at the National Academy of Design, of which he was soon to become an instructor, and left no stone unturned to perfect himself in all the branches of art pertaining to landscape painting.

> None of his compeers, perhaps, pursued the study of art technically with more ardour and enthusiasm. In his eagerness to acquire all that might add to his ability as an artist, he taxed his strength too severely, and as a result he fell ill and dyspeptic, and unable to work as hard as he had been doing. However, he had inherited a strong constitution, and by force of will succeeded in overcoming it to a certain degree. (*Life of Asher Durand.*)

It might be well to give some idea of the artistic circles in New York at this time, for they were certainly quaint and interesting.

In 1825 the students of art inhabiting New York formed an association for the practice of drawing. It was out of this association that the National Academy of Design sprang. To this group belonged not only artists but literary men. It was the fashion among artists in those days to depict Biblical scenes, to take subjects from legends and from Greek history, from scenes of ancient battlefields, scenes of heroic adventure; therefore literature mingled very potently with art, and was represented by men of learning. At the meetings friends of the members were often privileged to attend. This proved to be rather a disturbing privilege, especially to those who wished to devote themselves to drawing, and did not like the noise and chatter made by these outsiders. More than that, they began to be aware of a tendency to break away from the frugal repasts they enjoyed to something more costly and substantial. On this account the meetings were discontinued for awhile. Wishing, however, to establish some sort of club or association in which members must abide by stringent rules, thus obviating situations that had become embarrassing, a club was organized in 1825 called "The Sketch Club," and a set of by-laws were made out with great care. The third by-law was considered very important. It was intended to prevent any extravagant entertainments, "which if tolerated would set a bad example — defeat the object of the Club, and render it inaccessible to artists whose incomes did not warrant displays of this kind." (*Prehistoric Notes of the Century Club.*)

The meetings were to be held in the various houses of the associates.

In spite of all the rules that had been laid down and the care that had been taken to enforce them, a most unfortunate occurrence happened. When holding one of the meetings — this time at the house of a gentleman who liked to have things his own way — "Imagine the horror of the members when on opening the folding doors a superb supper appeared before them on a table at which they were expected to sit down!" Tradition says they refused to do so, declaring they would eat standing. Unfortunately for tradition, however, a printed record of the event is extant, declaring that the members concluded to take their seats — and be comfortable! Just the same, the honor of the club was outraged, and it was quietly arranged to get rid of this luxurious member by dissolving the club without more ado.

The members were somewhat discouraged by this time, but in 1830, after much deliberation, a new Sketch Club was organized, with even more stringent rules. They felt that these would accomplish their end. One thing looked ominous, and that was the introduction into the club of Mr. Luman Reed, a gentleman of simple and generous nature, who was most liberally encouraging artists in their endeavor to make a living by their art. Acceptance of him as a member showed the growing tendency of the times towards an infiltration of wealth which might seriously inhibit the desire for frugality which the members considered so important. The difficulty was that Mr. Reed was genuinely beloved by all the artists. They were indebted to him for so many acts of kindness that admitting him as a member was a necessity. The name of Luman Reed is interwoven in the life of art in New York during the period of the extraordinary success of the Hudson River painters. It is said that he was the first wealthy and intelligent connoisseur to encourage art in this country. It was in honor of him that four years after his death, the New York Gallery of Fine Arts came into being, showing the important position that the public accorded him.

But nothing daunted, another attempt was made to make drawing the most prominent feature of this newly organized club. It was attempted in all seriousness, with the assertion that the *literati* must manage to occupy themselves along their own lines. But in spite of rules, the laughing and joking still went on about them.

Now drawing is a thing of too serious and absorbing a nature for an artist to indulge in and at the same time control his nerves sufficiently to ignore the talk and laughter of those around him. Indeed, such is the verdict of the minutes of the club, especially as one sensitive artist member was reported as complaining that he became so nervously affected and diverted from the subject of his drawing that "for the last quarter of an hour [in the flowery language of the times] he had been sketching nothing but peanuts and sweet almond shells instead of 'Sweet Auburn, loveliest village of the plain.' "

For all this, the club hugely enjoyed itself. In the accounts given of the meetings of this new Sketch Club, songs and instrumental music are often recorded in the minutes, as well as story-telling, discussions, mirth, and philosophy. Also jokes and ridiculous remarks seem to have been in order and included in their mirth, sometimes of an order that would seem rather feeble mirth in these times, such as the remark made by a Mr. Brown "propounding a sage notion that perfection of bathing is to jump headforemost into a snow bank"! They evidently thought this wonderful, and it has come down to this day. Durand's biographer remarks that "it would take too much space to mention every instance of Sketch Club jollity."

"In 1831 the membership numbered thirteen artists including those with artistic pursuits. The rest were all literary men, such as William Cullen Bryant, John Howard Payne, Hamilton Fish, John Inmann, and others. . . . Later two or three lawyers and one merchant were taken into the Club, also two clergymen — Rev. Drs. Dewey and Bellows."

The result of all these changes was that in spite of the fact that Mr. Luman Reed was simple in his ways, though generous to a fault, very kindly, desirous of being only a helping hand regarding the growth of art in this country, insensibly the old frugal ways of conducting things disappeared one by one, and the club rose to a more impressive position in the community. It was from this Sketch Club, with its humble beginnings, that the famous Century Club emerged later on.

This, then, was the New York to which Asher Durand came from his quiet home among the hills of Hoboken. A man of simple tastes, loving the quiet of a small and unassuming place, he nevertheless braced himself to meet the larger life, and soon became the good friend and active contributor to the artist world in which he found himself.

It took no time at all for Mr. Luman Reed to discover Durand's great talents. The latter was devoting himself to portraiture at this time, finding he could make much more in that way than the landscape painters. These portraits were so much admired by Mr. Reed that in 1835 he commissioned him to go to Washington to paint a portrait of General Jackson — more than that, he gave him the tremendous order to paint the portraits of all the Presidents of the United States up to that day.

The series of portraits of the Presidents, ordered by Mr. Reed, was presented by him to the Museum and Library in the Brooklyn Navy Yard. Another series, duplicates, were kept by him for his own gallery. This demonstrates a habit then in vogue of ordering from an artist duplicates of any pictures by him that were admired and desired. This may have been acceptable and profitable to the artist, but it has often made the profession of collectors very confused in the years after all these artists had left this world for the next.

Having such an order as this on hand, Durand went to Washington, and as usual applied himself unstintingly to the job. But after awhile, being first and foremost a home-loving man, he began to long to return. He wrote to his friend and pupil Casilaer:

> I have seen everything in art and nature that the place affords, and there is much worth seeing. . . . I am getting homesick. But the remedy will be at hand in one week more, for I begin to see through my labours. If nothing interferes, I shall close, or very nearly so, this week. My work has been nearly double what I expected. . . . All pronounce my likenesses

"first rate." But however flattering their good opinions and the commissions may be, I still hope that I may not be induced to undertake others offered me, for I wish to be at home, and to that end every hour of the day is devoted to the completion of what I have on hand.

The happy day finally arrived when he could leave Washington, where he was only too well aware of being overworked, and go for a time to Boston, a city that always gave him a warm welcome and where he felt freer to live more quietly. Here he could devote himself to his work without the constant interruptions of his experience in Washington. As a matter of fact, he had very decidedly outstripped his strength by the work he had done there. He found himself looking at life in morbid dread of it, which was wholly unlike his natural point of view. Somewhat distressed by this, he sat down and wrote to Thomas Cole, with whom he had become on intimate terms. After some preamble he got down to the point of his letter. Since he had last seen him his whole mind was taken up with the painting of landscapes. The desire to take up that branch of the profession had been secretly luring him away from portraits. He found them stirring him with new enthusiasm, and he mentions it to his friend Cole: "Landscapes still occupy my attention. The vast range of this beautiful creation should be my dwelling place, the only portion of which I can at present avail myself being the neighborhood of Hoboken."

To which Thomas Cole replies:

> I am sorry that you are at times so depressed in spirits. You must come and live in the country. Nature is a sovereign remedy. Your depression is the result of debility; you require the pure air of heaven. You sit (I know you do) in a close airtight room, toiling, stagnating, and breeding dissatisfaction at all you do, when if you had the untainted breeze to breathe, your body would be invigorated, your spirits buoyant, and your pictures would even charm yourself. This is not exaggeration — there is much sober truth in it.
>
> You speak of the want of proper excitement. I am of the opinion that in the city more excitement is necessary than in the country. In the city we are surrounded by our fellow men, and we feel their presence; we labor

for their approbation, and require that stimulant frequently. But in the country we labor under more healthy influences. The desire to produce excellence feeds the flame of our enthusiasm. . . . You will think me sermonizing, but I merely wish to convince you that provided you could consistently leave the city, you would be better in health and spirits, and I am sure if you would pitch your tent near me, I should be benefited — so there you see I come in with a little selfishness at last.

But circumstances were against Durand's changing his home at Hoboken for the country life. His first wife having died, he now married Mary Frank, daughter of Jacob Frank, Esq., which altered his plans considerably. His biographer says:

> Always in quest of picturesque material in summer, and leading a sort of nomadic life for eight years — often separated from his children, and being the owner of a house, he was only too glad to return to it.
> Accordingly he took possession of his old home in 1838, where he was to remain for thirty-one years.
> Two years later he added a studio, and considered himself settled for life.

But he had been a nomad for too long a time, as it proved, to settle down entirely. His mind began to focus itself upon a visit to Europe. He reflected that many other artists were doing this. He felt that he should see the great paintings of the world that were on the other side, in order to do justice to the wealth of material on this side which it was his constant desire to portray. Moreover, some of his admirers urged him to go, and a wealthy friend of his, Mr. Jonathan Sturgis, a business partner of Mr. Luman Reed, offered to finance the trip.

Three of his artist friends, hearing of his plan, decided to accompany him. One was John Kensett, much younger than himself, but well on his way to a standing of importance in his profession as a landscape painter, John W. Casilaer, his former pupil who was now well launched as an important Hudson River artist, and Thomas P Rossiter, a well-known figure painter. The opportunity was too great a one to turn from, so Durand made his plans accordingly. It was arranged that they should sail for London in the steamer *British Queen* on June 1, 1840.

For four years now steamships instead of sailing vessels had been making the voyages across the Atlantic. The experience was such a new one to Durand that he felt almost bewildered by it. But his three younger companions kept everything tuning to a major key. It was also their first experience of an ocean voyage, and judging by their various temperaments, they must have thrown themselves into it with enthusiasm.

Fortunately Durand kept a journal, as well as copies of the letters he wrote home. Some of them give amusing descriptions of the days as they passed.

After studying the situation seriously he wrote:

> Really at a superficial glance this vessel appears to be little else than an immense cook shop and slaughter house afloat; the business of eating seems to take precedence of all others. . . . The dinner closes with songs and sentiments in the saloon; on deck the merry contagion spreads, and continues through the afternoon, when the evening closes in with dance and song among the sailors. All is joy and glee.

Here is another comment:

> It is said that a man of war at sea is a perfect despotism in miniature; not so with a steam packet. On the contrary, it is rather an example of perfect democracy. For instance, immediately in front, flat on the deck, on a small coiled rope, and squatted like a tailor, is George Combe, the phrenologist and philosopher. Near him, without even a coiled rope or seat of any kind other than the bare deck, two or three fashionable ladies; near them on a wooden bench sits an Italian Bishop surrounded by several of his confrères, consisting of priests and laymen, while all around in almost every possible position — sitting, standing, reclining, or stretched out at full length, appear ladies and gentlemen, soldiers and sailors, officers and crew, men and women of all nations and tongues, all apparently in full possession of equal rights and liberty of conscience.

When the day came that the steamer approached England, Durand was all filled with suppressed wonder and inward thrill. He was standing by the side of Mr. Combe, the philosopher. As the ship was gliding by the lovely and historic coast of England, he exclaimed with enthusiasm, "It is a beautiful world, Mr. Combe!"

The answer from this noted man came dreamily. "Yes," he said, "what a pity Man is not in harmony with it." A wet blanket if there ever was one!

When Durand and his three companions landed, they at once began to look for all the sights on their way up to London. All the galleries in that city were visited, the paintings carefully studied, while each made his comments on what he saw, and they saw about everything there was to see.

Durand's journal describes some of the sights of London apart from picture galleries and art exhibits. Here is an account of one of his experiences:

> In the evening [he says], having been complimented with a ticket, price one guinea, I attended a Masquerade Ball. Pursuant to regulations I provided myself with a black mask, to which my sense of propriety was much indebted, for I should have blushed to see my "natural face" in the glass as one of the motley throng assembled on this occasion in this scene of folly. There were about two or three hundred characters in the assemblage in various costumes — some of them in good taste, some in bad, and others in no taste. Some were masked without any other disguise. Of the female portion in particular the less said the better. I saw but one or two women whose countenances seemed at variance with the occasion, and one especially, whose soft pensive eyes and graceful brow revealed indeed "too much of heaven on earth to last — of too fair and delicate texture to sustain this folly."

The journal goes on to give some impressions of the English country:

> I have not seen one half of the city of London, but I have perhaps seen its fairest side. It seems to me a city of prosperity and abundance. Richness and variety strike one at every step through its principal streets, but it is only through these great thoroughfares that I have passed. That there are haunts of poverty and wretchedness equally startling, and perhaps more extended I well know, but I have not sought them — on the contrary, I have avoided them as unprofitable spectacles.

This last remark shows a very real side of Durand's character. The artist in him was always uppermost. Beauty meant everything to him, and was all he wished to see. Ugliness in anything was almost a sin. This did not mean that he was in any way lacking in sympathy with those in distress; on the contrary, it hurt him too much to see things that were unsightly which he was powerless to change.

The journal gives his impressions in detail of all he saw of the wonders of the Old World, but this short account of him cannot include them. He and his young friends — Casilaer and Kensett — made a tour of the art centers of Europe, enjoying some to the full, yet not being in sympathy with others. But it was Italy that their minds were continually yearning for. They were impatiently looking forward to seeing with their own eyes the old Italian masterpieces that were there. At that time the Mecca for all artists was Rome, where they could see statues by the great sculptors of antiquity, along with paintings by the equally great artists of all time. Durand had the supreme pleasure of staying under the roof of our American sculptor of fame at that period — Horatio Greenough, who made the design used afterwards for the construction of Bunker Hill Monument. He was living in Florence then. His enthusiasm for his branch of the arts was very inspiring to Durand. He awakened in his friend a wider and deeper appreciation of what Italy held that was beautiful, so that when the latter reached Rome his whole mind and spirit were filled to overflowing with wonder at what Man, through the ages, had accomplished. The ruins of the Colosseum — the sumptuous beauty of the Baths of Caracalla still holding up their columns, as if to challenge the modern world to create anything as majestic, gave Durand the sensation of looking into a dream world, wholly different from the one he was living in.

He said little of these sensations in his letters home. Being one of the exceptional men who have discovered that the intimate things of everyday life are what those at home desire most to hear, we find him writing these details while living among the ancient ruins of the past. His wife had not accompanied him on this journey because of the expenses involved, and he evidently knew that her first desire would be to know about his physical well-being. So he wrote:

Living is cheap. I pay eight dollars a month for my studio, including two small rooms besides, and six dollars per month for a bedroom at another place — very near and well furnished. I pay about seven cents for breakfast, which consists of tea or coffee, half milk, and a couple of rolls. I dine at half past four on two or three dishes, as it may be — good beefsteaks, puddings, etc. — which commonly cost about two cents each; then I generally lunch at noon for three or four cents more. (*Life of Asher Durand.*)

Thus he settled down for a winter's work, which is what he had planned to do, and which he did assiduously. He had separated now from Casilaer and Kensett who were eager to leave no stone unturned in seeing all that Italy had to offer, and the older man began at times to long for home, and his family, and neighbors, and the hills of Hoboken. He was not one to mix very freely with strangers. He was always civil and courteous with them, but was not one of those artists who throw themselves into the moods of other people. He was a quiet man at heart. He loved quiet places.

While working in his studio with these thoughts uppermost, an artist friend of his named F. W. Edmonds put new zest into his work, and suggested a short tour that he thought would cheer up his companion. Durand's son writes of this:

My father, it must be noted, was not fond of travel; its business details worried him, and moreover a journey for pleasure took time which he would rather devote to work. The whole tour, indeed, he regarded as an exile, and to be got through with as soon as possible. In his journal he often records a feeling of homesickness, but the company of a congenial companion, and the sights he was seeing drove it away for the time being. And then too, on his trip he made a great many pencil drawings of every place they visited, which kept him busy all the time.

But underneath it all the feeling persisted, for in a letter to his home written from Switzerland he says:

I wish to continue in Europe as long as it shall be pleasant, for the benefits it shall yield me as a landscape painter — for that object, no country in the world can equal it. But for purposes more important, and of higher interest that can be found in this or any other country, give me our own dear native land! I can look with admiration and wonder at the beauty and sublimity of the scenes now before me; I can look with gratification and advantage on the great works of art, as I have done in England and on the Continent and Italy, yet when all this looking and studying and admiring shall have an end, I am free to confess that I shall enjoy a sight of the signboards on the streets of New York more than all the pictures in Europe; and for real and unalloyed enjoyment of scenery, the rocks, trees, and green meadows of Hoboken will have a charm that all Switzerland cannot boast; only let me see them in the presence of family and friends, and they in health and prosperity.

"Swift fly around ye wheels of Time, and bring the welcome day!"

This was Asher Durand down to the very core. His love and loyalty to his country and to his home was so great that even the most famed centers of the world could not displace them.

His face showed it. His bearing showed it. Anyone who has seen a picture of him at this period of his life, a time when character imprints itself upon the features, can readily see in the clear-cut face, the natural power of the way he holds his head, and the quiet dignity of his expression, that here is a man who has planted deep roots in life, and who lives accordingly.

And now with Rome his European experience ended. He turned his face towards Hoboken.

On June 20, 1841, he was at Liverpool on board the steamship *Britannia,* bound for New York. Casilaer returned with him, but Rossiter and Kensett lingered on in Rome for two years longer, unable to tear themselves away from the artistic life of that golden city. In the meantime Durand was taking an important place in the artistic circles in New York. In 1845 he was elected president of the National Academy of Design, and unanimously re-elected until 1861. Honored as he felt at being given this important position, his troubles soon began on account of the rise of an institution called the "Art Union," which, though unable to live long on account of financial difficulties, formed a serious competition while it lasted, and the disagreements that arose in consequence made inroads on his health. It seemed to him that life under these circumstances was too complicated for him. A man with his artistic temperament, and the inborn love of peace and quiet, shrinks from anything like business turmoil and differences of opinion. His biographer writes of him: "Even in summer when he went into the country for rest, and to console himself as usual with the joy of studying and painting trees, which were his great delight, he was not left undisturbed."

In 1857 sorrow came to him again. His second wife died, and this left a blank in his life that nothing could fill. The buoyancy of life seemed to leave him. He felt unequal to going on with the presidency of the Academy of Design, and he resigned in 1861. His biographer wrote: "I am confident that he was happy and grateful for the opportunity for retiring."

Relieved now from cares of a public nature, Durand took his relaxation in traveling among out-of-the-way corners, of which he found many, and where he found subjects to paint without being molested. Encouraged by that, he spread his wings farther and advanced into wild regions before the railways had sought them out,

> where few scattered inhabitants could be found, almost as primitive as the forests, lakes, streams, and mountains around them. He visited, according to opportunity, every region in the North that was pictorially available, always branching off to escape civilization . . . stopping in the wilderness wherever the forms and colors of rocks, the trunks and branching of particular trees, the verdant masses of middle distances and the lines of the mountains answered to his search for the beautiful. . . . The banks of the Hudson came first in order, then further West, every nook, corner, and clove in the Catskill, Shandakin, and Shawangunk mountains — then to Lake George, Lake Champlain and its shores — the Adirondacks on one side and the mountains of Vermont on the other; then to the East — the White Mountains, North Conway, West Campton, the Berkshire hills in Massachusetts, the Valley of Connecticut . . . all so many haunts of nature. In the delineation of these beauties his brush never wearied. (*Life of Asher Durand*.)

At first his devoted pupil and friend Casilaer accompanied him. Then later, members of his family joined them, and later still younger artists like Kensett, Christopher Pearse Cranch, Hubbard and others, became members of the party.

With so many, there was difficulty in securing lodgings, and a headquarters was needed. Durand therefore purchased a house on the Hudson River near Newburgh, upon high ground overlooking "the vale of Avoca." The place chosen was a most beautiful spot, and the little group was enthusiastic about it, when to their dismay the lovely stream that wandered through it was taken by the railroad. The ground was turned up all along its banks and the dread fever-and-ague set in. The beautiful place which seemed to be everything they could desire had to be sold, and the sorrowing artists became nomads again.

Finally they stopped at the entrance of the Catskills, and in October, 1848, he wrote from Palensville. "The Clove is rich in beautiful wildness beyond all we have met heretofore." Here they settled for a while. Christopher Pearse Cranch mentions the fact of being there in a letter to John S. Dwight written in 1850. He says: "Spent the fall with Durand in the Catskill Clove." One of Durand's family who had joined the group wrote an amusing account of their life there.

The place was a small village, primitive in its ways, and the letter said:

> Besides Casilaer and Kensett we have next door Mr. Vilmering, the Dane, so we have plenty of talk — amusing bad English, and smoking every evening. You will see that although retired we are not lonesome . . . the bar room does all it can to lighten our troubles. Wet floors are disagreeable, and tobacco smoke in a close room unpleasant, but we all put on the best face, and contribute our mite to the general fund of amusement — playing cards indoors when it rains, and out of doors singing and guessing conundrums, our stock of which is so exhausted that we shall have to exercise our faculties in some other fashion. Our amusements are all of the quiet kind except one, with which every newcomer, friend or stranger, is, in our lawlessness, generally greeted. When one appears each of the party is assigned a separate syllable of a particular sound, which at a given signal is vociferously expressed, especially astonishing to strangers.
>
> I leave you to imagine what the effect would be were you to enter a room containing twelve or fifteen persons of different ages — some so quiet

and grave in appearance as to preclude the suspicion of a joke, and find them all at once joining in a deafening *sneeze* — then bursting into roars of laughter at your astonishment!

And now comes the period in Durand's life when these jaunts into the wilds had to be foregone. He felt unequal to tramping through the woods and up mountainsides in order to satisfy his desire for outlooks to paint. He was now seventy-three years old, and had worked hard all his life, and nature began to rebel. He felt that he needed a long rest and his family felt the same. The question was how to gently bring about the change to other surroundings. Fortunately the old family property at Jefferson Village, New Jersey, still belonged to him. The house had been burned to the ground, but they rebuilt it, and took pains to provide an even larger studio than he had ever had before. Here he took up his dwelling for the rest of his days, and it was not long before he could be found at his easel working with the same zest and enthusiasm that he had always experienced when his brush was in his hand with a canvas before him.

His son-in-law, Mr. George Woodman, built a house for himself close by so as to be near him and to enable him to see his daughter and grandchildren every day. His other children lived in the house with him, and relieved him of all household cares, thus giving him time to work without interruption, if he so wished.

He painted some of his most beautiful pictures during these quiet and undisturbed days. He was not only physically at rest but the serenity of his soul shone in his face, like the quiet waters of Lake George of which he had begun a landscape while in his former home, and which he now finished in his new studio. This picture is still in the possession of his family, by all accounts, and is the last picture of any size that he had strength enough to paint.

He painted a slightly smaller one sometime later called "Sunset on the Chocorua" which was purchased by Mr. J. B. Todd of Hoboken.

His very last picture he painted in 1879. It was called "Souvenir of the Adirondacks."

"As he made the last touches to this picture, with a hand enfeebled by the weight of eighty-three years, he laid down his palette and brushes forever, saying that his hand would no longer do what he wanted it to do."

But he was not disturbed by that fact. He accepted his limitations with calm equanimity, evidently feeling that he had done his best with the talents that had been given him, and so was willing to rest on his labors.

His friends and family had dreaded the time when he could no longer paint. They did not know what the effect would be on him, but they need not have feared. He took great pleasure in rambling through the woods and a little way up the mountain, communing with Nature, and experiencing the same thrill, and drawing from her the same inspiration he had felt when he was a boy.

His friends watched him with ever increasing admiration. They discussed together what they might do that would please him most by way of tribute. Already a proof of the devotion of his friends had taken shape in a service of plate for his daily use, but this time they wanted to make the tribute more personal.

A noted artist friend of his, Jervis McEntee, suggested a "surprise party," to be given in his honor in the woods of Maplewood, near-by, the guests being asked to bring food for the occasion. A committee was appointed for the arrangements. The members of it were Jervis McEntee, the artist Huntington, and his young friends, Kensett and Hall, and the eighth of June was selected for the occasion.

But as it so often happens at such times, they awoke to find a rainy day. It was impossible to think of going into the woods, but the house was quite a large one, with a fine piazza adjoining it where they decided to spread a table and make the best of the conditions as only those following the artistic life can do.

Mr. William Cullen Bryant was chosen as toastmaster. He had been a friend of Durand's for more than forty years, and he opened the festive occasion by delivering a most graceful and feeling address.

Asher Durand stood up and answered it. His strong, manly face, framed by long iron-gray hair reaching to his shoulders, made a deep

impression on those who heard him. He unconsciously made a picture long to be remembered.

There were many noted artists there of one kind or another. Mr.
and Mrs. Eastman Johnson were there, also Mr. and Mrs. Thomas
Hicks, Worthington Whittredge, Mr. and Mrs. William Cullen
Bryant, of course, and many others, besides Mr. and Mrs. William
Page, he being an ardent devotee of Shakespeare. Casilaer would certainly have been present, and Rossiter also if they had not been
away at the time. The artist John F. Weir regretted that he was
unable to attend the picnic, and wrote to McEntee as follows:

> I think we do too little, and cannot do too much to show our respect
> for the pioneers of our pathways which have become highways. I could
> sympathize with nothing more heartily than with this, and hope that
> you will not count me absent in spirit when you are deep in the "cham-
> pagne libations." . . . You are sure to have a glorious time, and in honor-
> ing Durand all you "Landscape fellows" honor yourselves.

The lunch proceeded with the usual toasts, speeches, and a general hilarity such as only happens in an informal gathering where
friends are present.

Mr. Page, the Shakespearean devotee, unwittingly provided a
source of amusement which was unlooked for and which threatened
seriously to hamper the schedule made out for the occasion. No
sooner did a pause of only a moment take place than he would
jump to his feet and start reciting one of Shakespeare's sonnets
which had no bearing whatsoever on the festivities at hand, so that
finally at the very moment another sonnet showed signs of coming,
Thomas Hicks and John Kensett would pounce upon him, in order
to hold him down in his seat. This caused great laughter, and added
much to the merriment of the assembled guests. Then other guests
contributed stories and souvenirs of the past, and two ladies played
several pieces on the piano in the drawing room.

After this the sun came out, and the party strolled through the
woodland on the mountain, until towards evening when, according
to Durand's biographer, "the party whirled off to the railway station

behind four-horse teams, giving loud cheers on bidding adieu to the venerable subject of their ovation."

McEntee wrote later to a friend: "The picnic was a perfect success. . . . It was a most satisfactory day, and I shall always remember my gratification that the suggestion was so heartily responded to, and that we were able to show in so fitting a way our veneration for the old man."

Time passes, and ninety years have come to Asher B. Durand. His body was free from the "ailments all flesh is akin to." Day after day passed tranquilly and happily. His serenity never left him. His children and grandchildren surrounded him with every comfort he could wish for, and gently and quietly the end came.

"Those who loved him had the satisfaction of knowing that his life ended in an honored, happy, and beautiful old age." (*Life and Times of Asher Durand.*)

Remarks:

"Of those who accepted Durand's point of view, and painted American scenery as they found it, Kensett is the most prominent. He too tried to give nature exactly, without reference to the way it had been arranged by other artists. (Samuel Isham.)

"Why," Durand asks, "should not the American landscape painter, in accordance with the principles of self-government, wholly originate a high and independent style, based on his own resources?

"Go first to Nature to learn to paint landscapes; and when you have learned to imitate them, you may study the pictures of great artists with benefit." (Tuckerman.)

"Durand's life was divided in three well-defined periods; first, from 1812 to 1832 was devoted to engraving. Second, from 1833 to 1838 to portraiture. Third, 1839 onward, to landscapes." (*Early American Portrait Draughtsmen in Crayon.*)

CHAPTER 6

Charles Codman
(1800–1842)

C HARLES CODMAN was an artist who made his way single-handed, with no help from anyone. He was born in Portland, Maine, in 1800. He began as a sign painter and was very proficient as one, so much so that Simon Willard, the famous New England maker of clocks, engaged him to paint the faces of his clocks with small landscapes on glass. He showed much skill and taste in doing so, and was of great assistance, therefore, to the success of his employer. From this work he was engaged to paint in "oil tapestry" one of the hotels in Portland. The work attracted the attention of art lovers, especially of John Neal, an artist in his day, who encouraged him to try painting on a more elevated scale; and Codman, who had a real love of art, began trying his hand and skill at marine painting. From that he went on to landscapes, showing such rare merit and individuality that he received many orders from all parts of the country, finally gaining such popularity that no local collection was considered complete without one or more of his pictures. Some of his pictures are real gems, and he continued to paint and improve until his death in 1842.

This is all that is to be found on the life of Charles Codman, and that after much searching. He has been a sort of shadowy adherent of the Hudson River School of Painting — one of them, but one who left no record of his life behind him. It is interesting to note how impossible it is to throw anything that is good into the discard with a belief that it will never reappear. Over a hundred years have passed since Codman was painting landscapes, and suddenly his pictures are reappearing, and collectors are adding them to their collections. At last they are taking their places where they rightly belong, and through them it can be surmised the type of man he was — full of talent and a sensitive appreciation of nature, with the gift of revealing its moods.

The information given was discovered in the *Maine Library Bulletin,* July-October, 1927.

The librarian of the Maine Historical Society sent this information with the following note attached: "The above is the best sketch of Charles Codman that I can find, as there is very little written about him."

CHAPTER 7

Thomas Cole
(1801–1848)

W E WILL NOW TELL ABOUT Asher B. Durand's great friend, Thomas Cole. He was an Englishman by birth, born at Bolton-le-moor, Lancaster, one of eight children. The Reverend Louis L. Noble, his biographer as well as his pastor and intimate friend, sums up his character thus: "Training had made Cole at home with difficulties. Obstacle was his stepping stone, and embarrassment his element, but he had energies which lifted his foot surely, if not quickly, upon the one, and moved him certainly, if not rapidly through the meshes of the other. . . . His was a lofty spirit, and there was a luminous chamber in his soul."

Around that sentence can be written Cole's life. The following account will show how true it was.

He was born on February 1, 1801. Undoubtedly all would have gone well with the Cole family if it had not been for the father's failure as a woolen manufacturer, a work for which he was by nature unfitted. Apparently he was a most kindly man, well-meaning in every respect and possessed of much poetic feeling, but never able to secure a position that suited him, and a complete loss as far as providing for his family went.

That was the atmosphere in which young Thomas grew up, and it seemed as if the weight of the family hung upon his boyish shoulders. At a very early age he was taken into a print works as a designer of calico, and this because he had shown a gift for mixing colors. But his temperament was such that he shrank from the coarseness of his fellow workers, and in the midst of numbers he remained alone. Almost his only friend there was a Scotsman who had the old Scottish ballads at his tongue tip, and told story after story about "the wild hills and blue lakes of his native land."

Such an association was of just the kind to stir the talents hidden within him. He was naturally a poet, and in his leisure moments wrote some lines that expressed his developing love of everything beautiful. It was his joy to wander off to some solitary place where he could be alone, and take his flute along with him, and mingle music with his poetical dreams. Sometimes his sister Sarah went with him, and while she sang he would accompany her on the flute. In later years the hours passed that way remained bright spots in his memory.

While living in these realms of fancy he got hold of a book telling of the beauty of American scenery. It fired his imagination. He talked about what he had read, he dreamed about it, his mind was full of it, so much so that his father, whose temperament loved change, especially that tinged with romance, at once set his mind on going to that new country where he felt sure he could repair his shattered fortune. So without more ado he gathered together all his effects and set out with his family on his voyage of discovery to America. That was in the spring of 1819.

After much consultation he decided upon Philadelphia as a likely place to get started in some sort of business, and they arrived there on the third of July of that year.

The new experiment lasted through the following summer. Then father Cole thought he would like to move again. This time his mind was set on going to the distant and romantic regions west of the Alleghenies. His fancy conjured up an Eldorado, where prosperity dwelt, and where he could gather some of it to himself, and they reached Pittsburgh late in the fall. But this did not turn out to be just what he was looking for, so he picked up his goods and chattels and family again, and moved to Steubenville.

Young Thomas did not go with them then. He had started to work in a wood-carving concern and remained into the winter to earn what he could towards the family support. The May following he first returned to Philadelphia and left a few months later to join his father at Steubenville. It was in the solitude of this secluded place that the artist in the soul of Thomas Cole was born. It came about in a peculiar way. A portrait painter named Stein arrived one day in the village. There was that about the man which inspired the younger Cole. "His conversation, the expression of his face, the witchery of the colours of his palette, above all, a book that he lent him — an English work on painting, illustrated with engravings, and treating of design, composition and colour, wrought like magic on his mind." (Louis L. Noble.)

The book was read and reread with an ever growing enthusiasm. In his mind there sprang up visions of a future of which he had never dreamed. Then and there he made the decision to become a painter, and through the canvas explain to the world the beauty in which it abounded.

His ardent desire was to paint landscapes, but portraits were then desired even in an out-of-the-way village like Steubenville, and as money was woefully needed he began his career as an artist by painting portraits. His biographer wrote: "Landscape was resigned with regret, and portraiture painting, a department of art for which he had neither taste nor ambition, was taken up with reluctance."

He started by painting members of his family. The results were considered good by them and by the neighbors, which gave him courage, and in February, 1822, Cole left his home to become an itinerant portrait painter. "With a green baize bag slung over his shoulder, containing a scanty stock of wearing apparel, his flute, colours, brushes, and a heavy stone-mumuler, he left his father's house, on foot, in the clear clean morning."

His experiences were varied, and the hardships he endured were very great. Some kind souls allowed him to paint their portraits but were willing to pay only a pittance for them. Others mocked at him, knowing nothing about art and considering it no sort of profession for a healthy young man to lead. But he could not be turned from his purpose. He plodded on from one village to another and was beginning to make some headway when word came from his family that his father had decided to move again. Thomas was quite in despair. He had seen no signs of such a decision when he left home, and it came upon him like a blow. He felt it necessary to return to Steubenville as quickly as possible, not knowing what conditions he might find there. But not before he had painted a picture of a style much to his liking; it depicted a feudal scene, moonlight, beacon fires blazing on the distant hill, in the foreground men in armor. His biographer states that at the time of writing, the picture was still in existence — "its manipulation as free and bold as many of his later works, with indications throughout of great invention and fine imagination."

On his arrival at Steubenville, he found the entire family waiting for him. His father had decided to go to Pittsburgh. Thomas managed to pack them off with all their belongings, but remained behind in order to earn some money to pay their expenses. He wrote to a friend, Mr. William A. Adams, on February 8, 1823: "My parents are at Pittsburgh, where I intend to go shortly. They did intend going over the mountains, but found they could not from inability in a pecuniary way. They intend residing in Pittsburgh; I hope they will succeed better than they have done here. But we have so often been disappointed that we dare not flatter ourselves. The gay and bright prospects I once pictured to myself are all faded except some faint lingering of hope."

So Cole went to join his parents and to help his father, who had involved himself in the manufacturing of floor cloths, and there this young lover of art and all things beautiful, from sheer affection and a sense of filial duty, tried to smother his dreams and work on what seemed to him as uninteresting a job as could possibly be found.

But he could not manage to smother his dreams. The situation made him think more clearly. He decided not to move too quickly, but to study nature with a new intensity, and as far as he was able without neglecting the help he was giving his father, to produce and produce, until he got paintings that suited him, after which he felt that he must try going his own way, and trust to his art to furnish him with the necessary funds to disentangle him from a very discouraging situation. He could already see that the manufacture

of floor cloths was something that his father could never make a success of. When he broached his decision to his father, the latter immediately disapproved, and "urged some more substantial calling,"
forgetting that his own "callings" so far had been anything but substantial. His mother, however, saw with clearer eyes and realized that
her son was giving his life to them, instead of having the freedom
to start out on his own career, in which she believed. This gave him
the encouragement he needed, and he decided to go back to Philadelphia, where he felt sure opportunities would open out in his favor.

He started off in November, 1823, with a small trunk as luggage,
a purse which contained only six dollars, and a cloth table cover
"which his mother drew from the table and threw about his shoulders with her blessing and her parting tears, to take the place of an
overcoat."

It was a long journey to make, but it was finally accomplished. His
biographer gives the following account of his arrival:

He was "a youthful stranger in a humble quarter of a great city,
in a little upper room, without bed, fire or furniture, save a few
articles needful for a painter; alive with sensibility, friendliness and
nearly penniless, with a baker's roll and a pitcher of water for refreshment by day, and the table-cloth for a cover by night. It is no exag-
gerated picture of Cole at the edge of that wider field of action to
which he had come with so much enthusiasm"; but nothing daunted
he was unremittingly industrious. He painted picture after picture,
sketched from nature. He also worked in the Academy.

Fortunately, Cole had a certain sense of humor, and he found by
chance that a picture the subject of which was more or less humorous was the only one he could quickly sell. Scenes of "frolic and
drinking would sell in a bar-room, a barber's shop and the oyster-
house, when simple representations of nature could not find a purchaser." It can be imagined how this went against Cole's sensitive
nature, but it had to be done. His body needed food and clothing,
as did his family.

But while he could sell these, he did not neglect his landscapes.
At this time he also indulged in a ready talent for writing poetry,

for which he had no mean gift, and this and his beloved flute kept his mind steady and his will power strong. To help make the two ends meet he wrote a tale entitled "Emma Morton" which he sold to the Philadelphia *Saturday Evening Post*.

Three years later, in 1825, Cole left Philadelphia for New York. In the meantime, father Cole had decided to move again with his family, and had also chosen New York to settle in; and having arrived in the city first and taken a forlorn house on Greenwich Street, his son Thomas had his studio for the first two years there in a room so narrow that he could scarcely move around in it. But seemingly out of the nowhere good fortune appeared and smiled on him. It came about thus.

All this time, Cole had been painting, despite his other duties, and he was now in a position to show what he had done. His aims were so lofty that nothing that he had so far accomplished came up to the standard he had set for himself, yet now that he had the opportunity to visit other studios and see the work of other artists, he realized that his paintings depicting nature should be of some value.

With some trepidation, however, he took five pictures to the art shop of a friend of his, a Mr. Dixey, who put them in his store window. They were characteristically marked in the simplest possible way. One was labeled "Composition"; his second was named "Composition — A Storm"; another "A Tree"; the fifth, "A Battle Scene." These were the first pictures of his that were exhibited in New York, and he anxiously watched for results.

Mr. Robert C. Bruen, who had studied engraving under P. Maverick, and also had worked with Asher B. Durand, and was now an engraver on his own metal, saw the paintings and was much struck by them. He recognized that the artist had unusual talent, and he bought three of them for the lump sum of twenty-one dollars. Mr. Dixey, who owned the shop, bought the fourth, and the remaining picture was sold to someone whose name was not recorded.

Small as this sum was, it spoke volumes to young Thomas Cole. He felt it might be the opening wedge to more substantial results, and as he had a number of pictures to draw from, his heart was full of hope.

There came still more results of those sales. Mr. Bruen, who had become a well-to-do man from his business of engraving, was sufficiently impressed by Cole's talent to offer to send him for a much-needed rest to the Catskills, where he told him he would find nature in its perfection, and where he could paint to his heart's content without the worry of all the duties that confronted him at home. Needless to say, Cole accepted his aid with a heart full of gratitude and at once made preparations to go. His biographer writes: "From the moment when his eye first caught the rural beauties clustered round the cliffs and Weehawken, and glanced up the distance of the Palisades, Cole's heart had been wandering in the Highlands, and nestling in the bosom of the Catskills."

The impression all that scenery made on him drew him back there the following autumn. That country "charmed his eye and took his soul captive. Wherever he travelled in after years, whether among the lakes and hills of Engand, the Alban heights or the Alps, up the sides of the Apennines or of Aetna, along the seashore, down the Rhone or the Rhine, he always turned to the Hudson, and the summits that pierce its clouds, and darken its blue skies, with the strength and tenderness of a first love."

After this trip, when he returned to New York, he put three paintings on sale. The locality of the first one was not listed, but it was labeled "Lake with Dead Trees"; another was a "View of Fort Putnam"; the third was "The Falls of the Catskills."

Now it so happened that Colonel Trumbull, himself a well-known artist, saw those paintings. He at once bought "The Falls of the Catskills," and hanging it up in his own studio, notified Durand of his discovery, asking him to come round to see it. Not only that, he invited him to meet the artist, who was to be at his studio at a certain hour. Always anxious to meet any young artists who often turned up, and might prove worthy of notice, Durand came as requested. Cole's biographer describes the visit:

> At the hour appointed, Cole came — a young man in appearance, not more than one and twenty, of slight form and medium height, soft brown hair, a face very pale (from agitation, no doubt), a fine forehead, and large blue eyes.

For the first few minutes a painful timidity indicated by quick nervous movements restricted all conversation on his part . . . but this subsided on account of a remark made by Col. Trumbull, who turned to him and said, "You surprise me at your age to paint like this. You have already done what I, with all my years and experience, am yet unable to do." Needless to say that Cole was overcome with joy at this praise, especially as it was followed up by the two remaining paintings being sold to Durand and Dunlap for the sum of twenty-five dollars apiece.

The news of this soon reached the art circles of New York, and suddenly Cole found himself in the limelight of that great city, with a fixed reputation as being among the young men "of whom our country had reason to be proud." (William Cullen Bryant's "Funeral Oration.")

In speaking of this dramatic discovery, Durand said to a friend many years afterwards, "His fame spread like fire."

All the landscapes which Cole had painted during his vacation in the Catskills, and those he had painted before now, had a ready sale. The more he placed before the public the faster his reputation as an artist of unusual merit grew. In a comparatively short time he became a member of the newly formed National Academy of Design; in fact, he was one of the founders of it. He described the Association as one made up of high-minded men, "distinguished as artists, and bound together by congenial feelings."

Another autumn comes and again he seeks the "joyous freedom of the romantic Catskills."

His biographer is again quoted, as through him Cole's character can best be exemplified. He says:

It is quite impossible to convey a true impression of that blissful feeling with which Cole both anticipated and enjoyed a season of retirement in the regions of the picturesque. Long companionship and sympathy with him could alone make the discovery. Religious fellowship with nature ever fills with an uncommunicable happiness, more especially the bosom of a true poet — and Cole walked with her as such, even while he looked and laboured as an artist. . . . It was an axiom with him, "To walk with nature as a poet is the necessary condition of a perfect artist."

In the quiet of the mountains he wrote in his journal the different impressions he received through the varied actions of nature. A quotation from one account of a storm describes the scene so perfectly that we place it here to show how he could paint in words as well as with the brush.

He describes the violence of the storm, the trees bent to earth, the wind howling, the mountains shrouded in unnatural darkness, the thunder, the flashes of lightning. It was at an hour when he knew the sun would soon be setting, and he hoped the storm had reached its peak when — "all at once a blast, with the voice and temper of a hurricane, swept up through the gulf, and lifted with magical swiftness the whole mass of clouds into the air. This was the signal for general dispersion. A flood of light burst in from the west, and jewelled the whole broad bosom of the mountain. The birds began to sing, and I saw in a neighboring dell the blue smoke curling up quietly from a cottage chimney. . . . "

It was here among the Catskills, when the first rush of joy over the beauty he found in nature swept over him, that a new element entered into his being, and into his deep appreciation of the wonders he saw with his physical eyes. There was something revealed to him more profound than what he saw. A consciousness of something beyond all that told him that to become the kind of artist he aspired to be, his paintings must reveal not only the beauty of scenery, but must convey to those able to sense it, an inner meaning and interpretation of the life of man on earth, as well as of the glories of the parable hidden behind all the physical structure of the universe, earth and its mountain peaks tinged by sunshine and shadow. His biographer says in regard to this: "Does not the theory find an exact correspondence in the fact that his pictures, for a season, were simple reproductions of the scenery with which he was captivated, and then began to speak a language strong, moral, and imaginative?"

From now on this thought possessed him.

It is evident that at this time Cole went through deep waters of thought. His paintings of the glories of our American scenery were receiving great praise from the critics, they were selling well, they would continue to sell well — he knew that. He knew also that landscapes painted with accuracy and true atmosphere by an artist who is an enthusiast in his love of nature was what his public wanted. Beyond that they would never be able to follow him, and if he kept to that, he would not have to worry about the wherewithal to live. Praise was pleasant to him as it is to everyone. He shrank from losing it. It was a difficult situation; Thomas Cole was going through the travail of the soul. Yet, "fond as he was of praise, he felt it was a smaller thing to sacrifice than the nobler vocation to which he aspired. Much as he really needed money, more for others who were dear to him and dependent than for himself, he could not dare to turn back from the ascending and original path upon which his vision had fastened, and content himself to walk in a lower and easier one, leading quickly to golden success.

"He pondered well on his setting out, and advanced boldly alone."

So Cole started on his experimental career. Among his pictures exhibited at the National Gallery in the spring of 1828 appeared the "Garden of Eden" and the "Expulsion."

Even the most ardent of his admirers feared that he was mistaken in swerving from what they thought was his only proper path, but now seeing that these two paintings had their admirers in spite of protests from others, they held their peace. And these others were those of the public who were startled by this innovation in opposition to the popular taste or conventionalism it was used to. It resented the audacity of an artist who had the daring to think for himself, and to paint according to his own views, which demanded too complex thinking on its part to please it. One result was that he found himself involved in lengthy correspondence that took up a great deal of his time.

> Thomas Cole to Mr. X —
> My dear Sir,
>   In your last letter you kindly intimated that a line from me would be acceptable.
>   The Exhibition of the Academy of Design is now open. It is perhaps the most numerous collection of the works of American artists that has been exhibited. Most of the pictures have been painted within the last

year — and amongst them are many of merit. Morse, Inman, Ingham, exhibit good pictures. Fisher and Doughty have several which are agreeable. I exhibit a number. Amongst them are two attempts at a higher style of landscape than I have hitherto tried. The subject of one picture is "The Garden of Eden." In this I have endeavored to conceive a happy spot wherein all the beautiful objects of nature were concentred. The subject of the other is "The Expulsion from the Garden." Here I have introduced the more terrible objects of nature, and have endeavored to heighten the effect by giving a glimpse of the Garden of Eden in its tranquillity. I wish you to consider that I have been speaking of what *I wished* to accomplish, rather than what *I have done*; for I may have failed in these efforts. . . . My going to Europe this fall depends in some measure on the sale of these two pictures. The price I ask for them is a high one. . . . In your last letter you made me a kind offer of assistance in case I should go to Europe. I hope I shall not find it necessary to tax your generosity. If the pictures now exhibiting sell, I shall be enabled, with economy, to study in Europe a year, or eighteen months.

I remain yours respectfully

Thomas Cole

It was on the first of June, 1829, that Cole set sail for England. In his journals at that time he gave some of his experiences:

To Sir Thomas Lawrence [he writes] I was introduced by a letter from Mr. Gilmore, of Baltimore. He treated me in a very friendly manner, was pleased with my pictures, and sent his carriage for me to come and breakfast with him. We breakfasted at eight, in a spacious apartment filled with works of art. We conversed on the Fine Arts of America. A short time after, I met him at the British Gallery, and he invited me to go with him to Sir Robert Peel's in a few days to see his collection. But death, whose hand was already upon him, deprived me of that pleasure. I lost a valuable acquaintance, and the world a distinguished man.

All Cole's experiences were interesting and new, but for some reason he did not feel easy in England. The climate depressed him, for one thing, and things were different from what he expected. He wrote from London to Mr. Thomas S. Cummings on October 19, 1830: "I must now desire you to remember me to Inman, Ingham,

Morton, Dunlap, Durand, Weir, and others, for whom you know I have a friendship, and tell them that to be with them, I, Thomas Cole, pant like the hart after water-brooks."

After this Cole visited the Continent and his journal gives an account of his impressions. It would be impossible to enter them all in this short article. Some of his impressions, however, are amusing, and here is one of them written about Genoa, in a letter to his parents:

> The approach to Genoa by sea is magnificent. It looks indeed like, as it has been called, a city of palaces. . . . I had always understood that Italy was the land of music; I did not however, imagine that I should be roused, at four o'clock in the morning, by a chorus of fifty asses, as I was, thanks to the market people.
>
> After breakfast I went to church, built after the model of St. Peter's, Rome. Some of the palaces of Genoa are superb, built in great measure of white marble. . . . Last night I went to the theatre, a grand and capacious building of white marble, larger, I think, than any theatre in London.
>
> The piece performing purported to be a tragedy — to me the strangest of all tragedies is a *sort* of opera. There they were, actors and actresses, singing and squalling at each other, through marvellously exciting scenes of the most burning love, most furious rage, the deepest despair, and here in the box was I, like a Goth, laughing when I should have wept. The most awful scene was one in which a tall fellow with a pigtail (in reality a courtier with a powdered queue, we take it) pinched the fingers of a little fat man in his snuff-box, upon offering him snuff. A fearful revenge truly for some tremendous wrong! In fact the tragedy was so deep and harrowing in its nature that it was necessary to resort to some pleasant expedient to prevent the house from becoming terribly affected. The expedient was a pantomime between acts, of sufficient length to allow the feelings and interests to cool. After all there was some tolerable singing, but as the audience kept up a continual talking all the while, as is usually the case in an Italian theatre, I could only catch a strain now and then.

But in spite of these humorous accounts that sometimes Cole delighted in as though to relieve some sense of strain in his system, he

took in all the beauty his eyes rested on at every turn. From Genoa
he went to Leghorn and then on to Florence, and wrote to his
parents:

> I have taken rooms in a house in which Mr. Greenough (the sculptor)
> had apartments. . . . My painting room is delightfully situated. From
> my window I have a fine view of Fiesole — a hill that Milton mentions
> in his "Paradise Lost." My bedroom is neat; and over my bed is a small
> picture covered with an embroidered curtain. It is "The true image of
> the Madonna of Comfort." . . .
>
> You cannot think how much I wish to be with you again — but I must
> go through this ordeal in order that I may have no further necessity of
> travelling. . . .
>
> I remain in good health and spirits
>
> Your affectionate son
Thomas Cole

All this time Cole was painting with a view to future pictures. His
sketches are carefully and accurately executed, and his portfolio was
filled with them. Everywhere he saw subjects for his symbolical
paintings, the thought of which absorbed him. In speaking of the
town of Volterra and the steep cliffs that form a part of the mountain with its wild and deep ravines: "What a study for a picture of
Elijah in the desert!" he exclaims in his journal. But there was so
much to see and to feel and delight in in spite of this, that he con-
fided this to his journal:

> Aug. 24th, 1831
>
> I am afraid that the days of romantic feeling are passing away. Con-
> verse with the world is daily deadening that sense of the beautiful in
> nature which has been through all my early life such a source of delight.
> Intercourse with men, I conceive, has induced this apathy, and yet I
> cannot see how it should have so benumbing an effect upon the soul. I
> have now been in Italy three months, and really how little I have felt.
> Italy! — where all beside me wrought to transport! I am grieved; still I
> hope to feel again; the dull cloud surely will pass over.

On the third of February, 1832, Cole left Florence for Rome,
where he first took rooms in the Via del Tritone, but soon changed

"for better lodgings on the Pincian Hill, and painted in an apartment which tradition has consecrated as the studio of Claude." (*Biography*.)

Here is an account of his everyday schedule:

> With the exception of short intervals given to reading, to the sunrise, to breakfast, always slight and simple — to watching from his windows the varying effect of the day upon the wonderful landscape — he painted till dinner, usually late, with an industry quite surprising to the easy Italians. "Ah, Madam," said a quiet old Roman with whom he took lodgings, while in conversation with an American lady about him, "he works like a crazy man."

In his dress he was perfectly neat, but plain, and without the least appearance of singularity. In nothing did he affect the artist and the genius. He was in Rome what he was at home — simply Cole.

In society, which he frequented but little, he was cheerful, though quiet and retiring, with an air of gravity, except when stirred by wit and humor, or overcome by the ridiculous, for which he had the keenest sense; then he resigned himself, for a moment, to the heartiest laughter.

Even in the clouded moments which attack every true artist at times, he never indulged in liquor of any kind in order to lift the cloud. He preferred to fight it out with himself. In fact, neither food nor drink made any great appeal to him. He lived sparingly, counting upon keeping the clear perception and lofty serenity of mind which he had gained in his wanderings among the Catskills, where his heart was.

It was here that Cole made one of his greatest pictures — he says of it in a letter to Mr. Gilmore when he had left Rome, and returned to Florence: "I am now engaged in a picture that is a view of the Campagna of Rome — broken aqueducts, etc. But I long for the wild mountains of the West."

The following October, 1832, Cole turned his face homeward, arriving in New York on November 25. He found rooms for painting, suitable for exhibiting his pictures as well, on the corner of Wall Street and Broadway.

It was here that one of the greatest incidents of his life occurred to promote his success. One day a gentleman well on in years appeared at his studio. He took rather a hasty view of the paintings, standing before each one in turn, but it was easy to see that he grasped the worth his eyes saw in them at a glance. To Cole's disappointment he turned and left the studio without saying a word. It was the great art collector, Luman Reed, known all over the country as a benefactor of the Arts, and a philanthropist. That he should have left the studio without comment was a severe blow to Cole's pride, but in the course of the winter he had a letter from him commissioning him to a large Italian landscape for a private gallery that he was thinking of building for himself.

This was the great turning point in Thomas Cole's life. He had longed for just such an opportunity, but never dared to think it possible that it could come true in any such way as this. He took advantage of it, and later, in answer to one of Mr. Reed's letters, he put forth his persistent idea.

My dear Sir: —

The desire you expressed that I should paint pictures to fill one of your rooms has given me much pleasure, and I have made some rough drawings (which I send you) of the arrangements that appear to me most, and in accordance with the subjects I would wish to paint. . . . I mentioned to you a favorite subject that I had been cherishing for several years with the faint hope that some day or other I might be able to embody it. . . .

In the drawings you will perceive that I have taken one side of the room for this subject.

A series of pictures might be painted that should illustrate the history of a natural scene, as well as an epitome of Man, showing the natural changes of landscape, and those effected by Man in his progress from barbarism to civilization — to luxury, to the vicious state or state of destruction, and to the state of ruin and desolation.

The philosophy of my subject is drawn from the history of the past, wherein we see how nations have risen from the savage state to that of power and glory, and then fallen, and become extinct. Natural scenery has also its changes — the hours of the day and seasons of the year, sunshine and storm. These justly applied will give expression to each picture of the series I would paint.

It will be well to have the same location in each picture. This location may be identified by the introduction of some striking object in each scene — a mountain of peculiar form, for instance.

He goes on to say that there must be the site of a seaport . . . a sea, a bay, rocks, waterfalls and woods.

Now, this description should be interesting to collectors, for it comes from Cole's own letter to Mr. Reed, and therefore discredits the various erroneous statements one comes across from many well-meaning persons who have not studied the question. Cole goes on to say:

The first picture, representing the savage state, must be of a wilderness — the sun rising from the sea, and the clouds of night retiring over the mountains. The figures must be savage, clothed in skins and occupied in the chase, and a spirit of motion pervading the scene, as though nature were just springing from chaos.

The second picture must be the pastoral state — the day further advanced — light clouds playing about the mountains — the land partly cultivated — a rude village near the bay — small vessels in the harbour — groups of peasants either pursuing their labours in the fields — watching their flocks, or engaged in some simple amusement.

The third must be a noonday — a great city girding the bay, gorgeous piles of architecture, bridges, aqueducts, temples, the port crowded with vessels, splendid processions, etc., all that can be combined to show the fulness of prosperity.

The fourth should be a tempest — a battle, and the burning of a city, towers falling, vessels wrecking the harbour. This is the scene of destruction, or the vicious state.

The fifth picture must be a sunset, the mountains riven, the city a desolate ruin, columns isolated amid the encroaching waters, ruined temples, broken bridges, fountains, sarcophagi, etc. — no human figure, a solitary bird perhaps: a calm and silent effect. This picture must be as a funeral knell of departed greatness, and may be called the state of Desolation. . . .

These five pictures, with three smaller ones above and two by the fireplace, will occupy all that side of the room. The three high pictures will be something in character with those over which they hang. . . .

To fill the other side of the room and the ends will require eighteen

or twenty pictures, five of which will be larger than the Italian Scene. . . .
For the completion of all these pictures I cannot reckon upon less than
two years' labour, and they may require more time. At all events, nothing should prevent me from using every means and exertion to make
the work satisfactory to you, and creditable to myself.

Cole then goes on to mention the price involved in this tremendous task:

For the ten pictures occupying the side with the fireplace I must ask
$2500. For the other side and the ends, five of which will be large pic-
tures, I cannot ask less, making $5000 for the completion of the whole
room. . . .

I am yours truly,

Thomas Cole

Mr. Reed caught Cole's enthusiasm. He not only ordered the pictures but doubled the price.

Consequently Cole repaired to the Catskills, where he ever found
inspiration, and it was here near Schroon Lake that he found "the
striking object in each scene — a mountain of peculiar form" which
he mentioned in his description he visioned in his letter to Mr. Reed.
An entry in his journal of October 7, 1835, states (after wandering
about Schroon Lake) : "In the distance mountains of remarkable
beauty bound the vision. Two summits in particular attracted my
attention: one of a serrated outline, and the other like a lofty pyra-
mid. At the time I saw them, they stood in the midst of the wilderness like peaks of sapphire." These are the two mountains that are
striking objects in "The Course of Empire," "The Voyage of Life,"
and "The Vision of Arcadia."

It was strange how vital the influence of Italy was upon these Hudson River artists. In composing this great series for Luman Reed,
Cole wished for one stirring impetus of Italy in composing the
details. He wished he was back again just for that. He had written
a letter to his artist friend Francis Alexander, with whom he had
often been during his visit to Rome. He made this remark:

Do you know I have been thinking of Italy of late? I do not know what has come over me; I feel as if I should go there again . . . you will think I am no wiser than when I used to put on the kettle for tea in never-to-be-forgotten Via del Tritone. Those were queer times. . . .

I hope you will go and see my big picture of the Angels ["The Angels Appearing to the Shepherds"], but will be indulgent. I painted it in about two months — I could not afford more.

During this period of painting the series of pictures for Luman Reed, he wrote in his journal:

I have had some little difficulty in finding at once a comprehensive and appropriate title for the Series of pictures I am now painting for Luman Reed. The one which I have at last adopted, although some may consider it lofty and ostentatious, appears very well to me. I call it "The Course of Empire."

To show the versatility of Cole, during these months of planning in detail his series of paintings for Mr. Luman Reed, he found time to write a dramatic poem called "The Spirits of the Wilderness," which two years later was rewritten, and prepared in a measure for publication, so claims his biographer. The scene of the poem is in the White Mountains.

It is a curious fact that even in the intimacy of his journal there is no mention of his having fallen in love. It is stated that a friend from a distant city turned up at his studio about this time, and his curiosity was stirred when he saw on the table there a beautiful bouquet of roses and other flowers which had just been delivered there, and which he recognized as the same bunch he had seen "in the hands of a beautiful lady as he came in by the shrubbery."

As Cole had never before shown signs of seeking a lady's hand in marriage, the friend felt he had discovered something exceedingly interesting, and when he returned to the hotel he was stopping at, he told one of his companions "that he had seen the lady that Cole would marry." He was right, and his predictions came true. The wedding took place in November in the year 1836, and at Cole's request the ceremony was performed up in the Catskills, the region he loved best of all, and where he built a home for himself and his beautiful wife.

But much happened before then which should be recorded. Cole was an artist first and last even if he had fallen in love like any other man, and the painting of "The Course of Empire" was just as absorbing in his life as it had been before he met his fate. On March 26, 1836, he wrote to Mr. Luman Reed:

> Formerly my love of approbation rendered me very sensitive to Newspaper praise . . . my love of approbation still exists, perhaps as strongly as ever; but the sources from which it is fed are changed. . . . I have ceased to labour to please the multitude of critics. . . . My stimulus to exertion is now the approbation of the few, in whose taste and judgment I have confidence, and the desire to obtain a lasting reputation. . . . Will you excuse me if I say I am afraid that you will be disappointed in the reception and notice my pictures will receive from the public, let them be exhibited to ever so good advantage? . . . Very few will understand the scheme of them, or the philosophy there may be in them. I hope I am prepared for all this. My leading hope is that when they have passed through the ordeal I shall find your esteem for them and myself undiminished.

How little we can foretell what lies ahead of us! Though Cole's last letter showed rather a somber state of mind, he was filled with enthusiasm nevertheless at the way the series of "The Course of Empire" was progressing, and was looking forward with keen enjoyment to its first appearance before the public, when a letter came to him from Asher B. Durand, containing a piece of news which seemed like the landing of a bombshell in the midst of all his hopes. The letter told of Mr. Luman Reed's sudden illness, but evidently trying to guard against upsetting his friend Cole in the midst of his work, he intimated that he understood their benefactor was better.

Of course this came as a great blow to Thomas Cole. In his acknowledgment of Durand's letter he wrote:

> I need not say how your intelligence affects me, for you feel as I do. But as Mr. Reed was better when you wrote, I hope there is no danger, and that our kindest, best friend will soon be restored to health. Do write immediately, for you know how anxious I shall be to hear of Mr. R.'s recovery.

On June 7, 1836, Cole wrote to Durand again — it was evidently about the latter's first landscape:

> I am pleased that you have attacked a landscape, and have no doubt that you will succeed to the satisfaction of all except yourself. In the hope that this will find you in good health and spirits, and that our friend is recovering rapidly, and that you have not forgotten you are to come here again shortly to gather up the flesh you dropped from your bones when last here, I remain, etc., etc.
>
> Thomas Cole

On that very same day the news reached Cole of Mr. Reed's death. On June 13 he wrote in his journal:

> On the 11th instant I returned from the city to which I had been called upon the melancholy occasion of the death of Mr. Reed, my best and kindest friend. He died on the morning of the seventh inst. after a sickness of five weeks. His mind was clear and calm to the last. In Mr. Reed I have lost a true, a generous, and noble friend. I could expatiate upon the grief. I feel at his departure, but words are poor things. I will simply say he was admired and beloved, and cannot be forgotten.

In spite of this shock and sorrow, Cole went bravely on with his "Course of Empire." His letter on the subject was very characteristic, written to Asher B. Durand. In it he says: "I have just about finished the picture (the last of the series). I did believe it was my best picture, but I took it down stairs and got rid of the notion." Cole was always that way.

Again in August, 1836, he wrote in his journal: "I have just returned from the city, where I have been with the series of pictures painted for Mr. Reed. When I took them I was fearful that they would disappoint the expectations of my friends. I have been greatly surprised, for they seem to give universal pleasure."

His biographer writes about this finishing of "The Course of Empire." He says, "We are now at the conclusion of Cole's first great work. It was completed in October, and shortly after exhibited by permission of the family of his lamented patron."

The group of these paintings, so novel in character, so elevated in purpose, so daring in conception for those times, made a great impression on those who understood their meaning. No less a critic than William Cullen Bryant said they "are among the most remarkable and characteristic of his works."

The noted novelist, James Fenimore Cooper, wrote this of them in a letter which Cole's biographer quotes:

> As an artist, I consider Cole one of the very first geniuses of the age. This has long been my opinion. "The Course of Empire" ought to make the reputation of any man. Cole improved vastly by his visit to Italy. This, however, was as an artist, rather than as a man of genius. The thought of the "Course of Empire" came from within. So far as my knowledge extends, he might have searched all the galleries of Europe for the conception in vain. The series is a great epic poem, in which the idea far surpasses the execution, though the last is generally fine. . . . I know of no painter whose works manifest such high poetic feeling of beauty as those of Cole.

Such was the nature of the impression his great serial made on those of especially high intellect.

It has been said that Cole's imagination was greatly fired by Bunyan's *Pilgrim's Progress,* and also by the works of Sir Walter Scott (*Art in America*), but there was a note in all his pictorial serials, something even more dramatic and new than these authors — that same something which about this time was seething in the mind of the great musical composer, Richard Wilhelm Wagner, when he was writing the script of *Tristan and Isolde, The Ring of the Nibelungen,* etc., the composition of which took twenty-five years, showing that this type of thought was generating in the minds of two men, far separated — belonging to different countries, working through different mediums, never having met, but belonging to the same race of imaginative thinkers.

After finishing the serial paintings of the "Course of Empire," and mourning over the death of his friend and patron, Mr. Luman Reed, and having seen the pictures he had ordered him to paint exhibited, and approved of by the public, Cole felt a great fatigue all through his body and mind, and, as was his wont, whenever exhaustion assailed him, he turned to his beloved Catskills for solace; and knowing that as yet his friend Durand had never seen the full grandeur of these picturesque mountains, he sought relief by prevailing on him to escort him there. Durand was in the full vigor of enthusiasm over having turned to landscape painting, and so it was arranged that Cole and Durand and their wives should have an outing away from the "milling crowds," and steep their souls among the solitudes of nature. On their return on July 8, 1837, Cole wrote in his journal that the scenery was entirely new to Durand and that he was happy in having been the means of introducing the rich and varied scenery of Schroon "to a true lover of nature."

It is interesting to find how at one these Hudson River artists were in sharing their findings of beautiful scenes that must surely fire the imagination, instead of keeping them secret for their own talents to draw on. In none of their lives can one find anything but a spirit of co-operation in their great determination to reveal to the public the beauties of our own country. It was the dominant idea that possessed them.

It was a little earlier than this visit to the Catskills that Cole received an order from William P. Van Rensselaer to paint a pair of pictures representing "Sunrise" and "Sunset." It is interesting to note, in Cole's answer to him, his description of the size he thought the pictures should be, for it shows the very decided tendency of the Hudson River artists to consider it well to produce works of an extreme size. He wrote:

"The size of the pictures you left in a measure to me; and I hope the canvas I have chosen will not be found too large, as I think the subjects require the size, which is about five feet long."

In Cole's serial paintings five feet seems to have been the usual size of his canvases. His individual paintings were executed on smaller ones.

Mr. Van Rensselaer was so pleased with the pictures "Sunrise" and "Sunset" that even before they were finished, he ordered two more pairs, Cole suggesting that he choose his own subjects, to which Mr. Van Rensselaer agreed. Whereupon Cole wrote to him of a subject that had been haunting him for some time. The subjects were supposed to belong to the thirteenth or fourteenth centuries, and he called them "The Departure" and "The Return." His description is so full of tragic imagination and the prevailing poetry of the times, that it is worth reading.

The first picture [he writes] depicts Morning, and I call it "The Departure." A dark and lofty castle stands on an eminence, embosomed in woods. The distance beyond is composed of cloud-capped mountains and cultivated lands, sloping down to the sea.

In the foreground is a sculptured Madonna, by which passes a road, winding beneath ancient trees, and crossing a stream by a Gothic bridge conducting to the gate of the castle.

From this gate has issued a troop of knights and soldiers in glittering armour; they are dashing down across the bridge and beneath the lofty trees in the foreground; and the principal figure, who may be considered the Lord of the Castle, reins in his charger, and turns with a look of pride and exultation at the castle of his fathers and his gallant retinue. He waves his sword as though saluting some fair lady, who from the battlement or window watches her lord's departure to the wars. The time is supposed to be early summer.

The second picture — "The Return" — is in early autumn. The spectator has his back to the castle. The sun is low; its yellow beams the pinnacles of an abbey standing in a shadowy wood. The Madonna stands a short distance from the foreground, and identifies the scene.

Near it, moving towards the castle, is a mournful procession — the lord is borne on a litter, dead or dying; his charger led behind, a single knight, and one or two attendants — all that war has spared of the once goodly company.

You will be inclined to think, perhaps, that this is a melancholy subject; but I hope that it will not, in consequence of that, be incapable of affording pleasure.

I will not trouble you with more than this hasty sketch of my labours. I have endeavored to tell the story in the richest and most picturesque manner that I could. And should there be no story understood, I trust that there will be sufficient truth and beauty found in the pictures to interest and please. . . .

Mr. Van Rensselaer evidently took to the idea of these pictures, for Cole completed them. And these show the change of thought between modern times and those of a hundred or more years ago. Today the thought that inspired them would undoubtedly be thought morbid, but not so in those days. It was an age of romance, when the lord of the castle, waving his sword to a beautiful lady on the terrace who responded with her lily-white hand, was considered the height of marital devotion, and his dead body returning was what balanced the picture in thought and deed.

It is a noticeable fact that Cole always balanced his pictures. Contrasts to him were one of the inevitable sequences of life. His titles alone show this. "Sunrise" and "Sunset" — "The Departure" and "The Return" — "The Course of Empire" with its start of beauty and sunshine amid savage customs and surroundings — the rural industry of the world — the peak of power and grandeur — the fall of nations, and the destruction of all that they strove for and fought for, was a longer theme, but the same thought is there. The love of these symbolical stories and paintings was very appealing to the public, and it ran for a considerable length of time.

It was some years afterwards that Tennyson was writing "Le Mort d'Arthur," which deals with practically the same theme as Cole's pictures of "The Departure" and "The Return."

To show how deeply the most intelligent people felt about portraying the balances of life both in poetry and art, William Cullen Bryant wrote of these particular paintings of Cole's: "There could not be a finer choice of circumstances, nor a more exquisite treatment of them than found in these pictures." And Buckingham, speaking of Cole and his works at some length in his writings on America, says of these paintings: "For beauty of composition, harmony of parts, accuracy of drawing, and power of effect, I have never seen any modern pictures that surpassed them." These were the opinions of the times in which Cole lived, that bespoke the trend in literature and art.

But there was one picture that Cole considered at length, which critics have placed among his serial paintings in spite of its having no resulting climax — his "Dream af Arcadia" which some have erroneously thought to be the second picture of "The Course of Empire," painted for Luman Reed. Cole had for some time dreamed of what an Arcadia would be like, and this picture stood by itself. It was his concrete ideal of a world at peace, where a sense of safety and joy abounded, where the happy inhabitants followed their own particular paths of enjoyment and industry without opposition — the children could gather water lilies in the pool — the youths and maidens could ride their horses without being molested (they can be seen crossing over the stone bridge) — the matrons could take their children out of the hot sun and watch them frolic under the shadows of ancient trees — damsels and swains could dance Greek dances and gain a thrill by so doing. In fact, it was the simple life amid the beauties of unspoiled nature which Cole wished evidently to depict. And it must be remembered that those days were the days of brigands, who wandered about the country robbing and stealing and terrifying the natives. Mothers feared to allow their daughters any freedom on lonely country roads — young men carried arms concealed about their persons, and were expected to do so. But not so in his dream. All fear had been removed, and all was beautiful and serene.

It will be noticed that the setting of the picture was in many respects the same as that of his serial pictures, and that may have led to misunderstandings. The two mountain peaks are the same. As you remember, he found these among the Catskills — the contour of the land is much the same. All his pictures of this type are like pictures in a dream. He did not hesitate to make them ideal, for his desire was to kindle in others the understanding of the truth underlying the painting, through beauty of the highest order, and he veiled this by giving the surroundings a Grecian atmosphere — a temple in which learning could be found, and in order to make the picture speak, there would be ruins in the distance, showing that all these things have been learned by the experiences of the past.

It is only in this way that one can read and understand the paintings of Thomas Cole, and the public at that time was deeply impressed, and enjoyed them.

It was in March, 1839, that a very important commission was given Cole by the then well-known and famous New York collector, Mr. Samuel Ward. He writes of it thus in his journal:

> I have received a noble commission from Mr. Samuel Ward to paint a series of pictures, the plan of which I conceived several years since, entitled "The Voyage of Life."
>
> I sincerely hope that I shall be able to execute the work in a manner worthy of Mr. Ward's liberality, and honorable to myself.
>
> The subject is an allegorical one, but perfectly intelligent, and capable of making a strong moral and religious impression.

During the following summer he went to the Genesee River to fill himself and his mind with beautiful and picturesque scenery, pending his work on the paintings which Mr. Ward had ordered of him. In writing to the latter he said:

> It has been difficult for me to overcome my impatience to commence the pictures before I had studied them with that care which I know to be necessary to ensure the production of a work of high excellence.
>
> The poetical conception of a subject may not be difficult, for it is spontaneous; but to imagine that which is to be embodied in light, and shadow and color — that which is strictly pictorial — is an accumulative work of the mind. . . . I have made some progress on the first picture, which is six feet six inches long.
>
> I am yours very respectfully
Thomas Cole

That very autumn the startling news came to Cole that Mr. Ward was dead! He wrote this in his journal: "Mr. Ward, who gave me the liberal commission for the 'Voyage of Life,' is dead. There would seem to be almost a fatality in these commissions. Mr. Reed died without seeing his series completed. Mr. Ward died soon after his was commenced."

Just as the year was ending he wrote this verse:

> Why do ye count your little months, your years,
> Or e'en your ages? They are naught; they are
> The measure of your feeble breath, your fears.

Ye are as misers, hoarding up with care
A glittering mass — a cold insensate dust
That ne'er to spirit can be changed; nor gold
Nor years are chattels of the soul; they rust
Or perish. Her possession is the trust
In God; the love which tongue hath never told;
And immortality which death shall soon unfold.

His biographer states:

Late in the autumn of 1840, Cole gave his second great series to the
public, and named it as was arranged: "The Voyage of Life." It depicts
Childhood.

From out of a cave glides a boat, whose prow and sides are sculptured
into figures of the Hours. Steered by an Angelic Form, it bears a laughing infant — the Voyager. On either hand the banks of the stream are
clothed in luxuriant herbage and flowers. The rising sun bathes the
mountains with rosy light.

The dark cavern is emblematic of our earthly origin, and the mysterious Past. The Boat, composed of figures of the Hours, images the
thought that we are borne on the hours down the Stream of Life. The
close banks, and the limited scope of the scene indicate the narrow experience of Childhood. The Egyptian Lotus in the foreground of the
picture is symbolical of human life.

The next of the series is Youth:

The infant of the former scene is become a Youth, on the verge of
Manhood. He is now alone in the Boat, and takes the helm himself . . .
and with eager expectation gazes up at a cloudy pile of architecture, an
air-built castle that rises dome upon dome in the far-off blue sky. The
Guardian Spirit stands on the bank of the stream, and with serious yet
benignant countenance seems to be bidding the impetuous Voyager Godspeed. . . . The gorgeous cloud-built palace, whose glorious domes seem
yet but half revealed to the eye, is emblematic of the day-dreams of
youth, its aspirations after glory and fame; and the dimly seen path on
the banks would intimate that Youth, in its impetuous career, is forgetful
that it is embarked on the Stream of Life, and that its current sweeps
along with resistless force, and increases its swiftness as it descends towards
the great ocean of Eternity.

Then comes Manhood.

> The Boat is there plunging amid the turbulent waves. The Voyager is now a man of middle age; the helm of the boat is gone, and he looks imploringly towards heaven; . . . The Guardian Spirit is watching with solicitude the affrighted Voyager. . . . Trouble is the characteristic of the period of Manhood. It is only when experience has taught us the realities of the world that we lift from our eyes the golden veil of early life. The Ocean which is dimly seen figures the end of life, which the Voyager is now approaching. The upward and imploring look of the Voyager shows his dependence on a superior Power — Old Age.

> A few barren rocks are seen through the gloom, the last shores of the world . . . The Boat, shattered by storms, its figures of the Hours broken and drooping, is seen gliding over the deep waters. The Stream of Life has now reached the Ocean to which all life is tending. The world to Old Age is destitute of interest . . . already the mind has glimpses of Immortal Life. The angelic figure, whose presence until now the Voyager has been unconscious of, is revealed to him . . . and shows to his wondering gaze scenes such as the eye of mortal has never beheld. (Cole's biographer.)

Now, the accounts and interpretation of the series of these pictures on which Cole made his great reputation are given here in part, because it seems they have been little understood, and no one can fairly judge of their worth unless he knows the inner meaning threaded in with the paint put on by a master's hand, and the vision of a thinker's mind.

One of their great values, apart from their artistic merit, is that they reveal to the generations coming after them the type of thought prevalent in those times. Those were the days of transcendentalism. Those were the days when vast numbers of the peoples of the world pondered over subjects like those that inspired the majestic paintings of Thomas Cole. That men like Luman Reed and Samuel Ward gave such large commissions to him, both of them being notable art collectors in New York, proves the estimate in which they were held.

Cole's biographer writes:

> It was Cole's aim, as we know, to give in all these serial landscapes that spiritual meaning which he himself drew from nature. How well he suc-

ceeded in this painting of "The Voyage of Life" an incident may serve
to illustrate:

Mr. Smillie, the distinguished engraver of the second of the series, going
early one morning into the exhibition room, found there a single person
only, a middle-aged man, seemingly lost in deep thought before these
pictures of Cole's. "Sir," he said at length, addressing the artist who had
been noticing his face, a striking one with a peculiarly melancholy air,
"I am a stranger in this city, and in great trouble of mind. But the sight
of these pictures has done me good. They have given me comfort. I go
away from this place quieted, and much strengthened to do my duty."

Bryant, in his funeral oration over the death of Cole, which was
some years later, calls the "Voyage of Life" "of simpler and less
elaborate design than the 'Course of Empire,' but more purely
imaginative. The conception of the series is a perfect poem, and
one of the most popular of Cole's compositions."

But of course any pictures painted outside the ordinary channels
are bound to have detractors, and Cole suffered from these more
than he should have. He was intensely sensitive to criticism. When
it was pointed against anything into which he had put his heart he
wilted under it. He had so many admirers that he should have ignored the others, but he seemed unable to throw off the effects of
adverse opinion, and while painting these pictures in a semi-exalted
state, and hoping that everyone would understand what they meant
and what he was aiming for, he found some to whom they seemed a
closed book — they were not able to take in his point of view, and the
result was disastrous to his health. Therefore, realizing that a change
of scene would probably restore it, he decided to visit Europe again,
and Rome in particular.

He wrote to his wife on November 9, 1841: "Rome . . . here I am
in the city of the soul."

It was while he was here that he had to make an important decision. Mr. Green, the American Consul, and a group of admirers and
friends urged him strongly to paint a duplicate of the "Voyage of
Life," as they felt sure it would sell at a large price, which was what
he was in need of. His biographer says on this subject: "Waiving

the considerations which made him feel at liberty to reproduce this work, he never would have done so in all probability, though he frequently meditated it, but for the influence of a kind and intimate friend, the American Consul at Rome, who commended the beauty and originality of its design, and its high artistic merit; and prophesied its great popularity, and probable sale to some of the English, or other travellers."

In one way Cole regretted agreeing to this, but the exigency of the case made him yield to the persuasions of his friends. He wrote to his wife about it, dating the letter Rome, November 30, 1841: "I shall surprise you perhaps — perhaps make you sorry — when I tell you that I am just beginning to paint the "Voyage of Life" over again. Mr. Green, the Consul, and several other persons have urged me strongly to do it, believing it will result greatly to my advantage. I intend to carry them through very speedily."

Now, during all this time Cole had been pondering on even deeper things than on the subjects of his paintings. He was thinking of becoming a member of the Episcopal Church. In dwelling upon semi-spiritual things, he found himself merging into spiritual states of mind and he began to read along these lines, and to study along these lines, and to paint along these lines, and his faith grew stronger and stronger. It seemed to possess him completely. While he had been unconsciously verging towards these spiritual convictions, his real conversion came during his short stay in London, when he went for a few days on a visit to relatives living some little way outside of the city.

A revival meeting was being held there, and more from curiosity probably than from any other feeling, Cole attended it. It so happened that the preacher who conducted the revival was a man of strength and power, who possessed the gift of putting forth his message of faith with conviction. It seemed as if all the questions that Cole had been asking himself were being answered. He left the meeting with his whole being awakened and transported into a new vision of Life and Death and the hereafter.

His biographer tells us that during his youth and his growing up, no definite instruction on religion had ever been given him. He might have been called a spiritually minded pagan, if such a combination could exist. It shows that the soil of his soul was ready for the sowing of the seed, and from that time on the way seemed clear to him. It was the turning point of his life.

So in viewing his paintings, especially after this experience, one can have no real understanding of them unless one looks beneath the surface to find the hidden truths they contain.

On January 31, 1842, he wrote a letter to his friend, Mr. Ver Bryck, from which the following extract is taken, which shows his love of home in spite of all the allurements of Rome:

> This Rome, this city of the soul is indeed a place that holds a man's heart like Mahomet's coffin suspended between earth and heaven. It is indeed the Mecca of the artist; and I am grieved that the most devout may not always be numbered among the pilgrims.
>
> Your company would be delightful here; your enjoyment of the beauties of Art and Nature would enhance mine. We could walk on the Pincian Hill together, and watch the sun set in gold behind the dome of St. Peter's, and talk of the Catskills — for every sunset takes my heart with it to my distant home.

He writes to his wife on February 6, 1842: he had received an invitation to attend a typical Roman party given by Prince Torlonia, and also one given by the French Ambassador. Knowing that letters containing news of this kind were especially enjoyed by his wife, rather than those on Roman art, he wrote an account of these entertainments to which he went in order to see how such functions were conducted in Italy. "I will give you a slight sketch of these parties, if this rascally Roman paper upon which I am writing will allow me," he wrote. He takes Prince Torlonia's party first:

> The company were invited at eight o'clock. The palace of Prince Torlonia, in which he gives his parties, is near St. Peter's.
>
> As we approached (I say we, for I went with several other persons in a carriage), the streets were lined with cavalry. After leaving the carriage, we ascended several long flights of carpeted steps, which led to a large entrance hall, in which guards and servants were placed; in the last hall

our names were announced by the servants, and we proceeded to the presentation chamber, where the Master of Ceremonies presented us to Prince and Princess, who stood in the middle of the room.

We bowed — a few words were passed — and we proceeded to the next room, which appeared to me badly lighted, but perhaps for effect. Here were ottomans in the centre of the room, and around it mirrors, pictures, and statues, and a brilliant assemblage of beauty and fashion. I saw more diamonds and emeralds in one hour than I ever saw in my whole life. Here we were regaled with delicious ices, and wandered about at our own sweet will. There were present a number of English nobility, as well as French and Italian.

The dancing continued until two o'clock, with intervals. The supper, cold of course, then came in, carried in tables ready set. I left after supper, but understood that the party did not break up until five in the morning.

Among the guests was the Countess Guiccioli. She is about forty years old, but a fine looking woman still, and I could not but look with interest on a woman whose name will ever be coupled with that of Byron.

The next that attracted the admiration of the company was the Princess Doria, the daughter of the English Earl of Shrewsbury. I never saw such a splendid display of dress and jewels.

The Princess Torlonia is decidedly one of the most beautiful women I ever saw — indeed I was never so struck with admiration before. This may partly be attributed to her family, and to the dignity consequent upon high station, in spite of republican notions to the contrary, and partly to being seen by candlelight. She is of the ancient Colonna family, about eighteen years of age, rather above middle height, her form graceful, face classic in its contour, a noble forehead, and fine large Italian eyes of pensive expression.

Her headdress consisted of a wreath of roses round the upper part of the head, a circlet of diamonds below, clasping the top of her forehead. The hair was brought down, as is the fashion here now — plain on each temple as low as the ear, and turned back.

She wore a necklace of splendid diamonds. Her dress was white satin, with a very thin lace-like skirt over it, with puffs of satin descending from her waist in diverging lines — the band at the waist was ornamented with a rose in front. She wore massive bracelets; and on the whole was elegantly and tastefully dressed.

It is not more than two years since she was married. She was then taken from the convent, and had never once seen her future husband.

After the presentations were over, the princess, accompanied by Prince Frederick of Prussia, led the way to the ballroom, which was brilliantly illuminated, the music from the orchestra struck up, and the dancing commenced.

The French Ambassador's party, at which I was last evening, was got up with more taste than Prince Torlonia's, and the party, though large, was far more select.

The lady of the Ambassador was present only for a short time, as she was an invalid. She was a very interesting looking person, about thirty years old, with a fine intellectual face. She sat all the time she was present.

Her attire struck my fancy exceedingly. She wore a sort of hat of crimson velvet, and ornamented with diamonds. Her dress was white satin with a sort of cape. I will stop by saying it reminded me of some of the most elegant costumes of the fifteenth century. . . .

How I long for you to talk with me in the grounds of the Villa Borghese, to see the warm sunlight streaming through the stately pines upon the rich grass, and to listen to the birds that are now singing like ours in May. . . .

The two descriptions given of those now historical parties, taking place in the luxurious days of Italian greatness as given to his wife, reveal one more interesting glimpse of Thomas Cole's character. From early childhood he had always thought of his family, and done whatever he could to make them happy — paid their bills when he could do so — helped to move them from place to place according to the whims of his charming but inconsequent father, and now in his letters to his wife he relates all the things that would interest her most, taking pains to notice the dresses of the ladies, and the jewels, and all the things that every real woman loves to hear about, right in the middle of the exalted state of his mind when his thoughts were dwelling on the sober things of life.

On March 20, 1842, he writes in his journal:

Yesterday I was gratified with a visit from Thorwaldsen. He is a grand old man. His remarks on the "Voyage of Life" were highly gratifying. He seized the allegory at once, and understood the whole intention of the artist. He said my work was entirely new and original in its conception, and executed in a masterly manner. He commended much the harmony of colour, and the adaptation of scenery and detail to the expression of the subject. He remained in my room some time, looking at the pictures.

"When he went away he thanked me for the great pleasure I had given him, and asked to come again."

In a letter from Mr. Green, the American Consul, he says about this visit:

> Cole was naturally anxious to have Thorwaldsen see "The Voyage of Life," and I arranged the interview.
>
> At the appointed hour, ten in the morning, the old gentleman came. The four pictures were standing in a row, the first three completed, the last still wanting in some finishing touches; but all that was essential to the story was there.
>
> I never saw Cole so nervous as when Thorwaldsen opened the door. Common criticisms he did not mind, but this was an ordeal to shake even his practised nerves. Thorwaldsen walked directly to the first piece, and taking the words from Cole's mouth as he began his explanation, went through the whole story — reading it from the canvas as readily as if the trees and flowers had been words.
>
> When he came to the last scene he paused, and stood silently before it, his eye resting with an expression of solemn musing on that cloud-veiled ocean upon which he too was to sail so soon. Twice he returned to gaze again at the closing scene with the same deep expression of earnest sympathy.
>
> I hardly ever passed an hour with him after that day but what he would bring in some mention of Cole. . . . What was he doing? — a great artist — what beauty of conception! What an admirable arrangement of parts! What an accurate study of nature! What truth of detail!
>
> I have often heard him speak of artists, friends and foes, the living and the dead, but never with such a glow of heartfelt enthusiasm as when he recalled his visit to the studio of Cole.

When April came the latter wrote to his wife regarding his copy of the "Voyage of Life." He said: "Won't you be glad when I tell you that the pictures are at length completed? And don't you think I

have worked hard to finish them in four months from the commencement? . . .

"A good number of persons have seen them, and I assure you I
have every reason to be satisfied with the impression they have made."

And now having finished the pictures his thoughts turned homeward. From his journal we find this: "*May 22, 1842.* In a few days
I leave Rome, in all probability for ever."

When he arrived home he wrote to Mr. Green, the American Consul at Rome:

> My dear Sir:
>
> I have now been nearly a month at home. You will, I know, be pleased
> to learn that I arrived in safety, and found my family in excellent health.
>
> Must I tell you that neither the Alps nor the Apennines, no — nor even
> Aetna itself have dimmed in my eyes the beauty of our own Catskills.
> It seems to me that I look on American scenery, if it were possible, with
> increased pleasure. It has its own peculiar charm — something not found
> elsewhere. I wish I could transport you here for a few days to enjoy
> these magnificent mountains. I know you would be willing to repay me
> in kind, and take me out of the Porta Pia to get a sight of Mont Albano.
>
> Yours truly
Thomas Cole

And now appears a short notice. I quote from his biographer: "A
subject which Cole had for some time been revolving in his mind
very prayerfully, but of which there is no record in his secret journal,
was that of his becoming a member of the Church."

The step was taken after his return from Europe, when he received
baptism, and the rite of confirmation, and came to the communion.
As far as can be judged, he never spoke to anyone of his decision
until the day came.

After this Cole gave all his energies to painting very large pictures
tinged with a wholly religious atmosphere.

On December 9, 1843, he held an exhibition of some of his pictures in Boston, where his work was always well received, and afterwards in New York. The following letter was written to his wife,
regarding the one in New York:

Since I wrote you I have been as busy as anybody possibly can be. Mrs. Reed could not let me have the "Course of Empire," which you know is a great disappointment, as it must diminish the effect of my exhibition. But I have determined to make up for it, and have commenced a large picture, larger than the "Angels Ministering to Christ," or of "Mount Aetna from Taormina." I have already finished two-thirds of it, and have only painted on it two days. I never painted so rapidly in my life.

The exhibitions were apparently successful, but in Cole's present state of mind, nothing satisfied him. It seemed to him that he could not convey the truth he was so eager to convey. He felt that the public failed to grasp the inner meaning that he tried to make evident. But there was one thing that was pending that gave him great satisfaction. Of this he speaks in a letter to his wife, dated New York, March 16, 1844, as follows: "Tonight there is a second meeting of gentlemen at Mr. Sturgis' on the subject of establishing a permanent gallery of pictures in the city of New York. The Reed Gallery is to be purchased as a commencement. The "Course of Empire" in such a case will be disposed of in a manner most agreeable to me."

On July 9, 1843, the art world was shocked at the news that Washington Allston had died. The American group of artists felt it keenly. Cole, writing in his journal, stated:

Allston is dead! As a man he was beloved by all who were so fortunate as to be acquainted with him. . . . He was truly a distinguished artist, and has executed works which will never cease to be highly prized, and considered great works of art. . . . His taste was pure and elevated far above that of most of his contemporaries. . . . His "Dead Man Restored by Touching the Bones of Elisha" and his "Miriam" may be considered among his finest works. His "Belshazzar" I have not seen.

Some of his small pictures painted in later years are exquisite.

Now, Cole never took pupils, but he made an exception to a young man in whom he recognized a superior talent. His name has become famous among our American artists — it was Frederick Church. This young man practically became a member of his household and looked upon Cole with a sort of filial affection, combined with an intense admiration for him as an artist, and the latter's interest in the young man was very genuine in return. "Church," he said, on several occasions, "has the finest eye for drawing in the world." He found comfort in having him about and giving him instruction, but during these days Cole was like one of the crusaders of old. He was impatient to draw people to this new vision he now had of life and death by the power of his brush and palette. Yet instead of feeling free to choose the subjects for his paintings, he found himself obliged, on account of financial difficulties, to produce some pictures which were pure landscapes with no story or moral attached to them. He resented having to give his time now to any kind of painting except that which preached the gospels, yet these very landscapes, painted in spite of himself with a master hand, gave the public once more a glimpse of the ineffable beauty of nature with no human incidents attached. They stand among his most valued productions, not only for this same beauty and the skill with which they are painted, but for another reason as well. They were not painted on the very large canvases on which his allegorical and religious pictures were painted, which could only hang on the walls of museums and large halls, but were of a size that could be enjoyed in the homes of his purchasers, and draw them away from the ordinary mundane run of life into a vision of the great outdoors, with its mountain peaks, peaceful lakes, golden sunshine, and swaying trees. While the public admired his great paintings with their esoteric meanings, and gazed upon them with a certain awe, these gave them an intimate enjoyment to which they were quick to respond. Here were the names of some of those executed during the period of 1845-46:

Twilight — a View up the Catskill River
The Cross in the Wilderness (the last hour of an autumnal day)
The Mountain Ford (wonderful for the vitality of its atmosphere)
Campagna di Roma (with moonlight stealing into the retiring twilight)
L'Allegro (a joyous picture of a rural scene in Italy)
Il Penseroso (Lake Nami after sunset)
The Picnic Party (a sylvan scene, all American)
Home in the Woods and The Hunter's Return (these were large pictures)
The Arch of Nero (another Roman picture)

Some of these were considered among his finest landscapes. These paintings brought him some of the pecuniary aid he was seeking, but he was restive under it all. On January 6, 1846, he wrote in his journal:

> I long for the time when I can paint whatever my imagination would dictate without fear of running into pecuniary difficulties. This painting for money, and to please the many, is sadly repulsive to me. . . . But I am about to venture. I have determined to commence a series of five pictures. The subject is "The Cross and the World," I have no commission for the work, and my means are scarcely competent for me to accomplish so great an undertaking. But the work I trust is a good one, and I will venture in faith and hope.

About this time Cole's health troubled him. He could hardly express what the trouble was, but he complained of feelings of weakness when he undertook to paint any very large picture. He took to wandering over the mountains for inspiration. Sometimes friends accompanied him. In order to give himself a mental tonic to strengthen him, he decided, notwithstanding the pecuniary difficulties which still oppressed him, to build a new studio attached to his Catskill home. It was constructed in the Italian villa style, and with reference to a spacious gallery, to accommodate the large works he contemplated painting. Its situation commanded a view of rarest beauty, showing the Catskill mountains fronting the Hudson River. Along the flowing outline of these, now behind one summit and then behind another, some of the finest sunsets could be seen . . . inexpressibly wild and gorgeous. (*Biography*.)

On Christmas Day, 1846, this is found in his journal:

"I am now sitting in my new studio. I have promised myself much enjoyment in it, in the prosecution of my art. But I ought ever to bear in mind that "the night cometh when no man can work." I pray to God that what I am permitted to accomplish here may be to his glory. If I produce fine works, I must ascribe the honor to the Giver of the gift. . . ."

Again the journal:

"*February 1, 1846*: My birthday. How they steal on! — one by one they come. O God, be thou my help, my support, when the last step is taken. This day I have painted the sky in the first picture of the Cross and the World."

January 1, 1848, journal:

"Of my series the last picture of 'The Pilgrim of the Cross' is about finished, and the second of 'The Pilgrim of the World' somewhat advanced. I am painting a smaller picture from a passage in the Psalms."

In a letter written from Catskill on February first to Mr. Falconer he writes:

> . . . I have very little to say about myself, only that I have been somewhat ailing of late. . . . An artist should be in the world, but not of it; its cares, its duties he must share with his contemporaries, but he must keep an eye steadfastly fixed upon his polar star, and steer by it whatever wind may blow. . . . And above all, if he would attain that serene atmosphere of mind in which float the highest conceptions of the soul, in which the sublimest works have been produced, he must be possessed of a holy and reasonable faith.
>
> Believe me very truly yours
> Thomas Cole

His biographer says:

> The powers of Cole had only now reached their maturity — a proof of their extent and greatness. Whatever may be said of his poetic, artistic, and religious life, prior to his last two or three years, must be said as of one yet in the progress of large developments. Pictures even such as the "Campagna di Roma," the "Mill at Sunset," "Home in the Woods," "The Mountain Ford," "The Hunter's Return," "The Arch of Nero," and others, awakening in his old admirers greater delight than ever, were productions not of the entirely unfolded, but still unfolding man. He had come to say, "O, that I had the Course of Empire yet to paint!" It was a theme upon which he felt he should love to exercise his powers, now ripened and seasoned with the Christian faith. It was not wholly a pleasing thought that he was leaving behind him a monument bearing his name, but not one symbol of that glorious faith affording the relief and consolation to which all should ever be pointed amid the crimes and desolations of the world.

But the time was short now. He knew it by intuition. He still took his long walks over the mountains. One day he went to the top of a huge precipice — a point visible from his house, and commanding a wonderful prospect. From this dizzy crag Cole took a long and silent look up and down his beloved valley of the Hudson. He had gazed upon it from other points unnumbered times, alone, and with companions, such as Bryant, Durand, Ver Bryck, and Huntington. It had filled his heart for years. This was his last look. . . .

It was while he was secretly bidding good-bye to the things he had loved in the world that he painted his last picture, what his biographer called "that most exquisite and most perfect of all his simple landscapes," founded on the opening of the twenty-third Psalm:

> The Lord is my Shepherd; I shall not want.
> He maketh me to lie down in green pastures;
> He leadeth me beside the still waters.

This was on Saturday, the fifth of February. He laid his remaining colors under water, cleansed his palette in his customary way, and left his studio. He never returned to it again. On Sunday he engaged in the services of the Church, and partook of the holy communion.

The following night he was stricken with inflammation of the lungs. He lingered until Friday of that week. In the evening of that day he felt that the end was near, and requested with great earnestness the immediate administration of the Lord's Supper. At the close of the service, through all of which he went with a deep serene devotion, he sank exhausted on his pillow, and said, "I want to be quiet." These were his last words. At eight o'clock he died, aged forty-seven years and a few days.

The following has been said of him: He proved "that landscape may be raised to the dignity of the historic; and that not only as a great designer, but as an originator of a new school of painting, he deserves today — what the future will surely award him — a place among the Spensers and Miltons of poetic art."

In his *Book of the Artists* Tuckerman gives a list of where some of Cole's most famous paintings went.

"The Course of Empire" is in the Gallery of the New York Historical Society.

One of the two series of "The Voyage of Life" belonged to J. Taylor Johnson, Esq., also "The Mountain Ford" and "Kenilworth Castle."

"The Tornado in an American Forest" belonged to R. M. Oliphant, Esq.

"The Expulsion from Eden" belonged to James Lenox, Esq.

"The Old Mill" and "A Landscape" belonged to Marshall O. Roberts, Esq.

"View on the Thames" and a smaller and larger landscape to Jonathan Sturgis, Esq.

"A View of the Roman Campagna" and "Catskill Creek at Sunset" to A. M. Cozzens, Esq., all of New York City.

"The Angels Appearing to the Shepherds" belongs to the Boston Athenaeum.

"A Cascade in the Catskills," "A View of the Northwest Bay on the Winnipesaukee Lake," and "A View of the White Mountains" are in the Wadsworth Gallery, Hartford, Connecticut, where also is Cole's large picture of Mount Etna — the view taken from Taormina, Sicily.

"The Voyage of Life" was first acquired by the American Art Union, and to show the estimate the public gave it, it was considered so irresistible a temptation to the subscribers of this organization that it increased the number from eight hundred to sixteen thousand. (From the *Art Bulletin* of 1853.)

This may be of service to someone: After "The Voyage of Life" had belonged to Mr. J. Taylor Johnson, he subsequently sold the series to Mr. Gorham D. Abbott who later either sold them or deposited them at the Springler Institute in New York in 1854.

It is said that this last Institute no longer exists.[1]

1 Harvard College Library.

CHAPTER 8

Frederick Edwin Church
(1826–1900)

I<small>T CAN SAFELY BE SAID THAT</small> Frederick Edwin Church first began to be conscious of all that art holds for a man who seeks it, when at the age of seventeen he was taken into the family life of the artist, Thomas Cole, as his one special pupil.

Before that he had passed through the stages of the usual disapprobation on the part of parents towards an artistic career for ablebodied sons. Fortunately for him he was the only son of a wealthy citizen of Hartford, Connecticut, Joseph Church, who, when he found distinct signs of genius appearing, let the boy go his own gait, even urging him to start right in his future profession by learning to draw before even touching palette and brush.

Young Church had a quick mind and saw the wisdom of this. He studied carefully and conscientiously with Benjamin A. Coe. From him he moved on to the well-known artist, A. H. Emmons, and studied color, and the application of it.

During this period his enthusiasm was increasing by leaps and bounds. He was receiving great encouragement from the sculptor, E. S. Bartholomew, who, seeing the unmistakable talent the young man possessed, drew to it the attention of Daniel Wadsworth, a great art critic of the time, who in turn persuaded Thomas Cole to take him as a pupil.

Cole had never taken any pupils and had never wanted any, but when he saw young Church and recognized the sincerity with which he desired to learn the art of painting, he gave in, and not only took him as a pupil but accepted him as a member of his household in his beautiful home on the Hudson River.

Up to this time young Church had thought himself absorbed in art. He had supposed all his ambition and all his hopes were focused upon it as a career. He loved Nature. He thought he knew her intimately — he felt sure of it — but the day he entered Thomas Cole's home on the Hudson River, life and art and the joy of beauty began, in the true sense of the word, for him. They all took on a different and deeper meaning to him. It would have been impossible for his sensitive make-up not to catch the fire that glowed in the soul of that searcher for truth in art, Thomas Cole, and as the boy gazed down the reaches of the Hudson River, and at the mountains rising from it on either side, with the wooded hillsides as yet untouched by the destructive hand of man, the beauty of the scene swept through him and over him, and he was like one looking out upon a new world.

This was in 1844. From then until the death of his beloved master in 1848, he was an inmate of his home and of his studio, and Cole treated him as a son.

This environment was a wonderful background for Church's future career, and he never lost the influence of it. Very soon he began to paint landscapes that attracted wide attention. One very beautiful one — "View of West Rock near New Haven" — made a great impression, and was bought by Cyrus W. Field, the noted art collector. He wandered up and down the Hudson choosing bits of nature for his brush that were striking and unusual. He painted sky effects that seized the imagination, such as masses of jagged rocks against a background of approaching storm. The daily intercourse with his master, Thomas Cole, awoke in him a love and understanding of the drama of nature; the mastery concealed behind the clouds; the sweep of rushing waters; the powerful effect of lights and shadows that made strong impressions upon his imagination.

He never acquired the spiritual quality that permeated the works of Cole, nor did the allegorical tendencies so dear to his master make any great appeal to him, but the same desire, so strong in the latter, to be true to the beauties and wonders of nature took firm root within him. He was loyal to that concept of art all through his life. But when Thomas Cole died, Church's outlook on life underwent a change. His horizons suddenly broadened. He became possessed with a desire to go to the far ends of the earth with his palette and brush, and bring back to civilization pictures revealing great mountain passes other than our own — views of thundering waterfalls, deep chasms yet to be discovered — there was no end to the visions that followed each other through his brain. He had become absorbed in the works of the great German naturalist and explorer, Frederick Humboldt. The accounts of what the latter found in his journeyings through the vast wildernesses of South America sounded like a call from the wilds to him. He knew he would never be satisfied with his life if he did not go there and experience for himself all the wonders that Humboldt had found and written about. So in 1853 he broke away from all his surroundings, and started out on his voyage of discovery.

What he brought back with him in the way of art is now well-known throughout the art world. He climbed to unbelievable heights in the Andes in order to perpetuate upon his canvas the wonders of the scenes he came upon. He stumbled through the tropical jungles for miles in search of points he was looking for that would reveal the almost terrible and beautiful wealth of vegetation that spread on all sides, so dense that man could easily be absorbed into it and never return.

At Quito, the capital of Ecuador, he hunted up the house in which Frederick Humboldt had lived fifty years before, summing up many of his most important wanderings, and Church took up his abode in it, following the example of the great naturalist. The fact of living within the very walls of the house where the latter had passed days and nights of study and reflection kindled Church's ardor threefold to leave to the world on canvas pictures as vivid and grand in subject as those the great naturalist and explorer had painted in words in his books.

But by that time he had amassed such a rich supply of studies and sketches that he decided to return to New York with them while the impression of all that he had seen was fresh in his mind. So he set forth on the home trek.

But when he got there he felt that he had returned too soon. There was much that he should have seen that he had allowed to escape him. Moreover, one or two of his pictures were seen and were received with such appreciation that he could hardly wait to go back and replenish his stock of sketches.

So in 1857 he returned to Ecuador, and to the house in which Humboldt had lived, where he could quietly assemble in his mind a list of what he wanted to see, and where he wanted to go, and add more of what he knew would be of value to his reputation as a landscape painter of renown. When he was satisfied that he had all the material necessary to achieve that end, he returned to New York again, and this time shut himself up in his studio with a clear vision of all that he had seen and learned.

He was a tremendous worker. One of his biographers writes of him: "Five hours of hard work before an easel any artist will admit is sufficient for a full day's work; but his indefatigable energy often held him to ten hours upon a canvas."

In spite of all this he managed to count time out to pay court to a charming girl named Isabel Mortimer, the daughter of Francis Carnes, who had been, or was at that time, a diplomat to the court of Louis Philippe in Paris. This fact is mentioned in only one account of him. It states that he was married in 1859, but no mention is made of his family life except that his wife bore him three sons and a daughter: Frederic Joseph, Theodore Winthrop, and Louis Palmer Church. Isabel Charlotte was the name of the daughter. She became the wife of Edward L. Howe of Princeton, New Jersey. (*National Cyclopedia*, Vol. 20, p. 14.)

But more happened than his marriage that very year. The art circles of New York were startled into a rush of enthusiasm when he exhibited his now famous pictures, "The Heart of the Andes," "Cotopaxi," "The Mountains of Ecuador," and other realistically painted tropical landscapes. The public flocked to see them. Here was a new star of the Hudson River School appearing upon the horizon to stay, with work to show such as had not been shown before, and Church's reputation soared to the skies.

But in spite of this he had not neglected the grandeur to be found in his own country. In 1857, before he returned to Ecuador, he visited Niagara Falls, not only on the American side but on the Canadian side as well. The now famous picture of the Falls on the American side was painted from near Table Rock on the Canadian side, on an oblong canvas. It was a huge painting — seven by three feet in size — a momentous piece of work.

In spite of the enthusiasm his tropical paintings evoked, his picture of Niagara Falls was considered his masterpiece, and has been so considered by many ever since. It was sent to the Paris Exhibition in 1867, where it was awarded a second medal, and produced a tremendous impression on the French public.

This newly born Hudson River School of painting was very intriguing to the art critics on both sides of the Atlantic. The audacity with which its members took hold of these great subjects which had never been successfully dealt with before made an electric appeal to the imagination.

It is interesting to know the way he accomplished this piece of work, for perfect as it is in all detail, it took him only six weeks to paint it. But before he started on the actual picture there was the work of innumerable sketches to be tested out, and that needed long hours of study. He prepared and set up two canvases of the same size. On one he experimented until he was satisfied with the results, and would then transfer it to the other. By so doing he got to know his subject so thoroughly that a long time afterwards he painted from memory the main Fall on a smaller canvas in seven hours, we are told.

The New York *Albion,* May, 1857, says this of the painting of the Falls: "Incontestably the finest oil-picture ever painted on this side of the Atlantic is now on exhibition on Broadway. It is a view of the great Horseshoe Falls of Niagara. We congratulate the artist on his brilliant success."

And from across the water comes this verdict from the London *Times*: "Mr. Church has painted this stupendous cataract with a quiet courage and a patient elaboration which leave us for the first time satisfied that even this awful reality is not beyond the range of human imitation." (August 7, 1857.)

On July 18, 1857, the art critic of the London *Athenaeum* wrote: "Mr. Church gives us with firmness and clear-sighted precision the tremendous level rush of the great line of water, as calmly, and with terrible calmness, it moves towards its grave in the great hell-pool from whence the rainbow springs with its celestial arch."

The Liverpool *Mercury*, July 16, 1858, says this of the picture: " . . . the excellency of the painting is the artist's wonderful conception and portrayal of the mighty waters in their everlasting turbulence and the fantastic play and dazzle of light upon them."

These excerpts from the press are enough to show the consideration given to Church's work by the newspapers here and abroad.

The painting was eventually sold from the collection of John Taylor Johnston for the Corcoran Gallery in Washington for the sum of twelve thousand five hundred dollars.

In 1859 the full exhibition of his tropical paintings took place in New York. It is recorded that the receipts at the door in a single day amounted to five hundred and thirty-eight dollars; and during the month of July, three thousand one hundred and seventy-two dollars.

In June the *Christian Intelligencer* made this comment on "The Heart of the Andes" which appeared in this exhibition: " 'The Heart of the Andes' is a complete condensation of South America into a single focus of magnificence."

The *New York Herald* of December 5, 1859, says this: "From the exhibition of Church's great picture, 'The Heart of the Andes,' may be dated the inauguration of a new art-epoch. That extraordinary picture may be said to embody all the peculiarities and excellencies which have given the stamp of originality to American art."

All the other great pictures received unlimited praise, and the exhibition was heralded all over the country by a laudatory press.

This recognition of his work gave Church supreme satisfaction, but it did not lessen his determination to suffer further hardships in order to reach the far-off goal of his ambition. He was a lover of contrasts. Having steeped his soul in the beauty of the tropics, with its perilous mountain passes and the danger of its mysterious jungles, he suddenly heard the North with its icebergs calling to him. He listened to that mysterious voice, and, filled with the anticipation of what this new experience might have in store for him, he set his compass towards Labrador. Out of it came his extraordinary painting of "The Icebergs," and another of "The Aurora Borealis as seen in the Arctic regions."

These were exhibited in 1861 in New York. Of "The Icebergs" the *New York Tribune* of April 24, 1861, says: "It is an absolutely wonderful picture, a work of genius that illustrates the time and the country producing it. The idea is grand, and the artist hand that has put it upon canvas is worthy of the artist mind that conceived it."

From England comes this estimate of it, from the columns of the London *Morning Star* of June 22, 1863: "We can believe that a truer picture was never painted."

The London *Post* gives the following account of his work: "Church is a delicate and accurate draughtsman, a patient student of Nature under her most difficult and perplexing aspects, a pure and brilliant colorist, and a master of that supreme art of composition which can never be taught, and never acquired."

A breathing space, in which he worked in his New York studio, was followed by another paroxysm of still unsatisfied ambition. In spite of all his success his goal seemed yet far off to him. Packing up his kit of palette and paints he set off for Jamaica, where he painted "The Vale of St. Thomas" and other West Indian subjects.

In the meantime he had been steeped in the books of Washington Irving, and 1871 found him in Greece painting "The Parthenon" very beautifully, as well as a picture of "The Aegean," both of which hang to this day in the Metropolitan Museum in New York.

Then came Palestine, with studies of Jerusalem and Damascus, and Turkey, and Persia with its touch of barbaric splendor.

Having again found his portfolio filled with sketches and studies, he turned his face homeward.

In the meantime his family had been coming and growing, and his mind began working upon a plan to build a home on the banks of the Hudson, among scenes which had surrounded him before he had set out on his wanderings. Like the rest of the Hudson River artists, there was where his heart abode, and there he wished his real home to be. A description of it is given here (Tuckerman, *Book of the Artists*):

> The house, or properly castle, with its towers, reserved balconies and pavilions, near Rip Van Winkle's Bed, is essentially one of his works of art. It stands opposite Catskill, three miles south of the city of Hudson, on a hill six hundred feet above the river. The site is the result of a careful study of river-banks, and commands so many views of varied beauty that all the glories of the Hudson may be said to circle it. No better spot could be found to keep fresh in mind an intimate knowledge of the clouds and atmosphere. The designs of the building were prepared by Church, assisted by the architect Mr. Vaux.
>
> It was Persian in style, provincialized only where necessity demanded it. The walls, two and a half feet thick, were of rough stone quarried on the spot, of a bluish tint, changing to a soft grey on the fracture. The cut work was of light brown and blue stone; the upper part of the principal tower was of red, yellow and black brick, arranged in a unique pattern, giving an impression of mosaic work.
>
> The main doorway was of light brown stone, surrounded by mosaic tiles. The wooden cornices were painted in Persian colors, low and soft, with an effect of quiet harmony throughout. The principal roofs were of red, green and black slates.
>
> Instead of the Persian court, a large hall, cruciform, formed the center of the building, from which opened the various rooms.
>
> The art gallery, with the ceilings eighteen feet high, was admirably lighted by four long windows on the north. The partitions were solid, and the whole was built on the foundation of mountain rock.
>
> The extensive grounds surrounding were in a constant state of arrangement under the supervision of the artist.

From now on this was the place of all others where he loved to do his work, though he still kept a studio in New York.

It was his habit to stand while painting, for this enabled him to step back quickly to view the progress of his work and inspect it from a distance.

"His gait, manner and use of the brush," so records one of his biographers, "all alike are indicative of the characteristic energy that marked his life."

But in spite of the tax he laid on his strength, he had certain methods of safeguarding it that seemed to him sufficient to keep his body in good repair. He took the precaution to walk during the hours he was not before his easel. Sometimes he walked as far as ten to fifteen miles at a stretch. These characteristics of the man showed themselves in his work. Resolution of purpose backed by tireless energy, and a strict honesty encircling his genius, resulted in a prominence gained without influence from the Old World and its famous old masters, for he never went abroad until his fame was firmly established in Europe as well as America. This was largely Cole's advice to him, and he followed it, firmly believing in its wisdom.

These were the days of his prosperity. This was his heyday, when Art accorded him a place in her inner circle. In recording them it was said, "In their time these paintings awoke the wildest admiration, and sold for extravagant prices, collectors in the United States and in Europe eagerly seeking them."

A picture made of him at this time gives the impression of a man driven by a force outside himself towards a goal all too comprehensive for the attainment of one individual. The eyes seemed to be boring into the future with too great intensity. It was as if every great picture that came from his brush left its mark upon his face, revealing the travail its perfection involved.

He was all unconscious of this. He kept hard at work without relaxation, planning this and planning that for future revelations of his genius until 1877, when a sinister cry of "Halt" broke in upon his work. His right arm and hand with which he had created his beautiful paintings had become useless!

The shock of it overwhelmed him. At the height of his career Fate called upon him to relinquish all that had made life worth while. Charles Dudley Warner wrote this of him in the catalogue of the great exhibition at the Metropolitan Museum of Art in New York in 1900: "The spirit made an heroic effort to conquer. The right hand refusing to work, he learned to paint with his left hand . . . but inflammatory rheumatism is a foe that the spirit fights in vain."

And so at the age of fifty-one Church's career was over — while he was still practically a young man in vigor of mind and spirit.

From that point on, history tells no more, except that he still lived in his beautiful home on the Hudson River during the summer, but his poor body could not stand the rigor of the northern winters, and he was sent to Mexico where the warmth of the southern sun might give him some comfort.

In 1899 a bereavement came to him. His wife died. It is a pity that nothing more is recorded of her. One likes to think of her as beautiful, and kind, and good. Instead she remains a misty figure in the records of the life of Church. His personality was so vital that those surrounding him seemed to fade so far into the background of his life as to become lost in it.

Nevertheless, one significant fact remains from which we may draw conclusions. He lingered barely a year after she had gone. After over twenty years of inactivity and suffering, on his return from a winter passed in Mexico to his home on the Hudson, he breathed his last. Perhaps he had now lost the incentive to live.

To quote again from Charles Dudley Warner: "Church had already while comparatively young attained a commanding eminence as a landscape artist, abroad as well as at home, and had done for American art, in his field, what Irving did for its literature."

And again:

> Mr. Church was a pioneer and adventurer. No other person of his own generation certainly, had such power of aerial perspective, or of giving the relative value of distances. These are achievements that no change in fashion can make obsolete. In his composition Mr. Church has shown the qualities of the great Masters — order, lucidity, and harmony of design, with the highest poetic sentiment. . . .
>
> In years of physical infirmity he was seventy-four. In his spirit and heroic cheerfulness he was still young, hopeful of the world, the most helpful of friends, and as clear and sweet in his Christian character as he was decided in his luminous rendition of the atmosphere, and of the distant mountains of his pictures.

He saw and felt the divinity in both worlds. We can scarcely over-estimate the debt of America to Mr. Church by his work at home and in tropical lands, in inculcating a taste, and arousing an enthusiasm for landscape art — that is, landscape art as an expression of the majesty and beauty of the divine manifestation in nature.

It has been said that "It is through suffering that we reach the stars." According to Charles Dudley Warner's estimate of his character, certainly Frederick Edwin Church had more than caught a glimpse of them.

CHAPTER 9

John William Casilaer
(1811–1893)

A TOUCH OF SPAIN can never be effaced in one born with Spanish blood in his veins. Some have hidden away in their make-up hints of the toreador, and the rugged fastnesses of the mountains of Spain. Others reveal glimpses of the sunshine, the music, the gaiety of that fascinating country.

Of such was the artist John William Casilaer. His paternal grandfather, Francisco Casilaer, came as a young man from Barcelona, Spain, to New York City. Whom he married is not recorded, but it is evident that he made himself of some account there, for when he died in 1796, he was buried in Saint Paul's churchyard.

His son (John William's father) evidently became a person of some consequence also, for he married into one of the prominent families of New Jersey — the Stevens family — and he and his wife, Rebecca Stevens, raised a large family of nine children of whom John William Casilaer was the third in number. He was born on June 25, 1811, in New York City.

He was fortunate enough to be brought up under circumstances which did not necessitate going through the hardships and self-sacrifices in early youth which most of the other Hudson River artists had to contend with. This fact, however, was no detriment to him. His nature was one that could not easily be spoiled. More than that, the American blood in him pushed him forward with the spirit of a true worker in the profession in which his ambition was to become eminent.

It has been said of him: "Like many artists of the Italian Renaissance period, a number of men who became eminent as painters in the United States through the first half of the nineteenth century found a safe starting point for their more ideal flights in the practice of engraving." (*Dictionary of American Biography*.)

Like many of those young men, when Casilaer became fifteen years old he began the study of that art under the well-known engraver, Peter Maverick. The latter died in 1831, at which time Casilaer entered the studio of Asher B. Durand and became his most eminent pupil. With Durand and his other pupils in engraving, Kensett and Rossiter, Casilaer made that ever-to-be-remembered trip to Europe which is spoken of in the article on Asher B. Durand, when he studied with enthusiasm all the masterpieces of Italian art in Rome. From this trip resulted one of the finest American engravings of the period — a reproduction of Daniel Huntington's "Sibyl," which was published by the American Art Union.

During this time his father had died, and now young Casilaer experienced the responsibility of caring for his widowed mother and his brother and sisters, for the difficulties of raising a large family had proved to be expensive beyond their expectations, and it became necessary to move with caution. The duty of carrying the family along fell on John William Casilaer's young shoulders.

He apparently was equal to the demands made on him. Also he had a level head upon his shoulders. He was going to attend to his duty to his family, but he also had a definite goal in view which he kept steadily before him — some day to become a landscape painter.

Before he could attain that goal, however, he knew he must stick to what was proving to be a very remunerative profession, and one that in those days stood in high repute all over the world. He put his mind seriously on how he could make it even more remunerative. So in perfecting his art along the same lines, he enlarged its scope by designing the medallions on bank notes so beautifully and artistically that the American Bank Note Company's attention was drawn to them, and it promptly sought him out and engaged him as a high-salaried designer. This proved to be a very successful move on his part.

His engraving of Daniel Huntington's noted painting "Sibyl," which he finished carefully on his return from his European trip, was a very great feather in his cap. The reviews in the newspapers were full of praise regarding it. His contemporary, Tuckerman, in his *Book of the American Artists,* called it: "A notable triumph of the burin; it has sharpness and decision of line worthy of the celebrated old engravers."

Then he opened a studio in New York in 1854 for more privacy in working. Having finally made himself financially secure, he resigned an interest he had acquired in the American Bank Note Company, in 1857, and went to Europe again with Asher B. Durand, and this time the artist Edmonds joined them.

Durand had by that time become a landscape painter, and Casilaer was his pupil along that line, as he had been before in the art of engraving.

On this trip he put his mind wholly upon studying the methods of the old masters of Europe, foregoing all outside pleasures. Durand was doing the same thing. Neither of them had any idea of copying these methods necessarily. They were eager to develop their own; at the same time they were fully aware that a well-rounded knowledge of the old and accepted use of paints and palette would count for more in developing and perfecting their own art, as they visioned it, than any other means.

On his return from Europe he settled down definitely to competing with the other landscape painters. Durand continued to pass judgment on his work, though he saw that his pupil was well able to take care of himself. And Casilaer had no sensitiveness about his doing so. On the contrary, he looked for the approbation of his erstwhile teacher with the same eagerness he had shown when he went to his studio to develop his knowledge of engraving, the foundations of which he had learned with Peter Maverick. He was a devoted admirer of Durand, ranking him among the finest of landscape painters, whose friendship meant everything to him. He followed him in one very special way by adopting the habit of painting as far as was possible from Nature herself, even finishing the picture in the open.

Thomas Cole also became interested in his work, and with the close friendship of these two great artists, Casilaer forged forward into the very heart of the art circles of New York. He was elected an Associate of the National Academy as far back as 1835, when he was known as an engraver, and was made an Academician in 1851. Now he became an Active Member of the Artist Fund Society, which gave yearly exhibitions.

Casilaer was a true and loyal friend to all those who cared for him, and in return was given real affection. Durand, Cole, Kensett, Rossiter, Huntington always gave him a warm welcome whenever he appeared in their company. He was a good companion. Differences of age did not mar his pleasure. He enjoyed the old as well as the young. All this appears in his paintings. His even, sunny nature reveals itself in his choice of subjects. His skies are luminous with sunshine. He loved the woods and the great shadows they cast on green meadows — he painted pools with white clouds mirrored in them, and sleepy cows at noontime wading in their cool depths. His paintings are very realistic. They take one right into the heart of nature as most people know it, and as those in the country have seen it and loved it all their lives.

The public enjoyed his work. They felt at home in it, as the following clipping from an article will show:

> As a whole Casilaer's pictures in subject and treatment harmonized with the even tenor of his life. At each succeeding exhibit of the National Academy of Design, his landscapes were remarked for their sunny skies, silvery clouds, quiet reaches of rivers and lakes between broad meadows and distant hills.
>
> His work was marked by careful finish. He was deeply in love with nature, which he approached with a reverent and poetic spirit. He produced pictures remarkable for their simple unaffected beauty, which has a definite place in the development of American landscape art. (*Dictionary of American Biography*.)

The *Art Journal* of 1876 said this:

> Casilaer's work is marked by a peculiarly silvery tone and delicacy of expression, which is in pleasant accord with nature in repose, and of his own poetically inclined feelings. . . . His pictures when sent from the

easel are as harmonious as a poem, and it is this perfect serenity in their handling which is so attractive to connoisseurs.

And this from the New York *Evening Post,* January 11, 1878:

> The small summer landscape of Casilaer, with its peaceful stream in a lush meadow under the golden radiance of a late afternoon, is interesting for its admirably apprehended and managed atmospheric effects. It is a very happy piece of composition also.

These excerpts were chosen as typical of the feelings of reviewers and the public regarding him.

Tuckerman says of him and his work: "The rectitude of his character and the refined accuracy of his original profession are exhibited in his pictures. They are finished with great care, and the subjects chosen with fastidious taste."

Casilaer married Ellen M. Howard of Tamworth, New Hampshire, in 1867. He had with her a peaceful, happy life. In his eighty-third year he took a trip with her to Saratoga, where he was suddenly stricken with apoplexy and died. He was buried from Doctor Houghton's church in Twenty-Ninth Street, New York City.

His paintings are now (1946) being eagerly sought by collectors.

Wisely, Casilaer did not undertake to paint the very large pictures that some of the Hudson River artists did, preferring them to be of moderate size, and putting into them all the care and skill he had acquired. They were highly considered by the critics as well as the public. His "Lake Lucerne" belonging to John Taylor Johnston sold for one thousand dollars in 1876, and probably his other paintings did likewise.

CHAPTER 10

John Frederick Kensett
(1818–1872)

O F ALL THE ARTISTS who formed the nucleus of the Hudson River School of painting, John F. Kensett was the most universally beloved. He was a quiet and retiring man, yet he possessed that rare faculty of stirring devotion towards himself even among newly found friends. His whole life bears witness of this.

He was born on March 22, 1818, in Cheshire, Connecticut. His father was an Englishman who came over to this country in 1812, having been an engraver at Hampton Court. A year after his arrival he married Elizabeth Gaggett, a granddaughter of the president of Yale College.

Like most of the artists of that period, Kensett followed his father's profession and became an engraver; in fact, he was so highly considered as such that he had been secured by the well-known American Bank Note Company and was in New York working for that firm when he made a sudden decision that changed the whole tenor of his life. He had become acquainted with a group of artists, Asher B. Durand, John W. Casilaer, and Thomas B. Rossiter. The latter he had known for some time, and he it was who urged Kensett to take up painting in oils. So it happened that after his office hours as an engraver he took to going to his friend's studio and trying his hand at landscape painting. He very soon became convinced that he could reveal his talents through that medium to better advantage than he could through that of engraving, and when these artist friends of his decided to go to England in 1840 to see what art meant over there, he seized the opportunity of joining them.

It was more of a revelation to him than he had expected. From the partially untamed beauty that then characterized vast tracts of the United States he found himself in a country where civilization was in evidence on all sides. He saw well-clipped hedgerows bordering pastures green with herbage. He saw neat thatched-roof cottages, each with little garden plots aglow with bloom. He caught glimpses of great estates with wide-spreading lawns shaded by ancient oak trees, and of castles with protecting moats surrounding them. It was all so different from what he had been accustomed to — so completely different from the new world across the Atlantic, which was still in the making, and where he was born.

He felt the urge to stop there and to paint some of the quiet pastoral scenes that made a strong appeal to him. He was eager, however, to gain an all-round knowledge of European art, so in 1841 he went to Paris, and there he found an artist whom he knew — Benjamin Champney of Boston, who had a studio in the Rue de l'Université. It was a great chance for him, as this friend allowed him to work there, and they made many excursions together through the Forest of Fontainebleau, taking their brushes and palettes along with them. After a while he went back to England and devoted himself to painting some of the scenes that had impressed him during his first visit. In referring to this period he wrote: "My real life commenced there, in the study of the stately woods of Windsor, and the famous beeches of Burnham, and the lovely and fascinating landscape that surrounds them." (Tuckerman.)

He made one more trip to Paris, and then returned to England where he remained for several years. He was repaid for doing so, for at the end of that time, when the Royal Academy held an exhibition of paintings in London, he entered a picture of Windsor Castle. Not only was it accepted, but it was selected as the best in the collection. This brought him very much to the fore in England, and from then on he was received there as an artist of note. The painting was purchased by a prize owner in the London Art Union.

But he wanted to see more of the art in other countries, so with his friend Champney he went to Germany. Here he examined the Düsseldorf School of painting sufficiently to know that it made no great appeal to him. His point in visiting these various countries, however, was to build up a groundwork of knowledge and experience in art on which he could stand with a sense of security.

It was in 1845 that his thoughts turned towards Rome. Every artist sooner or later turned his face in that direction. Finding that a small party was just starting out with the intention of ultimately reaching there, Kensett joined it and found himself on a prolonged tramp, extending even as far as Switzerland before it headed towards the "Eternal City." Kensett's friend Champney was one of the party, and that friend of all artists, George William Curtis, was another.

And now a word about George William Curtis, who was a very important part of the artist colony in Rome. He was well known in the history of his time, being a man of many parts. For one thing he was editor of *Harper's Weekly,* and was connected with the staff of the *New York Tribune.* As editor of the column "The Easy Chair" in *Harper's Magazine,* he wrote of the topics of the day with great verve and understanding. This column was eagerly read by the public. He was one of the Lyceum lecturers, and easily stood at the head of the list. At the time of the Civil War, which came later, he was one of our outstanding orators. In fact, there seemed no end to his talents, for in addition he was gifted with a fine baritone voice and was often called upon to sing, which, if for no other reason, made him socially a success in the most aristocratic circles as well as the simpler circle of artists, musicians, writers, and all the literary culture of Rome.

It sometimes happens that a man so versed in the ways of the big world will find himself singularly in accord with a person of a less sophisticated nature, and this happened to him in his friendship with Kensett. From the first glimpse he had of him he read behind the quiet and self-respecting but unassuming personality a strength of purpose and a high idealism such as he had rarely encountered. Curtis was something of an idealist himself. At one time he had been associated with the famous Brook Farm Colony, and with his talents and his exuberant nature had given the inmates such a good time that when he left it seemed as though the very life went out of the place.

It can easily be imagined that a friend like this was more than an asset to an artist like Kensett, coming as he did to a new place where all was strange to him. It stimulated him to be in Curtis's company. Somehow he felt in his presence as though everything was possible, and everything was worth while. So when he passed through the gates of the "Eternal City" his hopes ran high and his future seemed assured.

Another great friend, the artist Thomas Hicks, was there to greet him. Here again was another type of man on whom Kensett could rely, and with these two friends to back him, as well as Champney, it seemed certain that he was making a good start.

But no sooner had he entered the city than he discovered to his dismay that his indispensable though modest luggage which he had sent on before him had never turned up. While tramping along dusty highways day after day he had, in order to save his better clothes, worn a very old suit, much the worse for wear, which he hoped to cast off upon arriving. Now he found himself looking like a tramp, which, considering his position as an artist, was humiliating, to say the least, especially as time went on and no baggage appeared. His friends made a great joke of his dilemma, which did not help matters, but he took it all in such a kindly and at the same time sporting manner that they ceased to refer to it, and when, finally, after two months, his simple baggage appeared, the episode which had been so amusing to them at first was forgotten.

But it seemed as though the stars at that time were against him, for now a really serious setback came to mar his pleasure in all the interests that surrounded him. He fell ill with an attack of inflammatory rheumatism which prostrated him for several weeks, and stopped all the painting he depended upon doing. In this helpless position his friend Thomas Hicks came to his rescue, and with untiring devotion saw him through what turned out to be a very serious illness. Kensett's gratitude was very real, and when he had sufficiently recovered, these two friends had rooms together, ate together, and worked together all the rest of the time that Kensett was in Rome; and he was there for many months, in rooms on Via Margutta near the Piazza di Spagna. When finally he was able to take up his palette and brush he found to his distress that the concentration he had put into his study of English, French, and German art had somehow disintegrated his former completely individual style which was wholly American. In haste and with trepidation he set to work to regain what he had lost; therefore the real work he did while in Rome was an effort, and fortunately a successful effort, to win back his technique and his zeal for the reality of the beauties of nature, and to forget the many theories in regard to the methods of producing them on canvas.

It was while he was in Rome, after he had regained his former exquisite and individual style of painting, that Kensett sent to America several Italian landscapes, "which under the auspices of the Art Union first made his name and works familiar to his countrymen." (Tuckerman.)

The American press reviewed his work with deep appreciation. One critic said of his paintings, "The traveller feels at a glance how entirely the artist has discriminated in these and other landscapes drawn from European studies, between the forms and hues of nature in the Old and New World." He then sent many paintings to the New York exhibitions, and he found his reputation already won. The "View of Windsor Castle" which he had exhibited in London won especial praise.

He had now regained his balance and was painting freely. He was also enjoying the experience of life in Rome. It was full of American artists at that time, and no one could have failed to feel the exhilaration that flowed out from them. And Kensett went among them, and was welcome at every studio that he visited. It was said of him: "He was not a ready talker — his disposition was rather reserved; he often sat mute, but when he spoke it was with understanding, and even his silence diffused an atmosphere of friendliness about him." (Isham.)

Even those young artists who were just starting out were drawn to him; in fact, he was noted throughout the art circles as "the beginner's friend." Any one of them could go to him and gain valuable advice and encouragement. Up to that time he was a poor man, and he knew the difficulties of studying art and at the same time making the two ends meet. He could therefore sympathize with their periods of downheartedness, but nearly always he managed to drive the blues away and lighten their burdens for them by cheering them up. His appearance has been described as a "romantic-looking figure, with long dark hair, high forehead, straight nose, and sensitive expression, somewhat dreamy." One can surmise that from his landscapes — they too are often dreamy and imbued with poetic feeling and quiet beauty.

A few of the Hudson River artists in Rome around that time, with a certain leeway, for they were continually coming and going, were Thomas Cole, John F. Kensett, George Inness, John W. Casilaer, Jasper F. Cropsey, Frederick E. Church, Robert W. Weir, Thomas Hicks, Worthington Whittredge, H. K. Brown, Jervis McEntee, and Christopher Pearse Cranch, whose name is on many of the Hudson River lists. His work was frequently exhibited in the Paris Salon and in London, and he was so much a part of the artist life in Rome during those years that no account of it should be given without including him. Above all, he, like George William Curtis, reflected the interests of a world outside into the company of happy but hard-working artists, who after a day's study in some famous gallery met at a restaurant called "Trattoria, Le Lepre" or "The Hare Restaurant," where they dined, and afterwards went to a coffee house called the "Café Greco," for apparently coffee was not served at the restaurant.

These two popular places were the meeting grounds of all the artist colony in Rome, and their walls echoed with gay laughter and merry voices, and whenever Christopher Pearse Cranch, who was an intimate friend of George William Curtis, appeared in the doorway to join the diners, he was always acclaimed with a hearty welcome. He was sure to contribute some amusing experience that had happened to him during the day, or tell of some outside bit of news that bore recording.

A word more about him: Christopher Pearse Cranch (born 1813, died 1892) was an artist, a critic, a poet, and at one time a Unitarian minister (who had evidently retired before he became an artist). He and George William Curtis had been in sympathy with the experiment of Brook Farm, and had been frequent visitors there, and were friends of Ralph Waldo Emerson, Thoreau, and the other transcendentalists.

Since he had so many enlightening little glimpses of this period in Rome, let him tell a few of them here, in order to picture the scene more clearly, and show more definitely the atmosphere that surrounded Kensett.

From Cranch's diary, November 1846:

> We have a hive of artists here, of all nations too — Italian, French, German, Scotch, American. Besides there is a variety of music; there are three guitars, one grand piano, a violoncello, two flutes, and an accordion.
>
> Some mornings I hear the German in the room opposite sounding some fine chords on his piano, or playing some of the good German music which he plays finely. Then again I sit at my painting. Sometimes I hear a groaning and sighing of the Frenchman's violoncello upstairs; it sounds like a mighty musical wind blowing through the forests. In the afternoon the Scotchman's guitar tinkles an accompaniment to some pretty Neapolitan song that his master is teaching him. When Christopher comes in tired, he seizes his flute and warbles some sweet air upon it — some of Schubert's songs, or some sweet Italian air; so that we have music, painting, and sculpture in the house, two sculptors having their studio on the ground floor. Then George [George William Curtis] is the poet . . . so we have all the arts here. It is quite a little Parnassus.

December 30, 1846:

> Last night being a beautiful moonlight evening, I went with a party of gentlemen to see the Colosseum by moonlight. . . . Our party was entirely American. It consisted of George and his brother Burrill Curtis, the artist Hicks [and undoubtedly Kensett, since they had rooms together] and the artists Terry and Schlossen — all those whom I met every day at the Lepre.
>
> We went from the Lepre, where we dine daily at five, to the Café Nuovo, a large and handsome café where smoking is not allowed, and

after the gentlemen had taken their cup of "café Nero" we set out for the Colosseum, crossing the Capitoline Hill, down past the Forum, through the Arch of Titus, to the grandest of all ruins, which looked so desolate and grim in the moonlight — its time-worn arches and galleries speaking so strongly of the past that one could linger and dream there for hours.

Autobiography, 1848. Then Cranch goes to the Carnival:

> I enjoyed the festivities of the Carnival. With my linen blouse, scarlet neckhandkerchief and broad black hat looped up at the side with the tri-colored cockade and three feathers, I joined the throng in the crowded Corso — with a basket of bouquets in my hand and a pocket full of plaster confetti in case of attack. There were bright eyes and handsome faces enough; handsome dresses too, and grotesque ones. I had a deal of fun.

The great entertainers in Rome during those days were the William Storeys (he a sculptor) and they kept a sort of open house to the artist colony. Cranch, who always saw the humorous side of things, wrote thus about preparing to go to a grand ball they were giving to which he was invited. He evidently had some misgivings about the look of his hair, in spite of the fact that long hair was then universally the fashion among artists, musicians, and poets.

> Last Wednesday evening [he wrote to his wife] the Storeys gave a great ball, altogether the most brilliant party of the season. I went there yesterday for the address of a haircutter, and we had a discussion about my hair. It resulted in a capillary reform, by which I was assured I looked at least five years younger. My hair is cut, and I wear it henceforth parted in the middle, and my beard trimmed close at the sides and long in front. I wore it so last night, and two ladies complimented me on the change.

If Cranch told that bit of personal news to his friends at the Café Greco, one may imagine the uproar of jokes with which it was received!

At this time there happened to be a gentleman from New York who saw the picturesqueness of the artist life in Rome, and who wrote a book on the subject describing the hours of relaxation the artists enjoyed after the work of the day was over, to which he was an eye-witness. He writes thus of them:

> The Lepre [The Hare] is the most extensive trattoria [Restaurant] in Rome, and each of its numerous rooms is usually occupied almost exclusively by visitors of some one nation, and is named accordingly. The old waiter in the English room, Origlia by name, is somewhat of a character. He followed Napoleon to Moscow, where he suffered greatly, and even yet cannot bear to hear any jocose sounds like groans, as they remind him so painfully of the real ones which he heard there. All the rest of his life he has passed here, and has accumulated a little fortune out of the two cents, which is his regular fee from each guest. He is a great favorite with the young artists, to whom he often gives credit on his own responsibility for many weeks in succession when, as will sometimes happen, their funds have temporarily run out.
>
> From the Trattoria everybody adjourns to a Café, and directly opposite the Lepre is the Café Greco, the general rendezvous of the artists of all nations. It has existed two hundred years on the same spot and with the same name. When you enter, you find the smoke so dense that you can scarcely see across the room, but through it dimly appear the long beards, fierce moustaches, slouched hats, slashed velvet jackets, frogged coats, and wild but intellectual countenances which characterize most of the young artists of Rome. All are smoking or taking their after-dinner coffee, or talking in a confusion of languages, compared to which Babel was a deaf-and-dumb asylum.
>
> Though visitors of all degrees are attracted to the Café Greco by the excellence of its coffee (which the proprietor imports directly from Mocha), the majority of its habitual guests are artists, and in the company of some of them I adjourned thence one evening to a Ponte Molle or Artists' Festival. One of my companions was that night to be initiated into the general Association of Artists in Rome, the majority of whom are Germans, and who unite for mutual assistance and social enjoyment.
>
> The Ponte Molle is the bridge by which Northerners enter the city, and its name is therefore given to the Fête, which is the tax of the initiated.
>
> It was held in the trattoria Monte Citorio, behind the post-office; and about two hundred artists were assembled there in their most extravagantly picturesque costumes — most of them looking like Cavaliers of Charles I, and all busily eating, drinking and smoking. At the further

end of the chief room the President was selling at auction a collection of drawings, and paintings, etc., contributed by the more prosperous members of the Society, that the proceeds of the sale be applied to the relief of their poorer brethren in Art. All currencies were named at the biddings, and when an Austrian offered a zwanziger, an American paralleled it precisely with "a Yankee shilling."

The sale went off gaily and successfully. Some fine glees were then sung, all joining in the chorus and beating time with clashing glasses.

The initiation then took place. The doors of an adjoining room were thrown open, and displayed the tableau vivant of the candidate, wrapped in a scarlet mantle, and standing on a table, assuming successively the postures of the Apollo Belvedere, the Flying Mercury, and the like, as proofs of his artistic taste.

The assembly was then asked if they thought him worthy of being elected "Knight of the Baiocco." The response was a chorus of "Yes," "Oui," "Si," "Ya," and other affirmations, and he was immediately invested with the ribbon and medal of the Order, to wit, a new baiocco, or Roman cent; a democratic burlesque on the orders of knighthood, in token that artists should acknowledge the aristocracy of genius alone.

The new knight then received a horn of terra cotta, holding about a quart, as his Scandinavian drinking cup. He went the rounds of the room touching the glasses of everyone, and a German ode composed in honor of him and the Society was then sung.

The election of officers next took place, and finally the crowd dispersed in perfect harmony, having renewed and strengthened by their friendly festivities the fraternal ties which here unite into one brotherhood the thousands of every nation who congregate in Rome for the common pursuit of Art. (Rome as seen by a New Yorker in 1843-4.)

But there was another and more serious side, appreciated and enjoyed and reverently acknowledged by our artists. It is George William Curtis who tells of it in a few convincing sentences. Visualize him as standing on a balcony overlooking Saint Peter's and the Vatican Gardens:

I looked from a lofty balcony at the Vatican upon broad gardens [he writes] with evergreen palms and orange trees, in which gleamed the golden fruit and the rich rounding tufts of Italian pines; and the solemn shafts of cypress stood over fountains which spouted rainbows into the air which were silver clear and transparent, on which the outlines of the hills and foliage were drawn like a flame. Into the air rose floating the Dome of St. Peter's, which is not a nucleus of the city like the Duomo at Florence, but a crown more imposing, as one is further removed. . . .

Here he turns and goes into Saint Peter's. He hears a sound of distant singing, backed by the solemn notes of the organ. Deeply moved he listens:

Then from the high choir at the opposite side of the church, and far above our heads came swimming down the tremulous delicacy of the "Nun's Chant" like voices from Heaven. The sound pervaded the dim air of the church like a radiance too subtle to be seen, but warming and ennobling the soul with a sense of celestial splendor.

He now leaves the church and finds himself back in the open air once more. He continues:

The sun was setting as we came away after one of the aerially soft days with which our imaginations endow Italy. The rich golden flood streamed through the arches of the Colosseum, but could not unbend the stern gravity of its decay. It looked cold and still — the image of the destiny which consumes it. (*Life,* by Edward Cary.)

But to go back to our artists.

There was no studio more sought for than that of Kensett and Thomas Hicks on the Via Margutta near the Piazza di Spagna, up a long flight of stairs. There were no formalities there. Each one could speak out his thoughts and opinions without fear of being molested. He could play his flute or strum his guitar with an utter sense of freedom. An atmosphere of friendliness and ease pervaded the place that was remembered long afterwards.

All these descriptions, that have been quoted from sources of unquestioned authority, reveal in a measure the life and reactions of our American artists in those never-to-be-forgotten days in Rome, when they were young and full of ambitious hopes for the future.

It was in August, 1847, that Kensett left with George William Curtis for a trip through Germany. They returned for a few days to Italy before Kensett started on his way back to his home in America. He had accomplished the initial purpose of his stay in Europe. He had learned of the methods used in the various schools of art. He now returned with the conviction that art was the clearest and simplest medium by which the ideals of each country could be revealed. With this in mind he started with a deeper conception of the opportunity that was his, if he so willed it, to immortalize on canvas the mental states and the ideals of the land of his birth. He hired a studio in New York, and started with a new vigor and an even deeper enthusiasm to portray the free open spaces, the riversides and mountain tops, the green valleys and rolling uplands turning to red and yellow in the autumn — that meant America to him. He commenced a series of studies to enforce this idea of his. His paintings — "Sunset on the Adirondacks," "Scenes on the Genesee River," "Franconia Mountains," "Hudson River from Fort Putnam," "Lake George" — all these and many others of the same type were exhibited before the public, which took to them immediately. They became exceedingly popular, and made quick and ready sales, and were in constant demand.

In 1848 he became a member of the National Academy, and his studio was one of the great attractions in New York to all who loved the natural scenery as one sees it every day. He led Church and Bierstadt, those vital artists who demonstrated the grandeur of our great mountain passes and perilous ravines, our tropics of the South and our ice-fields of the North, and the untrodden places where as yet few men had penetrated, to show the country as they saw it and loved it. He chose to record on canvas scenes for those who prefer the familiar sights of every day.

Tuckerman says in his *Book of the Artists*:

> If we desired to carry abroad genuine memorials of our native scenery — to keep alive its impressions in a foreign land, we would select half a dozen of Kensett's landscapes.
>
> He loved to penetrate into the heart of our forests and paint bits of the rocky ledges on which dense clusters of trees clung, with dripping stones close to a waterfall on which grow lichens. These he portrayed with the literal minuteness of some of the old Flemish painters.

All sylvan subjects he painted to perfection. One of his reviewers wrote of him: "Mr. Kensett has long been accepted as a most consummate master of the treatment of subjects full of repose, and has a free individual method of painting certain facts of nature. . . . He has painted some of the most exquisite pictures that illustrate our art."

It has been stated by one of his biographers that "when one of Kensett's coast scenes was exhibited in Belgium, its strong, clear, and true traits formed so marked a contrast to the more vague and artificial landscapes around, that it became the center of attraction; the best critics awarded it the palm, and a score of eager amateurs beset our minister in Brussels, to whom the picture belonged, with their praises and orders." (Tuckerman.)

Kensett was a prolific painter, and all that came from his brush found an eager market. He was a poor man when he was in Rome. Now he found himself becoming exceedingly well off, and having no wife and family to provide for, he characteristically gave generously to the struggling artists who were going through the difficulties that he knew, but triumphed over, in his younger days.

Mr. Daniel Huntington, a member of the Century Club, said of him:

> As an artist his rank was of the highest. He had that rare assemblage of qualities which combine to make a great painter; an enthusiastic love of beauty, a marvellous eye for color, a clear conception of form, a passion for his art, sustained by a calm persistent patience in its pursuit, and a hand obedient to his trained eye — a hand which expressed his thought with wondrous spirit and felicity.
>
> It must be said that Kensett was not so romantic as Cole, nor had he the transfiguring imagination, and the grand historical vision of Turner, but in his paintings, so truthful of natural objects, so strong and faithful was his work, so affectionate in his temper and tone, that he became a classic among our artists, free from all the prevailing or tempting excesses. He had not the certain wearisome detail of the antique school, nor the dreamy indefiniteness of the new sentimentalism. He went on improving to the last, and those who will compare his pictures at the period when

he acquired his great reputation will see how much he grew in grace and unity — how wonderfully he harmonized and perfected his manner, and finished his pictures without finishing them away. . . . They are pencilled poems which will live. (*Tuttle Genealogy*.)

On July 6, 1859, George William Curtis wrote to Mr. Cranch: "Church is considered by the public — *King*. Then comes Kensett. They have plenty to do, and good pay."

It was in the summer of 1872, when Kensett's life and reputation were at their zenith, that he felt the lure of the Hudson River drawing him to its banks, and he and a close friend of his, Vincent Colyer, purchased a part of Contentment Island, in the Hudson River. There, away from the distractions of city life, he planned to give himself up to his work, with the luxurious feeling of being free from interruptions. Everything seemed to be going perfectly, when in the fall a terrible thing happened. Mr. Colyer's wife was drowned.

History gives no details of the tragic event as to how it happened, or why it happened. It merely states that Kensett plunged into the river and expended every ounce of his strength in an attempt to recover the body, and in so doing he contracted a chill which resulted in pneumonia. Against that disease, as it was in those days, he made a valiant fight for his life, and it seemed as if he had conquered. He was able to return to New York and settle himself in his studio in the Young Men's Christian Association. On Saturday morning he tried going out for a walk. On his return at noon a servant came to his studio door and asked him if he should bring his lunch up to him. Kensett had already seated himself at his easel, prepared to work. He answered "Yes" quite cheerfully and naturally, but when the man returned with his lunch on a tray, he found the artist sitting on the sofa, dead. This was on December 14, 1872. Thus quietly he went (*Arts and Artists in Connecticut*), leaving behind him his paintings and an exceedingly interesting work, though unpublished, on the legends of the Catskills.

His death made a sensation among his friends and admirers. The New York *Observer* wrote:

And thus closed one of the greatest and most evenly successful of artistic careers. An artist without enemies in his own guild is a rare man to find — but whoever spoke ill of Kensett? He looked, and was, a perfect gentleman, of kindly sentiment and genial culture, a friend to all good men, and an enemy to no one. Among all the guild of artists in the Century Club, in the Union League, and among a large circle of our best men and women, Kensett will be mourned with unaffected sorrow.

This feeling for him not only existed in this country but was felt by many across the Atlantic. George H. Broughton, writing from London, says: "As an artist and as a man, Kensett was as near perfection as possible. Others are left, kind and good and gifted, but he had his particular charm and value, and it died with him all too soon."

One could quote almost endlessly from articles and newspaper reviews like these, but it is not necessary to do so. These quite sufficiently tell the tale of the memory he left of himself.

And to prove how the public felt about his paintings, read this:

The results of Kensett's career from beginning to end are a wonderful example of the possibilities before an artist. He left six hundred studies, sketches, and finished pictures in his studio when he died, and being sold at auction in May, 1873, they brought over one hundred and fifty thousand dollars to add to an already ample fortune. It was the most remarkable sale on record. (*Art and Artists in Connecticut.*)

The following article, so full of charm and memory of the old Roman days when the Hudson River artists were young, was written by George William Curtis for *Harper's Magazine* after the death of Kensett (taken from the *Tuttle Genealogy*, 1883):

In the course of many years' monthly chatting and chronicling, the Easy Chair has had occasion often to speak a word of regretful farewell to some whom all men honored — and to some known only to a smaller circle. It is pleasant to think that on some day hereafter, when this century is ended and we are all gone, the new world that follows us will wonder over the quaint ways and amusing conceits of their ancestors. But gentle reader of that distant day, when your eyes fall upon this page, know that the few words which the Easy Chair is about to write cannot show you, as they fain would, the sweet and cheerful and serene soul which henceforth lives for us only in memory, and in his beautiful pictures.

Rome changes so little from year to year that the spacious studio in which the Easy Chair first saw Kensett doubtless still remains, and is occupied perhaps by some young worker at the easel, who hears the same old constant ringing of church bells, and who climbs the hill over the studio at evening to see the sun setting, and St. Peter's steeped in the rosy light. It was upon the Via Margutta, a little back from the street, that Kensett shared the studio with his lifelong friend, Thomas Hicks. There in the happy days they studied and painted, and there was always the lively welcome for the mere loungers, youths making the grand tour, and excellent seniors who came to Rome with families and traveling carriages, the bland dispensers of commissions. All that Kensett was in the latter days — ever bright, tranquil, sympathetic, modest, generous, manly — he was in the Roman days, more than twenty years ago. Never peevish, never selfish, scorning to solicit in any way, self-reliant, trusting himself and the future, how plainly he seems to stand at this moment, stepping back a little from the easel, turning his head and studying the effect of every touch, while a soft, lovely landscape of summer peace brightens his canvas.

There was the usual sign of artists of all kinds in Rome, one of whom, the oldest resident, Robert Macpherson, who married Mrs. Jameson's niece, and who chanced upon the famous Sebastian del Piombo, died just before Kensett. We all dined at the Lepre and probably ate more than our peck of — ? But what a flavor it had! Hark! That is the "boss" waiter. "Ecco! Signore, vengo, vengo! Eccomi qua!"

What guests does the bustling Muzio serve now? and what viands? Do the unwary still expect broth when they order Zuppa Inglese? Does the tradition of Mezzo Sbrinzo yet linger? And Calcedonio, with his smooth, fair face, who needed only the heavy vine chaplet to be Antinous himself, in what celestial trattorio does he now come smiling in, holding huge piles of plates aloft?

From the Lepre we crossed to the Café Greco. It was famous ground, for Thorwaldsen had sat there sipping his black coffee, and Gibson was sometimes seen in our day. We sat in the narrow, dark room called the omnibus. We paid two baiocchi or pennies for a tumbler of coffee. How we smoked! How we talked and laughed! What good things were said at the Lepre! Because there was a Mermaid, shall there be no other cakes and ale?

How plain it was! How dingy! And were ever more satisfaction, more pleasure, and richer memories bought at a cheaper rate? And among all the famous loiterers at the Greco was there ever a kinder, simpler, sweeter companion than Kensett? He was not fluent. He told few stories. But his generous sympathy, his interested attention, was inspiration. He made a sunshine that harmonized and softened all. Is there a Greco still? The old dingy room must have gone. But if by any chance it remains, let its frequenters of to-day cherish it more because of that gentle presence long ago.

Was it to the Piazza and to the round game of pool at the billiard table that we afterward repaired? There is not a gilded fledgling of a New York club that would not have smiled at our small skill. But the Easy Chair watches the splendid games of to-day and sees no gayer players. There are jokes, there are incidents from those old games of pool still current among those innocent gamesters grown gray. There are characters, figures, movements, that are still irresistible in memory. Those Roman hours of youth are bonds still among men whose lives are widely severed and who have no other interests in common. Christopher Sly and old John Naps of Greece are names merely — so are Leafchild and the fat British troubadour. He played the guitar and threw up his round, blue eyes and his pudgy fingers as he trolled a sentimental ditty. And what awful stories he told afterward! That fat troubadour told tales of English social life which, if they were true, are such as Mrs. Aphra Behn would have delighted to record, but which, probably for the honor of human nature, none of the hearers believed.

There were tea-parties, also, in the rooms of the bachelors up many and many a flight of stone stairs. The nearer the roof the nearer heaven. Nor was there any disturbing fear, as in the splendid modern cities. There was no burning in Rome, that is, no burning of houses. There had been other kinds formerly, and according to some sermons preached, there was immense preparation for firing up hereafter. There were bachelor tea-parties; tea, with a "leetle" hot spiced wine; simple wine, you understand — Velletri, and other vineyards of the neighboring hills. Not one of that set of foreign Romans did the Easy Chair ever see as he should not be, by reason of wine. One night there was a symposium at the rooms of Kensett and Hicks. It was a pleasant, merry, singing, not roistering, feast; tea in large cups, without milk, and a dash of Velletri somewhere during the evening. And somehow it came to be midnight, and as Time is always pushing on, he began to mow the tender stalks of morning hours, and still the tea was hot, and still there was one more glass of spiced Velletri, and another song when there was a knock at the door.

It was an hour when only doctors or the police knock, and there was some wonder. But the youngest comer said quietly, "I think that must be Cousin Timothy." The youngest comer was new to Rome, and was stopping with his cousin, who served the god of regularity, and who, vexed and alarmed by the nocturnal truancy of a tyro, came forth to seek him. When the door was opened the admonishing figure of Timothy appeared, holding a coil of wax taper in his hand to light his way, and it also revealed the spruce trimness of his attire. "It's time to come home," said Timothy gravely — and he was in the right. But the youngest comer replied calmly, "Cousin Timothy, henceforth I think that all baggage had better be at the risk of the owner." It was decisive. Timothy politely withdrew and hunted no more erring lambs before light.

From Rome there was a long and happy journey with Kensett to Naples, and Paestum, and Amalfi, Ischia, and the Blue Grotto. Then again for a few summer days to Rome, and slowly northward to Florence. After a month at Florence, where Mr. and Mrs. Browning then were, we passed across the Apennines by Bologna and Ferrara to Venice. In September we came through Lombardy, and one soft evening, at Verona, Kensett climbed into the banquette of the diligence, and reaching down his hand, we who remained shook it heartily and bade him Godspeed for America.

During all that Italian time, Kensett was constantly at work, and with wonderful little waste. He would pass a day faithfully studying and painting a mullein. His sketches were so vivid and faithful and delicate that afterward there was no wall in New York so beautiful as that of his old studio, at the top of the Waverley House, on the corner of Broadway and Fourth Street, upon which they were hung in a solid mass.

He returned home to a series of noiseless victories. He was a recognized master of landscape, and all his pictures are biographical, for they reveal the fidelity, the tenderness, and the sweet serenity of his nature. Universally beloved, he was always welcome. He did not live to be an old man; but although he had turned the half-century corner, he seemed no older in heart and sympathy and the fresh faith that illuminates life with celestial radiance, in the studio upon the Fourth Avenue and Twenty-Third Street where he died, than in the old Roman room in the Via Margutta long ago. Somewhat lonely he must sometimes have been, but no one probably ever heard from him a sigh of regret, or the least impatient wish that life might have been different. As those who personally knew him die, his eventless life will pass from memory, but his lovely character will still live on in his pictures, and mingle unconsciously, to those who grow beneath the spell of their beauty, with other lives and characters in a hundred homes. So the influence of a good man is not lost; and so will it forever inspire that faith in the divine goodness which was peculiarly that of this beloved artist.

Kensett was buried in the Greenwood Cemetery in New York.

Cranch's visit to Robert Browning and his wife on December 20, 1848, in Rome is so interesting that the chapter should not close without including it. He writes:

> We called yesterday at the Casa Guidi to see Robert Browning and his wife, Elizabeth Barrett Browning. Found her a small, delicate, not handsome invalid, who did not impress me at all at first as the poetess and woman of learning and genius that she is, till she warmed into conversation on some interesting theme, such as Italy and the Pope and France — then her eyes shone with a true inward lustre. Her enthusiasm in speaking of children and her general goodness of heart impressed me most. I thought her somewhat diffident, and like one who had lived in retirement most of her life.
>
> Browning is very different; he seems like a man who had lived in society, a true, social, healthy, open, frank nature, entering into life and associating with men, while inwardly delicate and poetic.

CHAPTER II

Robert Walter Weir

(1803–1889)

As Robert Walter Weir was also one of the landscape painters who had memories of the picturesque colony of Hudson River artists in Rome, it is his right to tell of his life among them, and though it does not differ greatly from the accounts already given in the article on John Frederick Kensett, at the same time each account is a contribution, and gives additional color and illumination to the whole episode.

But before giving his account of it, which is very short, his nationality must be recorded. He was the son of a Scotsman for whom he was named, who came over from Paisley in 1790, and settled in New York. Mercantile and shipping pursuits were his interests, in which he was very successful for a time, even to maintaining a country-seat in New Rochelle. The boy Robert therefore was brought up in affluence until he was ten years old, when his father met with financial reverses, and young as he was he was placed in a cotton factory, where he worked for twelve years.

An uncle of his undertook to give him an education, and took him to Albany where he was placed in a school, with certain studies given him in New York. It did not work out at all well and he was very unhappy every moment of the time. In fact he relates to Dunlap (*Arts of Design*) that the misery he suffered was indescribable, and his father, becoming aware of his son's unhappiness, sent for him to come home.

It is interesting to notice by what quirks of fate a life is led. Weir, having learned practically nothing during the few months under his uncle's supervision, began going to school again.

Now, opposite the schoolhouse the artist John Wesley Jarvis had his studio, and when young Weir was not studying he was apt to linger about the door, hoping to get a glimpse of this noted artist at work. In spite of his many attempts he did not succeed, and one day a thought entered his head that revealed the tenacity of his Scottish blood. He boldly entered the studio. Mr. Jarvis happened to be absent, but nothing abashed, the boy addressed a student who was working there, and asked him what the cost would be to have his portrait painted by Jarvis. The pupil was somewhat taken by surprise, but answered him solemnly and very politely, stating the various prices according to size, and going so far as to offer to sketch his head for the sum of five dollars.

These few moments of conversation brought about a friendship that proved valuable to young Weir, as the pupil was none other than the future well-known artist, Henry Inman, who was then studying under Jarvis and later became one of our noted portrait painters.

This episode stirred a love of art in Weir's breast without his fully realizing the strength of it, but it led decisively to a desire to know more on the subject, and he relates a fact to prove it. "The first book on painting that fell in my way," he writes, "was Dryden's translation of Du Fresnoy, with notes by De Piles. I read it with enthusiastic delight; every word sank deep within me, and caused tears of joy and shouts of ecstasy at every page. My soul swelled with pure zeal for the art, and when finished I felt better and happier, and resolved to be a painter."

But trying to make his way in the world in order to help out the sad and unfortunate situation in which his father was placed had to be his first consideration, and in the fall of 1817 a situation opened for him in a French mercantile firm in the South. Eighteen months later he was offered the position of head clerk in a mercantile office in New York, which he accepted, and after three years was offered a partnership in the firm. He refused this offer. He seemed to feel himself incapable of becoming an established businessman and making a fortune, so the artistic feeling which had been stirred in him by his experience in the office of John Wesley Jarvis, and his subsequent friendship with Inman, which seemed long ago to him in one way but fresh in another, came to the fore. He therefore broke away from a business career and looked about him for a teacher in art. He got in touch with an Englishman who offered to give him lessons, but Weir soon became convinced that the man lacked the groundwork which he desired most earnestly to attain, so he left him. Being of necessity short of funds, as he had his father to support, he decided to let the spirit of Art itself lead him, and in the fall of 1821 he set himself seriously to work and made a small sketch of "Paul preaching at Athens."

He received some praise for this painting, and immediately became ambitious to paint this subject lifesize, in accordance with some of the very large paintings which were finding favor with the public and were the fashion of the day.

He was then in his nineteenth year and at an age when nothing daunted him, but it was an exceedingly laborious undertaking, occupying every available moment for nine months, during which time, he writes to Dunlap, "I was beating about through a sea of trouble, sometimes rubbing out whole platoons of figures."

He did this monumental work in the attic of an old almshouse, where he was continually being dunned for rent. It was indeed a dreary place. If a friend desired to see how the work was progressing, he had to climb up ladders, push his way through trapdoors, and plow through heaps of rubbish which was stowed away in the garret before he could reach the place where Weir was making a temporary studio for himself.

At last the picture was finished and exhibited in Washington Hall. It created a good deal of attention, so much so that he felt himself fully justified in pursuing the profession he had chosen. But he realized that he must perfect himself in anatomy, though in so doing he considered himself injured not only physically but nervously. Weir was temperamental in his make-up. Things out of the ordinary made a deep impression on him. He tells of one experience he had when he first began a course under a Doctor Post, who gave him late one afternoon half of a human head to take home with him, wrapping it in Weir's handkerchief as an easy way to carry it. The latter writes:

> The novelty of carrying such a commodity set my imagination to working, so that before reaching my father's house my feverish fancy was much excited. Having reached my bedchamber I deposited my troublesome burden in my trunk and crept into bed — but not to sleep, for my thoughts which had possessed my brain pursued me, and after tossing about until two in the morning, I determined to get up and carry it back. In my anxiety I had forgotten that every house must be shut at that time, and I wandered the silent and deserted streets until daylight.

Weir had two very distinct sides to his character. On one side was the grim determination of a Scotsman, and on the other was a gay prankish side, more or less like that of a small boy. He recognized this himself, and he relates an anecdote to his friend Dunlap that reveals it. Here it is:

> It had been an amusement for me occasionally to paint a picture, and nearly obliterating it with dirt, to put it in the way of some would-be connoisseur, who after examining it attentively would pronounce it an undoubted work of some one of the old masters.

Here he tells of a hoax he played on a fellow artist which nearly cost him his friendship:

> I had called one morning and found him delightfully employed in copying one of my antiques (?).
>
> "What are you about, Tom?" I exclaimed.
>
> "Ah!" was his reply — "there is a jewel for you! — that's an undoubted original of Annibale Carracci!"
>
> "An undoubted humbug," was my rejoinder.
>
> Tom turned his dark eyes fiercely on me, repeating, "Do you doubt it? Do you doubt it? Why, Mr. P. lent it to me yesterday, and at the same time told me that it cost him $300."
>
> "Well, Tom, I can only say if you take that picture out of the frame, you will find on the lower edge of the panel the initials of my name." To satisfy himself he took it out, and there the little telltales were. The next day Tom sent the picture home with many thanks to the owner, and at the same time threw his copy into the fire.

Time of course took away any desire to perform such pranks, and Weir turned his attention to learning Italian. Then came the same longing which at some time or other attacked the artists of those days to see Rome, and all the beauty and art and antiquity that were centered there.

On the fifteenth of December, 1824, he bade adieu to his friends and to his native land and sailed for Leghorn. It took him sixty days to get there. During the passage he illustrated the greater part of Dante's *Inferno,* not wishing to waste any time.

This trip of his was made possible by the generosity of Mr. Henry Carey, and Weir felt doubly anxious to take advantage of the unexpected opportunity to enlarge his knowledge of art, and the world, and all the beauty it contained. He stopped at Florence and became a pupil of Pietro Benvenuti, who was frescoing the Pitti Palace, but it was not for long — it was Rome he wanted, and he hastened there. He had in some way become a friend of the sculptor Greenough, and he knew that through him the treasures of the great city would be open to him. With a feeling of almost overpowering anticipation he wrote of this experience to his friend Dunlap:

My face was set towards Rome, my heart many leagues in advance. [The following is a description of his arrival] A few days brought me to the gates of the great city of art, where I entered most unpropitiously amid hail and rain, but it did not prevent me from seeing the Colosseum and some works of art before I retired for the night. Here I found our friend Greenough who had lately arrived, and we soon agreed to take rooms together, which we happily procured on the Pincian Hill. Our home was situated opposite to that which had been occupied by Claude Lorrain and between those known as Salvator Rosa's and Nicolas Poussin's.

You may imagine that in the midst of such, to us, "holy ground" our enthusiasm was not a little excited. There we set ourselves most industriously to work, and as you wished me to detail to you our mode of study, I will attempt it:

We rose tolerably early, and either pursued some study in our own room, or went to the French Academy and drew from the antique until breakfast time, after which we separated — Greenough to his studio, whilst

I went to the Vatican or the Sistine Chapel, or some of the private galleries that are liberally thrown open for the purpose of study. There I worked away until three o'clock, at which time they closed. I then took a lunch, and either strolled through St. Peter's or the antique galleries of the Vatican, or went to the French Academy and drew from casts, or to my own room, or in the fields, and drew from nature until six, which was our dinner hour.

We then assembled at the Bacco dí Lione, a famous eating house, the dining hall of which had been the painting room of Pompio Battoni. It was in this room where he received Reynolds with the pompous salutation: "Well, young man, walk in — walk in — you shall see Pompio Battoni paint!"

It served our imagination, and formed a part of that atmosphere of art which surrounds the student in Rome, and makes his lamp burn bright and his enthusiasm strong.

After dinner, or rather after supper, all the artists met at a place called the Greek Coffee House (Café Greco) where we had our coffee, and chatted until seven, at which hour the life school opened, and we separated — some to the French or Italian, and Greenough and myself to the English, where we studied from life until nine o'clock, and then if the night proved fine and the moon shone bright, we formed small parties to go and dream among the ruins of Imperial Rome.

This formed our round of daily occupation; we lived and moved in art; it was our food, ready at all times — we had but to stretch out our hands and pluck what we wanted.

In the midst of this artists' paradise it was easy for them to live in a sort of unreal world, and to become somewhat vague in regard to money, and such realities. This happened to Weir. One day he saw a complete suit or armor that filled his eye. He wanted it — he wanted to own it — it tempted him though he had no business to allow it to do so; finally it was too much for him and he bought it. The natural result was that he found himself entirely out of funds, so much so that he had to manage to live on ten cents a day, so he states, for nearly a month before he could resume his normal way of living.

But now the course of study that Weir and Greenough had laid out for themselves proved to be too strenuous, for the latter's health began to break under it, and he was obliged to leave Rome and rest for awhile. This left Weir responsible for the apartment which was far too high in price for him to carry on alone, costing as it did ten dollars a month, so he sought one in a less fashionable quarter, and found one for four dollars a month, which suited his purse better, and which in those days was considered a high enough price for an artist to pay.

Shortly after that he met an English architect, with whom he had expected to walk to Venice and make sketches on the way, when suddenly word reached him that his friend Greenough was in bad shape and very ill. Weir immediately gave up all his plans and hastened to him, finding him not only ill but very low in his mind. All zest for life seemed to have left him. His doctor ordered a change of scene, and Weir took him to Naples, thinking a view of the bay of that beautiful city, with Vesuvius beyond, would calm him and restore him. But he did not improve there, and Weir, taking sole charge of his friend with complete devotion, which involved giving up all his plans for the future, insisted upon returning with him to America. The voyage seemed to restore him, and Weir was able to deliver him to his family greatly relieved in body and mind.

In the meantime Weir's father had died, and he was obliged to settle the latter's affairs, and though when he left Italy he had cherished the hope of returning to complete the course of studies he was taking there, he found it necessary to remain on this side of the water, so he opened a studio in New York. This was in 1827.

It was in 1829 that he married Louise Ferguson, and in that same year he was elected a member of the National Academy of Design. His name was now well to the fore in the art world, and things were going finely when in 1834 a new avenue to success opened for him. He took Charles Leslie's place as instructor in drawing at the United States Military Academy at West Point, where in 1846 he was made a full professor.

This was a very fortunate move for him. Among his many distinguished pupils whose names became famous in after life were

Generals Grant, Lee, Sherman, and others, including the artist Whistler.

While the duties in this new position were arduous, he was able to continue as a painter of pictures, and, living as he did in full sight of the Hudson River, he devoted himself largely to landscape painting, which revealed his innate knowledge of nature in her various moods, and won the approbation of the public. However, he did not neglect his historical paintings, for between 1836 and 1840 he was painting "The Embarkation of the Pilgrims" for the rotunda of the Capitol at Washington.

About this time sorrow came to him with the death of two of his children. Using the ten-thousand-dollar commission he had received, he designed and had built a memorial chapel in their memory at Highland Falls, near West Point, which was known as "The Church of the Holy Innocents."

Then another sorrow came to him in the death of his wife. Being the sort of man who could not live happily without the comfort of a near companionship, in 1846 he married Susan Bayard. In all he was the father of sixteen children. He had the unique experience among the group of Hudson River artists of passing on to two of his children his artistic talent, so that they became well-known artists in their own right. One son, John Ferguson Weir, became a member of the National Academy of Design in 1866, and a director of the Yale University Art School in 1868. His other artist son, Julian Alden Weir, studied under his father, and became a distinguished landscape painter, and a painter of portraits as well. (*Encyclopaedia Britannica.*)

Like all the artists of his time Robert Walter Weir was very much influenced by its literature. The novels of Sir Walter Scott and of James Fenimore Cooper made a deep impression on his imagination and contributed unconsciously to his work. The Bible also was a never ending source of inspiration to his more serious side, and many of his early pictures depicted scenes therefrom. It must have been noticed that, one may say, all of these artists inclined towards spiritual things. It can be seen in their high idealism, and the single-minded manner in which they strove to attain their goal.

The two places where the most vital periods of Weir's life were lived were the Hudson River, and the Eternal City — Rome. They were marked in italics on his heart.

To show how versatile were his talents, he designed an altarpiece for the Church of the Holy Cross in Troy, New York. He designed stained-glass windows for Trinity Chapel and Calvary Church in New York City, and the altarpiece descriptive of "Peace" and "War" in the old chapel at West Point.

His vital personality, his qualities of sound judgment, his keen and idealistic imagination awoke the lasting affection of the generation of students he instructed at West Point, and his friendliness to all his fellow artists is frequently mentioned by his biographers, especially by his friend William Dunlap.

After a period of forty-two years he retired from his duties at West Point. That was in 1876, but from then on to the day of his death on May 1, 1889, he maintained a studio in New York where he worked with his accustomed vigor. It was characteristic of him that he died, so to speak, in harness, according to his desire.

Weir's portrait painted by Daniel Huntington hangs in the Library of the United States Military Academy at West Point, New York.

CHAPTER 12

William Louis Sonntag, N.A.
(1822–1900)

WILLIAM LOUIS SONNTAG is one of the few highlights of the Hudson River School of painting who has left to posterity beautiful pictures to guard and cherish, but has left no word regarding himself to place him alongside the varied characters that made up that interesting group of early landscape painters of American art. There have been searchings on every side for some clue of his life, but all that can be found is a short notice of his birth and death, and the dates of his visits to Europe, and a long list of the pictures he painted.

This much is known: He was born at East Liberty, near Pittsburgh, Pennsylvania, on March 2, 1822. He was self-taught in his chosen profession, and did much of his early work in Cincinnati. Then he moved to New York, where he became much sought after. He seems to have been an eager and ambitious worker. His trips to Europe were in 1853, 1856, 1860, and 1862.

He was evidently a very self-contained individual and not one to associate with his fellow artists beyond a certain point, for one never finds his name linked with others in taking walking trips through the mountains of Switzerland, etc., as so many did, thus enjoying companionship, as well as making sketches of the scenery. One does not hear of him with the others enjoying the hospitality of the Café Greco in Rome.

It seems a pity that his character, which must have been endowed with strength and decision, if one can judge by his paintings, should not be revealed to the public. Perhaps he had no relative who would take the time to do this. As a result, all that can be done to understand the traits of his character is to study his work.

He died in 1900, a member of the National Academy.

CHAPTER 13

Albert Bierstadt
(1830–1902)

THE STRONG PERSONALITY of Albert Bierstadt stands out by itself, and has its own place among the artists of the Hudson River group. He was of the rugged type, one who had fought in the Peninsular War.

His father was by profession a German soldier, whose native home was in Düsseldorf, one of the art centers of Germany. His son Albert was born just two years before he and his family emigrated to the United States and settled in New Bedford, Massachusetts.

The love of the beautiful does not come suddenly into the life of a true artist. Signs of it are sure to manifest themselves during childhood, and so it was with young Bierstadt. All during his schooldays even, while he watched the sailing ships coming and going to and from the busy wharfs of New Bedford, a longing was taking hold of him. As usual, his father's friends and relatives at once tried to destroy this longing which they could see taking possession of him, by putting forward all the objections they could think of. But he came of determined stock, and while to all appearances he was giving some attention to the various business professions with which they thought to tempt him, he was making up his own mind as to the path he intended to follow.

As yet he had not shown any definite or unusual signs of an artistic nature to warrant any drastic methods of determining his future, but it was some really clever sketches in crayon which, as youth developed into manhood, he frequently executed that caused them real anxiety.

He moved cautiously, and it was not until his twenty-third year

(1851) that he openly began to paint in oils, in order to accumulate sufficient funds to enable him to visit his native city of Düsseldorf, and incidentally a cousin of his, an eminent artist of genre paintings, which were exceedingly popular in this country. Accordingly he packed his few belongings in 1853, and set his face towards Düsseldorf.

He thought — and his family agreed to this — that his cousin's influence would give him an assistance with which none of the other young American artists had been blessed. To his great disappointment, however, he discovered upon his arrival in what had been his "home town" that Hazenclever had died within a short time. He felt stranded for a moment. But with the tenacity and dogged determination of his race, he started right away to make friends.

It so happened that Worthington Whittredge, our well-known Hudson River artist, who was there making a study of the Düsseldorf methods of painting — for the Academy was admittedly famous for its own technique in the art, and also for the artist Leutze and a few others — took him into their circle, which showed the natural attraction of his strong personality, and under their advice he began receiving instruction from the artists belonging to the Academy, giving some promise of becoming a true follower of the Hudson River group. But under the complicated and technical methods of the German School he became restless, so much so that in the matter of painting he "gave no striking proof of individual merit"; though doubtless he acquired much technical aptitude by his drawing and color practice, and from the criticisms of his more experienced companions.

In this, as in so many other instances of the Hudson River artists, the true development in landscape art "was gained away from the studio, by the personal and independent study of Nature herself." (Tuckerman.)

And so he broke away from Düsseldorf to seek inspiration from other sources. He first went on a pedestrian tour through Westphalia, then the next year he went on a tour through Hesse-Cassel. This last tour gave him a subject to paint that started him on his way to fame. He was much struck, one afternoon while tramping along shouldering his painting kit, with a "beautiful effect of light and shade on the mossy massive front and low arched door of a quaint mediaeval church, with a wide-spreading venerable tree, beside the wall, and an old woman seated by the gateway. The whole scene was full of mellow, time-honored and consecrated repose." (Tuckerman.) Bierstadt caught the spirit of the scene perfectly — the arched door of the ancient church, the old peasant sitting quietly near, under the shade of the protecting tree. He called the picture "Sunshine and Shadow."

With his skill and natural ability for detail, the painting was so realistic and so true to nature that the public took to it at once — the papers commented most favorably upon it, and looked for more from his brush.

Now, his experience at Düsseldorf brought into his life something he greatly prized, and that was his friendship with Whittredge. The latter's quiet ways acted as a balancing influence on the tremendous vigor of Bierstadt's temperament, and on leaving the German art center they decided to go to Rome for the winter.

The wonders of the "Eternal City" with its traditions, its great collections of famous paintings, the beauty of its ancient ruins, filled them, as it did all the artists who went there, with a very special enthusiasm, but Bierstadt's mind was ever on his longing to leave the past with all the history attached to it, and to plunge into the yet unknown regions of our own land, and show forth the marvels hidden there. It was with this purpose in view that he studied carefully the Old-World paintings to which he gave all reverence, with the hope that he might enlarge and intensify his love of beauty in whatever phase he found it, so that he could reveal the wonders of his own adopted land more perfectly.

When spring came a young artist turned up who was already on his way to claim association with the Hudson River group. His name was R. Sanford Gifford. He was anxious to make a pedestrian tour through the Apennines, to get sketches for future development from among those mountains. Bierstadt, always ready to plunge into new experiences, arranged to go with him, and they set off with packs on their backs. It was a fine experience for Bierstadt, but it was a still greater one for Gifford. That young artist probably never realized the vigor, the versatility, the inborn enthusiasm of a man like Bierstadt, who was eager to climb to the highest peaks and sketch at seemingly impossible angles. In looking back at that tour after many years they undoubtedly put a red letter next it in their memories.

On their return to Rome he found Whittredge eager to get hold of him for a sojourn in Switzerland and a trip down the Rhine with the addition of the artist Haseltine. This made a strong appeal to Bierstadt, who was not sure of ever getting so tempting an opportunity again, so in spite of the strenuous mountain-climbing he had done recently, off he went. These trips enlarged his powers of observation, and filled his portfolio with treasures in the way of sketches he could not have acquired in any other way, so that when he returned to his New Bedford home in 1857, he had a wealth of material to work upon. A quotation is given here:

> Among the works which our artist elaborated from his careful European studies, is a most effective picture of the "Bay of Sorrento," one of the "Arch of Octavian," a "Street Scene in Rome," and "Lake Lucerne," each of which, for accuracy of local details, still life, atmospheric effects, tints of earth and water, character of accessories, and in every essential feature, is an eloquent epitome of its subject, and transports the spectator to the fairest environs of Naples — to the heart of Switzerland, or to the centre of the "Eternal City." (Tuckerman.)

It was no wonder that these artists, bound together by the same vivid interests, should have finished these tours with minds stimulated and refreshed, filled with new ideas, and a memory of happy days.

The aforesaid paintings, exhibited to show what Bierstadt had seen and studied and digested from his travels in the Old World, were quickly sold, and absorbed mostly into private collections; therefore they disappeared more or less from public view. But the painting "Sunshine and Shadow," which had so taken the public fancy when it was exhibited on the other side, now appeared prom-

inently in many exhibitions on this side of the water, and was looked
upon as his best work, for his great achievements in the West were
yet to come.

Tuckerman says in his valuable *Book of the Artists*:

> Adventure is an element in American artist-life which gives it singular
> zest and interest. . . . A few years ago [he was writing thus in 1867] the
> idea of a carefully studied, faithfully composed, and admirably executed
> landscape of Rocky Mountain scenery would have been deemed chimer-
> ical, involving as it must long and isolated journeys, and no ordinary risk
> and privation. And yet the American work of art which attracted most
> attention, and afforded the greatest promise and pleasure in the spring of
> 1863 was such a picture.

At that time Bierstadt decided to become truly adventurous, so
he joined General Lander's now famous expedition into the unbroken West. It meant months away from civilization, but that did
not retard him — on the contrary, it seemed to beckon to him, and
he entered the experience with the ardor of a boy.

There are long accounts given of the trip with its vicissitudes, and
its inspiring pleasures, and its perilous escapes, and victorious
achievements, which hardly belong to this article. Suffice it to say
that after a time he and a few others left Lander's party still on the
great cliffs of as yet untrodden mountains, and set out for home.

"They reached Fort Laramie in safety, after a journey of many
days through a country perilous even for a body of armed troops."

"What a contrast to the artist-life of Rome and Paris in this fresh
and free search for the picturesque in the remote and solitary heart
of nature!"

But Bierstadt was so concentrated on how he was to demonstrate
on canvas the marvels of what he had seen that he took no time out
for comparisons.

The results make interesting reading. He held an exhibition of
the scenery of those wonderful creations of nature. People flocked
from long distances to see them. The fact that they were for sale
added to the interest.

The finest picture of all was called "The Rocky Mountains —

Lander's Peak," six by ten feet in size. Sold to James McHenry, Esq., for twenty-five thousand dollars.

"Estes Park." Sold to the Earl of Dunraven.

"Storm in the Rocky Mountains — Mount Rosalie," owner T. W. Kennard, Esq.; twelve by seven feet in size, valued at thirty-five thousand dollars.

"The Domes of the Yosemite," owner Le Grand Lockwood, Esq.

"Looking down the Yosemite," owner U. H. Crosby.

"Laramie Peak," belonging to the Buffalo Academy of Fine Arts.

"Valley of the Yosemite," owner James Lenox, Esq., of New York, etc.

These were pictures of enormous size, as is seen. But there were smaller ones which were eagerly sought by the public and which also commanded high prices. The list is too long to record.

In writing about the "Storm in the Rocky Mountains," the London *Saturday Review* stated: "The qualities which strike us in Mr. Bierstadt, as an artist, are first, a great audacity, justified by perfect ability to accomplish all that he intends. He is not a mere copyist of nature, but an artist having definite artistic intentions, and carrying them out with care and resolution."

Another writer says: "No more genuine and grand American work has been produced in landscape art than Bierstadt's 'Rocky Mountains.'" (Tuckerman.)

He was sometimes described as a true representative of the Düsseldorf School of painting, which means that, in spite of himself, he had imbibed certain methods of theirs though his desire was to keep his own particular American methods. It was also said that the Düsseldorf methods were a novelty in this country, though familiar abroad, and that this accounted somewhat for his tremendous success. In fact, our art centers were greatly stirred by his productions and discussed them at length. What he had done was something entirely out of the ordinary.

Henry T. Tuckerman, whose *Book of the Artists* has been frequently quoted, and who was a contemporary of Bierstadt's, says in it:

"We are glad to have the Düsseldorf school so emphatically represented; . . . It is admirably adapted to some scenes and subjects; it
adds to the variety and the popularity of our landscape art; its contrasts are desirable; and it appeals to an order of minds comparatively
insensible to more vague and latent art-language."

The size of some of Bierstadt's paintings, while very dramatic and
very beautiful, excludes them from very many exhibition halls. One
account of it says:

"The painting 'The Domes of the Yosemite' is panoramic in size;
it is a wildly magnificent and unique scene, drawn with singular
fidelity from the solitary heart of the Rocky Mountains."

The owner, Le Grand Lockwood, Esq., must have had an enor-
mously high gallery to hang it in!

The art world was stirred by these great paintings of Albert Bierstadt's, not only in America but also in Europe. The audacity of the
artist made a great appeal. His paintings showed a vitality and zest
that made his western landscapes of the Rocky Mountains very
striking, and often in size and coloring somewhat breath-taking. Of
the two styles of painting the public in its heart preferred the dreamy
romantic style of Doughty, Durand — the dramatic art of Thomas
Cole, and those who followed them — but the subjects they chose to
paint were wholly different from the awe-inspiring scenes of the
Rocky Mountains, which needed the temperament and majestic conception of grandeur of a Bierstadt to put convincingly their giant
proportions, lofty heights, and cavernous depths before it. But in
certain moods he could turn about and paint in a quieter vein when
he chose to, and in these moods he took smaller canvases to paint on
which made them available to the homes of the people. These had
the same realistic qualities of his larger paintings, softened and mel-
lowed, however, by his return to rural scenes of a quieter kind.

Another quotation is given here from the London *Saturday Review* which shows the international quality of his reputation as an
artist:

> In an age when some hold the theory that art may be dispensed with,
> and that mere copyism is enough, we welcome a man like Bierstadt, who,

as devoted a lover of the grandest scenes in nature as any painter who ever lived, is at the same time plotting and planning for purely artistic ends. He is always trying for luminous gradations and useful oppositions, and reaches what he tries for . . . we believe that in art of this kind, when the object is to produce a powerful impression of overwhelming grandeur, a painter must employ all the resources possible to him.

In 1860 he was made a member of the National Academy of Design, and in 1867 he was sent to Europe upon a government commission to make studies for a painting of the "Discovery of the North River" by Hendrick Hudson — a subject "admirably adapted to his pencil and to national historic landscape." (*Artists of the Nineteenth Century; Book of the Artists.*)

It was during this trip (1867) that France conferred upon him the distinguished tribute of making him a Chevalier of the Legion of Honor. In 1869 Austria made him a member of the Order of Saint Stanislas, and Germany, Bavaria, and Belgium granted him distinguished medals. (*Dictionary of American Biography*, Allen Johnson and Dumas Malone.)

Bierstadt was now thirty-seven years old, and was at the height of his strength and vigor. He traveled all over the country, discovering places as yet unknown to the public though sometimes near at hand. He went among the Western Indians and painted them at their various occupations — he sketched wherever he could bring new knowledge of the out-of-the-way places to the public. More and more he became convinced that the only vital school of landscape art was the patient and faithful study of nature, and this conviction was carried out in no halfhearted way.

Bierstadt now became anxious to own a home, and like so many of the other Hudson River landscape painters he chose the site of it on the banks of the Hudson, and his spacious studio, like that of Cole's, commanded a beautiful and extensive view of the river nearing the Palisades. There he worked assiduously.

One day while walking near Bierstadt's beautiful villa, Tuckerman, his contemporary, and the friend who was with him, stood looking in admiration at the sunset. The sky was like an opal. All the colors of the rainbow were melting together, and the friend said:

"If it were possible to transfer these brilliant hues and this wonderful cloud-picture to canvas, how few would regard the work as a genuine reflex of a sublime natural fact!"

"And yet," replied Tuckerman, "its very unique loveliness is the best reason for preserving as far as possible its evanescent glory."

Just at that moment they turned the angle of an orchard, and suddenly came in sight of Bierstadt, seated on a campstool, rapidly, and with skillful eagerness, sketching the marvelous sunset with its wealth of color, as a study for a larger picture. The incident was another proof of his firm belief, to which he was faithful, in seeking both his subject and his inspiration from Nature herself, and from no other medium.

It was not until 1886 that he seriously turned his thoughts to matrimony. He was fifty-seven years old when he married Rosalie Osborne. Seven years later she died. Probably fearing to find himself facing the rest of his life alone, he married the widow of David Stewart the following year of 1894.

Bierstadt had many friends among his fellow artists. It is on record that he was a very handsome man, of great distinction in bearing and manner. He looked the part evidently of a man who could push his way to the top of the highest mountain and keep his equilibrium. Tall and broad-shouldered, he had a commanding presence, and it has been suggested that those attributes helped him face the world with assurance, which he did with such success.

But there came a time when his great vigor began to lessen, and towards the end of his life his pictures lacked the earlier fire and verve. He had gone to Europe again in 1878, and then again in 1894. On this last visit something seemed to have gone from him — the paint was carelessly applied to the canvas of his pictures — the old wonderful detail was no longer there. The public noticed this, and Bierstadt felt it. That moment of realization is one of the bitterest in life to him who has climbed the mountain peaks and begins to slip downwards. To a man of Bierstadt's temperament this was especially tragic. Picture lovers began to turn spontaneously to the landscape painters "gifted with deeper mentality and equipped with stronger technique."

His formal dignity, and the size of the canvases he covered, as well as the convincing quality of his address in explaining the goal he was seeking, had made a great impression upon his contemporaries. Now the huge canvases seemed oppressive in size. The great buildings which the artists of that day hoped to see materialize failed to appear, and left some of these mammoth pictures without walls to rest on. They were entered in exhibitions, and for a number of years were greatly admired, and were looked upon with a certain amount of awe, but it was upon the canvases of moderate size that the Hudson River artists painted their most beautiful pictures, and to these the public turned, with a certain sense of relief.

To add to his troubles, his large and beautiful studio, which he had built with so much care at his villa at Irvington-on-the-Hudson, right in the midst of the scenery which he loved, was burned down in 1882. He felt it too late to rebuild, so he opened a studio in New York City and, nothing daunted, and in spite of handicaps, continued to paint. For the Capitol at Washington he painted "The Discovery of the Hudson River." Still others appeared, but when 1885 came and he was starting upon a huge landscape of the "Wilds of North America" his brush began to falter. His life of overexertion and strain was demanding toll. He died on February 18, 1902, at the age of seventy-two.

A dynamic and picturesque character.

CHAPTER 14

T. Worthington Whittredge
(1820–1910)

To WORTHINGTON WHITTREDGE's father was one of those Massachusetts men who followed the long trail of those who moved to the West to seek a fortune. He got as far as Ohio and there he pitched his tent, figuratively speaking. He had been a sea captain most of his previous life, and was always spoken of as Captain Joseph Whittredge. He must have had some Scottish blood in his veins and have inherited some of the quaint Highland independence of an uncle of his in Scotland who conceived the idea that the name Whittredge written out might be simplified by dropping one *t* and changing *e* to *i* and thereupon took the habit of signing his name Whitridge. That he carried influence with his people is shown by the fact that even his relatives on this side of the water adopted the habit, presumably in order to please him; but in the fifties they returned to the original spelling. Undoubtedly the old gentleman had passed on and had taken his vagaries with him, thus leaving them free to follow their own inclinations.

This fact is especially mentioned because it has sometimes caused confusion in verifying the signatures of the artist T. Worthington Whittredge, who later became one of the Hudson River group of painters. Though he is usually spoken of as Worthington Whittredge, his paintings were entered in the exhibitions of the Academy of Design when he started exhibiting them as T. Worthington Whittredge, showing that that was his real name, and some of his pictures even were signed that way. Later he dropped the *T*.

Young Whittredge was born on a farm in Ohio in 1820, the fifth of a large family. At an early age he tried his hand at making a living but made no great success of it. When things were getting pretty bad, he picked up his small belongings and made his way to Cincinnati where one of his sisters had a home. His brother-in-law set him to learning a trade, but the more he worked at it the more he became convinced that a business career for him was out of the question. As a first attempt he took to sign painting, at which he won some applause. He took to painting the head of General Harrison on banners pending his election as President, and as many told him that the heads were fine likenesses, he ventured to paint portraits of some of the local people. This went on quite satisfactorily, until the day came when he wanted to move on and attempt greater things, but lacked the funds to do them.

Now, in 1839 Louis Jacques Daguerre came to this country from France with his invention of making daguerreotypes. The initial cost of the necessary materials and paraphernalia was heavy, but it was discovered that there was money in it and studios where these new likenesses were taken cropped up all over the country. Whittredge had made friends with a young man who suggested that they should join forces and open just such a studio. But they were novices in the ways of business, and before they knew it they were in debt, and had to sell out. This worked badly for Whittredge. He worried himself into a state of ill health, and it happened that he was in Indianapolis when he actually took to his bed. One never knows when experiences of great interest are going to happen, and one of these came to Whittredge as a result of his illness. He tells about it in his *Autobiography* as follows:

Henry Ward Beecher had recently come (1830) to Indianapolis as a young man of twenty-six, and was hewing his way to that great eminence as a preacher which he afterwards obtained. I had known him and all the Beecher family back in Cincinnati from my earliest days. My sister and all her family went to his father's Second Presbyterian Church and I had gone with them. I associated intimately with the young people of the church. Mrs. Stowe and all her family were familiar with our raids upon them at Walnut Hills where they lived. On cold nights in winter the whole choir of the church often went in sleighs to visit them.

Henry, as we all familiarly called him, soon found out that I was sick and lying in a miserable room over the restaurant. . . . He came with his wife and removed me to his home — a very small house, but they found a room to put me in. It was a very concrete form of Christian charity. In due time I recovered sufficiently to do a little painting, and I accordingly undertook portraits of all the family.

Whittredge lived a year in Henry Ward Beecher's home and was familiar with the formation of the story of *Uncle Tom's Cabin*. It so happened that there was an old doctor at the seminary on Walnut Hills who was very much addicted to writing "Round Robin" letters. They touched on all kinds of subjects, and he would get various people to write in them. While young Whittredge was living with the Beechers he heard read some of these letters, which were sure to arrive once a month. All the topics of the day appeared in them, and when the question of slavery came up, the Round Robin letters were full of it.

Whittredge says in his *Autobiography*:

It was from one of these Round Robins that Harriet Beecher Stowe got the story of Uncle Tom. All the art of this wonderful story, however, is Mrs. Stowe's. No other member of the family could have written it. She was romantic as well as serious, and had an artist's eye for all that was picturesque in human nature which none of the members possessed to the same degree. But the book, after all, may be viewed in a great measure as the joint product of this remarkable family.

Among the portraits that Whittredge undertook at that time was that of a very beautiful woman, the wife of an ex-Congressman. She apparently was very much considered in Washington. And here is an anecdote about her which he tells with great feeling:

I used to choose my seat in church where I could scan her beautiful face. A very eloquent divine used to preach every Sunday. I do not remember what he said, but I recall her features still. She was then about thirty years of age, more beautiful, probably, than she was when a girl. Her graceful movements, her rich though delicate color, her fascinating manners, together with her soft Southern accent and singularly frank speech, were well calculated to captivate a Northern born painter boy.

It appears that Whittredge managed to get an introduction, and it was she who suggested to him that he paint her portrait. Of course he was overcome with joy at the prospect, but unfortunately he was not satisfied with the way it progressed and grew melancholy, going about town with his eyes on the pavement. The picture of the beautiful woman grew more unsatisfactory each day, while to his enamoured eyes she grew more beautiful. Being an artist and therefore exceedingly temperamental, and feeling disturbed in his mind, he went one evening to his studio. The picture was on his easel and he sat and contemplated it. It was unsatisfactory; there was no question about it. There was no life in it. He writes: "It became a corpse before me. I held a solitary wake over it till midnight, when I stripped it from the stretcher and committed it to the flames. . . . This episode of Charleston closed my portrait painting career and led to my taking up landscape instead."

He went abroad in 1849. The lure of travel attacked him, as it had all the other artists in the group. His first landing was at Drachenfels, and all the while he kept murmuring to himself Byron's famous poem beginning, "The castled crag of Drachenfels." But he did not find the blue-eyed girls about whom the poet wrote. Anyone who has seen Drachenfels towering above the Rhine never forgets it. All the romance of the centuries is gathered around it.

After traveling about here, there, and everywhere, Whittredge turned up in Paris, but that gay city made no special appeal to him then. He saw only the outside of it and had not time to take in its wonderfully interesting art collections. The more he thought over what he ought to do, the more he felt that he should go to Düsseldorf. So he left Paris and went to see what he could learn in this school of art. Leutze was working there at the time, and soon Albert Bierstadt arrived. This was the period in which Leutze was in his prime, and he was just contemplating his famous picture of "Washington Crossing the Delaware."

It was to be painted on a very large canvas, twenty feet by sixteen, and the figures were life size, as those who have seen it at the Metropolitan Museum, New York, can verify. It was with great difficulty that this artist got models for the many figures that are in it, especially as none of the German models could fill Washington's clothes. (Through the influence of Mr. Steward, a suit had been procured from the Patent Office in Washington.) Also he had great difficulty in finding American types for the heads and figures for the various characters he wished to have impersonated. Therefore he tried to press into service as a model every American who came along. One gentleman, a man over six feet, he attacked at once and secured. When Whittredge arrived he was seized upon and made to pose as model for two of the characters in the picture. One was the steersman of the boat, and the other was Washington himself. He stood for two hours without moving. This was in order that the cloak of Washington could be painted at a single sitting. The *Autobiography* says: "Clad in Washington's full uniform, heavy chapeau and all, spyglass in one hand and the other on my knee, I was nearly dead when the operation was over. They poured champagne down my throat and I lived through it."

In order to get a perfect likeness of the face, Leutze chose to copy that from Houdon's bust. The famous French sculptor was in America at that time, commissioned by the State of Virginia to do a portrait statue of Washington, which is now at the Louvre.

A friend of Whittredge who, he says, "was a thin sickly looking man — in fact all his life a half-invalid — was seized also, a bandage put around his head, and was the model for the wounded man lying prostrate in the boat."

"Leutze mixed the colors for it overnight," so says the *Autobiography,* "and invited Andreas Achenbach, a German artist, and myself to help him cover the bare canvas the next day, it being necessary to blend the colors easily to cover it all over in one day."

While Whittredge did some valuable studying at Düsseldorf, he rebelled against the restrictions they put upon him. There were certain rules of painting which he was obliged to follow, and this was exactly what he did not want to do. He longed to be able to paint as he liked and at the same time have the advantages of the Düsseldorf methods, some of which he could take and some of which he could forego. It created a certain amount of discussion, and he came to the conclusion that he was better off following his own bent than following the prescribed methods of any school of art.

Having heard much of Rome, he began to make plans for going there. He had painted a number of pictures and sent them all to a friend of his at Scarborough, New York, in order to pay for the trip. He makes this remark in his *Autobiography*: "I soon prepared to change my domicile. One more sketching trip in Germany and then I was to be off for the Eternal City." And the following is his account of his experiences there:

> Rome in 1850 was not the Rome of today. When I visited the city the old Café Greco was still in existence, 86 Via Condotti. It was a place where from time immemorial great men of all sorts, poets, painters, sculptors, and philosophers, had assembled morning and evening to get their *café latte* and chat together. Persons all over the world intending to go to Rome were making a kind of post office of the Café Greco and having their letters addressed there. This ancient café was a very insignificant affair compared with the glittering splendor of the great saloons so common to our eyes now in New York. At best there were but three little rooms in it, the first, a sort of bar without many bottles in sight where the letters were kept in a cigar box which was handed out to everybody who inquired for it. The next, a very small interior room, and the last, a long narrow room with fixed seats on the sides and lighted by a skylight and called the "Omnibus." My letters had been addressed there, and I rose early the following morning to go and get them. I found seats in the "Omnibus" pretty well filled . . . among them were several English artists, as I soon discovered from their speech, when suddenly there stepped into view my hero of yesterday. Half a dozen Englishmen jumped to their feet and cried, *"Leighton,"* and came nearer embracing him than I ever before observed Englishmen in the habit of doing on such occasions. This was Leighton, the Pre-Raphaelite, or at that time, said to be one who, with Rossetti and others, was kicking up such a fuss in London.

Apparently there were but two landscape painters at this time in Rome; they were Brown and Tilton, and they were making Rome a permanent residence. But there were a number of sculptors. Among them were Crawford, Story, Rogers, Rinehart, Mozier, Ives, and

Bartholomew — he writes, "a solemn lot of very serious people for a landscape painter to mingle with."

Whittredge remained in Rome for four winters, and Rome was very gay all that time, and the artists found it necessary to mix with the gay world as much as possible in order to make the acquaintance of all the strangers who came there and who would be likely to buy their pictures. They found it a very lucrative way of disposing of their work, and it was a delightful way, too, for they made many friends as well as purchasers. They even took lessons in dancing in order to qualify as partners at balls or receptions. Mr. Case, the American Minister at Rome, was a great entertainer, as were a number of other prominent personages, and the artists paid their five *scudi* in order to attend the great annual function at the Palazzo Doria, which was about the same as the yearly charitable balls in New York. On these occasions there was some dancing, but "the greatest interest," he writes, "centered in the spacious chamber where were seated all the aristocracy of Rome, at which we were permitted to glance as we passed through the room. This assemblage did not pretend to leave the room. They had not come to see but to be seen, and sat there in various graceful attitudes, chatting away in the most lively manner, the ladies glittering with diamonds and the men in costumes denoting their rank or office which, with an occasional sight of some prince or princess we had heard of, was what we came to see, and having once seen were perfectly satisfied."

Towards spring there was always a danger of Roman fever, and many went away at that time. But there were others who seemed to be immune from it. Robert Browning, the poet, and Mrs. Browning were among the latter. Whittredge did not see them very often, but he met them once or twice at the house of Mozier, the sculptor. He gives his view, which is interesting to hear, of Mrs. Browning. He said she had a sweet face covered up mostly with curls. Of Browning his remark was that "he looked very little like a poet, and at that time I confess I had hard work to find out from his writings that he was a poet. He was a huge mass of a man, and apparently he had learned the trick of pouring his great vitality into his work; whether one admired (or understood) his poetry did not seem so important as the fact that we all realized, even at that time, that he was truly a *great* poet. Yet he never affected any of the tricks of greatness, and was indeed a remarkably pleasant, simple spoken man who worked as hard as any of us in creating his works of art."

Among other people whom Whittredge spoke of was Hawthorne, who was there writing his *Marble Faun*. "He was even shyer than the Brownings. I caught a glimpse of him once near the Tarpeian Rock but he disappeared in a moment like a buck in a forest. We knew nothing about the 'Marble Faun' at that time, and he had come to the place to study it a little and to use it for the most tragic scene in his novel."

Whittredge's summers were usually passed in the Alban or Sabine Mountains, and in October he returned to Rome and was smitten with Roman fever most unexpectedly. His account of it is amusing. He says:

> I grew worse daily, and my dear friends Gifford and Church gave up all hope of saving my life. They nursed me tenderly, but I sank steadily under their eyes. At last they gathered in my rooms to wait out the last vigil with me. I lay in one little room to the side, unconscious with fever and exhaustion; they sat gloomily in my studio, discussing, as they afterwards told me, plans for my burial. At last unable to stand the strain any longer, one of them said, "Come, let's have a game of poker." They dealt out the cards and started to play. A mournful game it must have been, with me dying in the next room. About midnight I woke from my coma; the crisis had passed and my fever had abated. I gazed out into the studio and saw my friends gathered around the table playing my favorite game of poker. I cried out, "Bring the cards in here." Amazed, they came in and, thinking me delirious, tried to soothe me, but I soon showed them I was not delirious. They dealt out the cards on the bedspread for the first hand. I won that hand with three aces. Two hands later I had a straight flush and it was not on my cheeks. To make a long story short, I cleaned them out every penny and rose the next morning perfectly well.

Whittredge makes an interesting remark in his *Autobiography* about the effect of life in foreign cities. He says this:

It was then and is now and probably always will be a question whether our students going abroad to study art are likely to make better artists than if they stayed at home. Frankly, I doubt the desirability of long foreign study. A flying visit across the water is not objectionable but rather to be commended, but to go abroad and to become so fascinated with the art life in Paris and other great centers as to take up permanent abode there is not everywhere believed to be the best thing for an American artist. We are looking and hoping for something distinctive in the art of our country, something which shall receive a new tinge from our peculiar form of government, from our position on the globe, or something peculiar to our people, to distinguish it from the art of other nations and to enable us to pronounce without shame the oft-repeated phrase of *American art*. If Shakespeare when a boy had crossed the channel and got safely into France without being seasick and had lived in Paris all his life, he would never have been the immortal English bard that he is.

These questions were troubling Whittredge, and he said that he had now been nearly ten years in Europe and began to long for the United States and his home. One August morning in 1859 he made up his mind to lose no time in returning. One of the first things he did in New York was to visit the Historical Society. He wanted to see Cole's "Voyage of Life" and "Course of Empire," and also Durand's "Thanatopsis."

"I may have been a little nervous," he says in his *Autobiography*, "I cannot say; but when I looked at Durand's truly American landscape, so delicate and refined, such a faithful, if in some parts somber, delineation of our own hills and valleys, I confess the tears came to my eyes."

When the Civil War broke out Whittredge cast his profession aside, secured a uniform and the greater part of an equipment, and went to enlist in the Seventh Regiment which was just about to start off, but to his bitter disappointment he found that the regiment quota was full and they could take no more into it. He made various attempts which failed, but even so his ardor never flagged, and he threw himself into doing all he could on the home front; and he apparently did it successfully.

At the close of the war General Pope invited him to go in a civilian capacity on a tour of inspection through the Rocky Mountains and New Mexico, probably with an eye to his painting some of the scenery they would pass through. Two of Whittredge's artist friends — Gifford and John R. Kensett — were also of the party. It gave them a wonderful opportunity to realize the vast open spaces — the mountainous districts — the virgin forests of the land they lived in, but for Whittredge, now that he had returned to his native land, it was the woods and streams of New York State and New England that he loved best. So when the tour was over he had made his decision — his home was to be in New York.

He secured a studio on Tenth Street, which was at that time the quarter occupied by the artist world; then, it being near Christmas, he went to Cincinnati to pass the holidays with his old-time friend Joseph Longworth, who had a lovely home there. Every sort of argument was used to induce him to make his home again in that attractive city, but Whittredge wanted something entirely new for his surroundings. He was eager to arrange his new studio. An exhibition of the Academy of Design was near at hand and he just had time to enter his picture of the "Roman Campagna," which he had finished with the greatest care before leaving Rome. When the exhibition opened, on entering he found it, to his supreme pleasure, "hung on the line" and creating much admiration from the public. As a result he was elected an Associate Member of the Academy. That was in 1861, and in 1865 he served as president of that organization.

Cupid with his bow then came on the scene, and on October 16, 1867, Whittredge married a young girl named Euphemia Foote. The wedding took place at Geneva, New York. Life was now full of promise, and he entered into it with eager interest. His chief desire now was to devote his art to truly American scenes, so he went to the Catskills and painted some successful pictures there, three of which he sent to the annual exhibition of the Academy. It was his great desire to do his part in revealing to the world at large the beauties of American scenery. but he chose the gentler aspects of nature, the peaceful scenes that quiet the soul instead of stirring it. He strove too to represent exactly what he saw, and after the tumult and the heartaches following the trail of the Civil War, his pictures were most acceptable to the war-weary public, for he painted with intelligence and charm.

In 1868, soon after his marriage, a number of people, mostly young people with families, begged Mr. Rutherford Stuyvesant of New York to build an apartment house where they could have suitable accommodations. Whittredge was one of the first to subscribe to an apartment. The building was to be erected in Eighteenth Street near Third Avenue and Stuyvesant Square. This was the only apartment house in New York at that time, except a very small one that was owned by a Frenchman.

Some time after that, Whittredge, liking change, took an apartment in one of Mr. Astor's apartment houses in Forty-Fourth Street that had grown up after Mr. Stuyvesant's venture. He lived there some time, but longing for the quiet of the country, he chose New Jersey for his dwelling place — still keeping his studio, however, in New York. He bought land in Summit, from where he could see rich meadows and forest lands and pastoral scenes that he loved. He lived there with his wife and three daughters for the rest of his life, happy and contented.

On his eightieth birthday came a surprise. All the neighbors from near and far crowded to his house to do him honor, as well as many of his artist friends from New York, and many old friends from the city. A beautifully wrought loving cup was presented to him, and the whole occasion was one long to be remembered.

On his eighty-eighth birthday his Summit friends gave him a dinner to which John Burroughs, the poet, came, and F. Hopkinson Smith, John W. Alexander, Homer Davenport, and Frederick Dielman. He was happy to be so recognized, but on his eighty-ninth birthday a home celebration was all he could safely go through. He died in 1910, three months before his ninetieth birthday.

Of his paintings Whittredge says that along the banks of Lake George and the Hudson River he found many of the subjects of his pictures. "I have tried anything and everything which has struck me as interesting — coast scenes, brook scenes, scenes on the plains — moonlight, firelight, and every picturesque feature that presented itself."

His paintings are to be seen in all the prominent museums in the country.

CHAPTER 15

Jasper F. Cropsey
(1823–1900)

Jasper F. Cropsey began life as a boy with a handicap. He was delicate in health. His parents were very worthy people — industrious and self-respecting, but comparatively poor. But they believed that their son was gifted, so they never stood in his way. Their great concern was how to further his chances for development along the line of art. It was indeed a notty question to consider, and they had to feel their way along once they made up their minds that he knew what he wanted.

Young Cropsey had two strains of blood in his veins, and both of them could be recognized in his character. The first Cropseys who emigrated to this country came from Holland, but history states that they really were German. Cropsey's grandmother was of French Huguenot blood. The second generation — Jasper's father and mother — were both of them born on Staten Island, and it was there that he first saw the light, on February 18, 1823.

In childhood he received his education at the country school. In those days such schools were pretty strenuous for any child but one in robust health. They were draughty, and often damp and ill-lighted, and in spite of the rod of the country schoolmaster the pupils were inclined to be unruly and boisterous. A boy of sensitive nature had little chance among them.

Whether he stayed at the school and took lessons in mechanics is doubtful, for no country school had a curriculum including so advanced a study in those days, but we find that at the age of twelve he made a model of a highly finished and elaborate country dwelling — and the tools he used were of his own making.

This model came under the observation of men higher up in the line of education, the result being that this small boy received a diploma from the Mechanics' Institute — certainly a very unusual honor for one so young. Under whose tuition he received the knowledge to obtain it we do not know, but it evidently convinced his parents that their son was gifted, and instead of deterring him from working along this line they encouraged him to enter an architect's office to perfect what he had learned thus far. In the second year of work there he received a diploma from the American Institute for the "best specimens of architectural drawing."

This aroused his ambition to such an extent that at the end of two years he was completely overworked, and his health failed him, so that he was obliged to go to the country for a complete rest.

One can never tell into what paths circumstances will lead one. They led Jasper Cropsey into the profession of his life — that of becoming a landscape painter.

It happened this way. During his apprenticeship in the architect's office, a certain amount of encouragement had been given to his love of painting. From the very first he had fostered this love secretly in his heart, and so during his convalescence he indulged it whenever his health allowed him to. The habit grew and became all-absorbing.

When he had sufficiently regained his strength he returned to the office, but his employer soon saw that a change had come over him — the young man's mind was on painting, and not on architectural drawings. This caused trouble. The end of it was that he left the office permanently and went back to Staten Island.

He remained there for the winter with his parents, but not in idleness. In fact, his temperament was such that he could not remain idle and be happy. He had to be accomplishing something. So he painted an architectural landscape and called it an "Italian Composition," which was remarkable, as he had never been in Italy. But he had learned much through reading, for among other things he strove for self-culture, not having opportunity for acquiring knowledge in any other way. Probably his reading had drawn him to accounts of Italy which he had absorbed with all the romance of his youth. That he had a keen mind and a shrewd one as well, is evident, for he had already learned that if he executed a piece of work that he suspected to be good, it was wise to let it be known; and he had done so in this case, with the result that this first "Composition" of his was favorably hung at the National Academy — another honor that came to him. More than that, a gentleman by the name of L. H. Cortelyou of Staten Island thought so much of the canvas that he gave Cropsey an order to paint a picture of his own house and place. He had bought the latter's exhibit at the Academy, and wanted this one as a companion to it, to hang on the walls of his home.

All this was very encouraging, so the next year Cropsey had the temerity to hang out his sign as an architect, and this resulted in an order to design not only a dwelling house but a church, which was to stand in the center of the cemetery at New Dorp.

This sounded very fine, but he struck a snag. It was difficult to find workmen capable of carrying out plans of this kind, and though he managed to push this job through it was a hazardous undertaking; and when he received another order to design a small Gothic church at Rossville, these same builders made a complete mess of it, so that when it was finished it was "sadly mutilated" — so says one of his biographers.

This misfortune certainly hurt his future as an architect. Up to that time he had suspected that architecture was a much more remunerative branch of art than picture painting, so he had felt obliged to follow it if he could do so successfully, in order to be independent and not a drain on his parents, but now he felt at liberty to make a change, and to devote himself to the profession he really loved — that of landscape painting.

It was soon after this that he had the good fortune to meet Mr. J. P. Ridner, who advised him to go to New Jersey where he was sure to find scenery that would make an appeal to the homeloving public of the Eastern states — pastoral scenes with which the people were surrounded, and which spelled home to them.

Cropsey accepted the idea, and thought it was a good one. The scenery which Mr. Ridner especially advocated was in Orange

County. There the young would-be artist found the country exceedingly picturesque around Greenwood Lake, and he at once started in to paint.

His ambition was so thoroughly aroused that he secured a canvas three by five feet in size, and with that he persevered until he had painted a picture that surprised even himself. A number of his friends saw it. Even the artist Inman got wind of it and went to see it. The latter was so much impressed by it that he made a request that it be sent to the Academy, which was done, and to Cropsey's supreme satisfaction his painting "Greenwood Lake, Orange County" was the means of his being made an Associate Member of that august organization.

After this he devoted himself to hard study for three or four years, dividing his time between Connecticut, Hudson River, and again Greenwood Lake.

This last place had an attraction for him that took him back there again and again. But it was not only the lovely lake, nor was it the green banks that bordered it, nor the blue sky that shone over it. There was something more — it was the sweet-faced daughter of the Honorable J. P. Cooley, who lived on the borders of it, and glorified the scene to him.

The courtship began when he was half through painting along the shores of that romantic sheet of water which had started him on a successful career. Small wonder that the spot was a hallowed one for him. The wedding took place in 1847.

In the meantime the painting "Greenwood Lake, Orange County" had appeared in the 1844 exhibition of the National Academy of Design. It was thought highly of, so much so that in 1851 he became a full-fledged Academician.

But to go back to 1847. The time now came which sooner or later came to all the Hudson River landscape artists, when Cropsey felt a longing to spread his wings to other climes — to have the chance to see what the rest of the world was like, to try to understand the thoughts of other nations on art, and to study the goal they were striving to reach.

It was here that his German blood showed itself and came to his aid. In order to leave his studio in perfect order, he collected all the paintings and sketches he had on hand and put them on exhibition, planning to hold a sale, the results of which he hoped would help defray some of his traveling expenses. He expected to be gone several years. It was a good deal of a venture, but to him it was worth it. He was convinced that a certain period of time must be given to absorbing completely the knowledge he wished to acquire.

The sale took place just before he and his bride sailed for England in May, 1847. The results of it outreached his fondest hopes. Not only was it highly remunerative, but his prestige as an artist was greatly enhanced by it. The popularity of his paintings had been increasing steadily with the public, and this demonstration of it made him light of heart, and they set forth on their travels with easy minds.

At that time there was quite a group of artists devoted to study at Kensington, close to London. The latter great and important city seemed too big a place in which to begin his career in England. He felt it wiser to feel his way towards it instead of attempting to force his way immediately into the center of it. Moreover, the thought of joining a group of artists made a great appeal to the Cropseys, and on arriving in England they turned their faces towards Kensington.

It was a wise move. There they made several lifelong friends, who proved helpful in starting them on the right road, for in any country on the other side of the water a stranger needs a certain amount of backing at the beginning.

Cropsey had a gift for making acquaintances as well as friends. He was genial and what is commonly called a "good mixer" and people liked him. And then too he stuck to his job. He was an indefatigable worker, though it was a constant fight with him to save his health, a thing which he more than often forgot to do. If ill health got the better of him, he fought it vigorously, and was up and about and at his work again before even his friends knew what he had been through.

But even so, sometimes his work showed it. When he was in good health, he painted not only with skill and assurance, but with a distinct understanding and intimate feeling with nature, which always made its appeal. Every now and then a painting of his would appear that was more crude in technique, and a bit more careless in detail than his usual work, and it puzzled the public. But those paintings were few and far between, and if any appeared, the art critics grew to understand the reasons for it and passed them by. His best works were always sought after with eagerness.

While at Kensington, Cropsey and his wife went into London and saw the sights there. The London season was still in full swing. They must have looked with amazement at the equipages — the powdered wigs on the coachmen — the thoroughbred horses — the gay trappings, and inside, beautiful English women with great ostrich plumes on their hats that waved in the breeze as they drove towards the Park. Certainly a far cry from Greenwood Lake!

But first and foremost, of course, were the visits to the National Gallery and every other place where they could see pictures. And here a very strong feeling towards English art took hold of Cropsey. He understood it. It was more like home to him than the specimens of foreign art of which he had as yet seen only engravings.

Now he wanted to see more of England. He had heard of the great oak trees beautifying their parks. People had told him of the long hedges of may (hawthorn) in full bloom that bordered great stretches of pastures in the country districts. They were a bit too late to see the bloom, but the hedges alone were typical of England. And there were places he wanted to visit — Stratford-on-Avon, and then Kenilworth Castle, and Loch Lomond in Scotland, where he wanted to paint a picture of the lake to send to the Art Union. Finally they went to Paris, after which they made their way down to Rome — the place of all others where he wished to study, and for that purpose proposed to spend the winter there.

It was a type of honeymoon that any artist would long for, and the Cropseys were granted this great opportunity. Taking advantage of this good fortune, they seized upon it to treasure in memory the rest of their lives.

When they reached Rome they were fortunate enough to be able to hire the studio on the Via Barbuino that had once been occupied by Thomas Cole during one of the latter's visits to Rome.

That was inspiration enough for Cropsey, who looked upon Cole as one of our greatest artists, and with a spurt of enthusiasm he set to work as soon as his luggage was unpacked. But he was too eager — his make-up was too delicate — he gave himself no time for relaxation, and that, with the discovery that traveling in Europe was much more expensive than he had anticipated and had caused an uncomfortable financial situation, began to prey on him and brought on an illness. He was prostrated for some weeks, and had to give up his work as a result.

The following spring when the weather was warm his ambition began to stir again. He wanted to see more, and to meet interesting people in his profession. They heard that the American sculptor, William Wetmore Story, whose statues of Cleopatra and the Sibyl placed him in the first ranks of art in those days, was passing the summer at Sorrento, with occasional visits to Amalfi. So Cropsey and his wife decided to go there. They were able to secure rooms in the same house as Mr. and Mrs. Story, which proved to be a most agreeable arrangement, and bound the cords of friendship together so that when they all returned to Rome in the fall, the Storys introduced the Cropseys to a very select group of artistic people, where they became much liked.

Near them at Sorrento, indeed almost next door, was a Hudson River artist who was practically the center of every artistic group in Rome. His name was Christopher Pearse Cranch, a most versatile and interesting character, as I have said earlier. He also became their friend. Before leaving Sorrento, Cropsey painted two successful landscapes: one was a view of that romantic spot, and the other was of the island of Capri, which was purchased by the Art Union, in New York.

When the fall came and they returned to Rome, he painted one of his most important pictures. It was of the "Pontine Marshes," and measured four by six feet. Later it was presented to the New York Academy, and afterwards was sold to the Art Union. From that organization it came into the possession of Mr. William H. Appleton of New York.

This was the Cropseys' second visit to Rome, and he and his wife found themselves taken into what might be called the fellowship of the artist life there. They were agreeable and intelligent companions, and could be counted on to add to the simple gaieties that spread from studio to studio, when the work of the day was done.

It was a new outlook on life for them, and they drew a great inspiration from it. But things came to disturb the pleasant life they were leading. Towards the spring of 1849 there were civic troubles in Rome, and a general air of distrust and mystery prevailed. The peaceful atmosphere of the "Eternal City" was disturbed. Art, for the time being, seemed sidetracked, and Cropsey thought it better to turn his face homeward.

He managed to stop over in Paris in order to make some sketches at Barbizon and the forest of Fontainebleau in company with Thomas Hicks, the American artist, and George William Curtis whom he had met in Rome, and who was intimately associated with the colony of artists there.

Cropsey and his wife arrived at their home in the United States in July, 1849.

And now after all his European experiences Cropsey was glad to settle down to several years of concentrated work. His summer studio was at Greenwood Lake, where there was a leafy glen near-by, and there he passed many a dreamy hour, going over all he had seen on the other side, as well as pondering over the possibilities hidden in the future.

Life had been very kind to him in many ways. In spite of delicate health he had forged his way into a prominent position as an American artist of the Hudson River group of landscape painters, and was recognized as such on both sides of the Atlantic; yet somehow he was not satisfied — he wanted more, and to accomplish more.

It was at this period that he painted a picture called "Sybil's Temple" which was thought highly of, so much so that he received six orders for replicas.

This was a common custom of that time. If anyone liked a paint-ing, it was considered perfectly proper to go to the artist who painted it and give him an order for a copy. This was done quite frequently, and has caused much confusion in art circles as a consequence, as the artists consenting to do this rarely left any record of so doing for the benefit of those coming after them.

Seven years went by, and Cropsey painted many landscapes — typical views of our own country — when a sudden desire for change again assailed him. There seemed always to be an unseen force push-ing him forward throughout his life, and this time it was England that he felt calling him. So in the spring of 1856 he and his wife set sail again for those shores, but when they arrived this time they went straight to London. As before, he sold all his sketches and paintings on leaving home except those he intended to take with him, in order to leave himself free to stay as long or as short a time as he wished without having to worry about things he had left behind him.

In 1862, after a period of hard work, a picture of his called "Autumn on the Hudson" was exhibited at the great London Inter-national Exhibition and was favorably mentioned by John Ruskin. It also brought forth a highly complimentary notice in the London *Times,* a portion of which is as follows:

> American artists are rapidly making the untravelled portion of the English public familiar with the scenery of the Western Continent. Mr. Church's "Falls of Niagara," and the "Heart of the Andes" recently ex-hibited here, have found a companion picture in Mr. Cropsey's "Autumn on the Hudson River," now on view. The painting is a perfectly faithful view of the locality. The singularly vivid colors of an American autumn scene — the endless contrasts of purples and yellows, scarlets and browns, running into every conceivable shade between the extremes — might easily tempt a painter to exaggerate or revel in variety of hue and effect, like a Turner of the forest. But Mr. Cropsey has resisted the temptation and even a little tempered the capricious tinting of nature; his autumn is still brilliant, but not quite lost to sobriety, as we have sometimes, we think, seen in that Western world. The result is a fine picture, full of points that are new, without being wholly foreign to the European eye.

The success of "Autumn on the Hudson" gave Cropsey the idea of painting a companion picture to it of a typical English landscape, and after much searching for a scene that would be wholly English in character but historic as well, he chose Richmond Hill, painting it in the glow of summer sunshine, as a contrast to the other.

The London *Builder* said in a review of this picture:

> Mr. Cropsey, the American landscape painter, whose "Autumn on the Hudson" was the great adornment of the United States Department of the International Exhibition, sought for a corresponding view to show Summer in England, and finding it on Richmond Hill — "loved by the Muses" — has painted a parallel picture of great size. He has chosen well. Everyone knows Royal Richmond . . . where Edward III, Henry VII, and Queen Elizabeth died; where Henry VIII jousted; where the Queen of George II received Jeanie Deans; where Reynolds and Gainsborough lived; and which has been sung by Pope and Thomson.
>
> We congratulate Mr. Cropsey on having produced a charming picture of a charming spot. The picture is now at Mr. Henry Graves' in Pall-Mall, and is to be forthwith engraved by Mr. Robert Wallis.

The aforesaid reviewer apparently went later to Cropsey's studio. Concerning it he says:

> During this half hour in Cropsey's studio I have been lured to Rome, to the Catskills, and the Passaic, to the Ramapo Valley, and to Newport. and each locality, besides refreshing my eye with natural beauty, has awakened fond reminiscences.

Another comment in the newspapers in London is of interest. It is as follows:

> A picture of paramount interest in London was the large picture of "Autumn on the Hudson River," five by nine feet. This attracted unusual notice from all parts of the country. It was exhibited at the great London International Exhibition of 1862, especial attention being directed to it by the Royal Commissioners, on account of services the artist rendered in the American Department, for which he afterwards received a medal. It was sold out of the Exhibition to an English gentleman.

The Cropseys resided in London from 1856 to 1863. Cropsey's paintings were exhibited regularly at the Royal Academy. He was elected a member of the London Society of Arts, as well as being elected a complimentary member of the London Athenaeum Club.

A very delightful memory of his sojourn in London during those years was the day when he was presented at the Court of Queen Victoria by our United States Minister, Charles Francis Adams. There he had the opportunity of getting a near view of the pomp and magnificence of the English court life of those days.

Trouble at home decided Cropsey to return at once to the United States after seven pleasant and gratifying years in London. The following comment on his sudden departure appeared in a newspaper there: "During his stay here he gained 'social and artistic position,' receiving many attentions, and having great inducements to make this city his home for life; but the Slaveholder's Rebellion broke out in the United States, and the artist's intense love of home and country induced him to return."

Before Cropsey left London he received a commission from the publishers, E. B. Cambert & Company, for thirty-six pictures intended for publication. After sixteen of these had been painted, the order had to be terminated on account of the financial difficulties of 1857.

This shows how popular Cropsey's paintings were at that time. When the Cropseys reached the United States they did not go back to Greenwood Lake. To own a home on the Hudson River, where he could devote himself to the beauty of the Catskill Mountains, and the graceful windings of the river surrounded by the picturesqueness that Nature had so lavishly bestowed upon that region, had taken hold of his imagination. He found this home at Hastings-on-the-Hudson, New York, and like so many of the Hudson River landscape painters he passed all his declining years there, imbued with the beauties of his own country as never before.

He died there in 1900 — the same year that Thomas Cole died, and on the banks of the selfsame river.

CHAPTER 16

Thomas Hewes Hinckley
(1813–1896)

A PAINTER OF ANIMALS was something out of the ordinary when Thomas Hewes Hinckley took up his brush to make that his profession. He was born in Milton, Massachusetts, and to show how ingrained was his love of animals from earliest childhood up, there were found among his father's papers, after the latter had died, two very creditable drawings of a pig and a dog, marked "T. H. H., aged four."

Apparently that was enough to cause dismay in the father's heart, for in order to eradicate signs of an artistic tendency in his son, he sent him to Philadelphia to learn a trade. It so happened, however, that there was an artist named Mason who held evening classes in drawing there in his own home, and into these classes drifted young Hinckley. Mason was evidently a very conscientious teacher, for his methods were adopted later by the Lowell Institute of Boston, and from him the young man received a most valuable and thorough training in the matter of perspective and the mingling of lights and shades, etc. As it turned out, this was the only instruction he ever received.

His father died in 1833 and young Hinckley then took matters into his own hands. He gave up the work in which he was engaged, and not knowing how to start on an artistic career, launched out as a "sign and fancy painter." He was quite successful at it, and becoming ambitious he tried his hand at painting portraits. But that was not what he wanted. He wanted to paint animals, and finally found a most congenial field in this branch of the profession.

He started out by painting a picture of a spaniel in 1838 which was thought well of, but the first picture to attract the public and make his work well known was one named "A Setter and Pups." This was painted in 1843 and was purchased by Lucius Manlius Sargent, Esq. Other paintings followed in quick succession after this, so that in 1845 he built a studio in Milton. The building was no sooner finished than he received an order from Daniel Webster to make drawings of his famous Ayrshire herd at Marshfield. The sketches of these beautiful animals proved to be a valuable mine of wealth to draw upon, for they furnished material for innumerable paintings during the following years. Most of these pictures were bought by the American Art Union. Among them was a painting called "The Rabbit Hunter" which was drawn to the attention of the great singer, Jenny Lind, who was making a sensation with her marvelous voice at that time, and she tried in every way to persuade the Art Union to sell it to her. But they refused, showing the value they put on Hinckley's work. When during the following years that institution became involved in difficulties, the picture was bought at the closing sale by Smith Van Buren, Esq.

More and more opportunities were showered on Hinckley from lovers of animals. When he painted an animal, he did so against a beautiful background of New England scenery, surrounded by fertile pastures with trees and streams and flowering marshlands, or on rocky promontories where the wild deer call for their mates. Because of the beauty of the settings, his pictures were bought by fastidious art lovers all over the country.

William W. Swain, Esq., of Naushon, familiarly known as "The Governor," made everything easy for him to study the deer on his island. Hinckley took full advantage of his generosity, and produced some beautiful pictures of those graceful and stately animals. He also frequented the Adirondack Mountains, and penetrated the forests around Moosehead Lake where he could watch their habits unseen by them. His understanding of the creatures of the woods was limitless. He loved them, and they in return loved him.

In 1851 he made his first trip to Europe in order to study the paintings of Landseer in England, and also of the Flemish painters, all of whom stood high in the art world, and in 1858 two of his paintings were exhibited in the Royal Academy Exhibition of that year. After that, in 1870, he went to California to make studies of the elk. His picture called "The Single Elk" was promptly sold in New York, and there were many others, one of which was sold to Russell Sturgis, Esq., of London.

The great Centennial Exhibition took place at Philadelphia in 1876. To that he sent a picture called "The End of the Chase," which attracted much attention. His work was unique in its way. It emphasized his love of animals and their beauty, making them form a part of the natural scenery, and though apparently it has not been suggested before, it is fully possible that during those years he was sowing some of the seeds that have budded and flowered into the many organizations that for some years now have received the enthusiastic support of the public. A love of animals and a concern for their welfare has, happily, grown to be a requirement in these days of modern civilization.

The technique of his paintings was that of the Hudson River School, and though he was not exclusively a landscape painter, there was a great deal of landscape in his pictures; therefore it could be claimed that in a way he belonged to that school, though he disclaimed any suggestion that he followed any school of art, but sought to paint only what he saw. That, however, was the fundamental theory of our first school of art, the Hudson River School.

He lived to be eighty-three years old, and died in 1896, painting up to the end, finding that the beautiful surroundings of his home in Milton furnished all the necessary material.

His paintings hang in the galleries of all the principal cities of the United States.

CHAPTER 17

François Régis Gignoux

(1816–1882)

A<small>T THIS TIME</small> a number of foreign artists came over here — became naturalized and were intimately associated with the artistic element of the country. François Régis Gignoux was one of these. Born in the city of Lyons, France, in 1816, he emigrated here in 1844, and took a prominent position at once. What gave him a firm standing in the estimation of the public, besides the excellence of his own paintings, was that he was the only artist of whom George Inness was a pupil. Gignoux's temperament was particularly adapted to influencing the somewhat chaotic nature of George Inness, who remained his devoted friend. Gignoux had a real gift for teaching and a manner of inspiring confidence in his methods and opinions. He had all the gay mannerisms of a Frenchman. He could laugh heartily and enliven any assemblage of artists, however despondent and discouraged they might be. Tuckerman says of him that this made him a complete contrast "with the more serious of our painters in the same sphere, and adds another element of variety to the versatile group of the American School of landscape painting." His debonair attitude towards life in general must have been a great refreshment to those artists who were worrying about the future. He had intended to devote himself entirely to historical paintings, but when he came to this country he became fascinated by the sight of our winter scenes. He loved to see the fields and the hills and the valleys covered with snow, bright and glistening in the sunshine, and his paintings of these were the first that the public knew of. They kept to the beauty of nature and were realistic; in fact, "it has been said that some of them are so truthful that they would allure a snow-bunting from the sky." (Tuckerman.) It is also said of his work that these winter scenes were so esteemed that lovers of art felt that one of Gignoux's winter scenes must be added to their collection and "orders flowed in upon him far beyond his ability to execute." To show his versatile capacity, each one of his American landscape experiments received the same popularity. Then came his autumnal views and they acquired the same success. Then he tried something more ambitious. His "Niagara in Winter" and his "Virginia in Indian Summer" were both eagerly sought after and he received application for works like them as well as duplicates of the originals. It is well to quote here again from Tuckerman's estimate of him, as follows: "He was a genial man and a cheerful worker; he carried into his observation of nature no morbid feeling, but catches her pleasantest language and delights in reproducing her salient effects. His landscape indicates accuracy of tone, a legitimate feeling for color, and a sympathy for the picturesque."

He was elected a member of the Academy of Design in 1851 and was the first president of the Brooklyn Art Academy. A very noted series that he painted was "The Four Seasons in America" belonging to Baron Rothschild, Paris; and another was "The Dismal Swamp" which was the property of the Earl of Ellesmere. He returned to France in 1870. He was a prolific artist and his works are rapidly coming to the fore, especially as he depicted the American scenes as they were in those days. Therefore they have historical value as well as an artistic one.

Though Gignoux painted moderate-sized pictures of winter scenes and the like, he sometimes, as did most of the artists of those days, painted on a large scale. These reveal the versatility of his hand and mind. A very beautiful one, called "A Mountain View," is reproduced in this book.

In his youth he had studied painting in the School of Fine Arts in Paris and had also been a pupil of the prominent artist, Delaroche. Therefore he brought with him an accuracy of style that enabled him to reproduce the scenes he saw with truth and vigor. And though a foreigner, he intuitively showed forth the salient characteristics of American scenery.

CHAPTER 18

George Inness
(1825–1894)

IN ONE SHORT PARAGRAPH the *Dictionary of American Biography* sums up the personality of George Inness better than anything else could do it.

> Inness was always a mystic, and he loved metaphysical speculation. Beginning as a Baptist, he went over to Methodism, and at last became a Swedenborgian. His three hobbies were art, religion, and the single tax. "He was," says Van Dyke, "supertemperamental even for an artist. His personal appearance bore out these psychological qualities. He looked like a fanatic. With his piercing gaze, his long hair, the intensity of his expression, and the nervous energy that marked his action, he was a formidable person."

That was a true picture of George Inness. But of course there was much more to say about him than that. There were the highlights of his life, and the low depressions. He aspired to high goals that were inaccessible. "His pictures breathed forth the poetic side of all he saw, but his special interest was for the elusive beauties of lights and shades, of atmospheric conditions, and above all for the rich, full, throbbing life of earth and sky."

Moreover, and apart from that, he was a man with man's shortcomings, but a genius withal.

To begin with, he was a nervous, delicate child, the fifth of thirteen brothers and sisters, but he was strong of will and impetuous, and from his earliest years ambitious for something even his family could not fathom, for he was not one to confide his innermost thoughts to even those near and dear to him. He was a dreamer, an idealist. It was natural to him. He was born that way.

His father was a prosperous merchant of Scottish descent, and tremendously keen about having his son follow in his footsteps. He bought a farm near Newburgh, New York, and there on May 1, 1825, George Inness was born. Later he moved to Newark, New Jersey, with his family.

It was a great mortification and sorrow to this man when he first became aware that he had a son who was definitely inclined towards art — so much so that he could not be made to study at school. Our country at that time was too young for the field of art to have any merit as a profession. To the general public a picture painter was beyond the pale. An artist in a family was little short of a disgrace. Therefore the boy was admittedly a disappointment to his family during the years of his growing up.

Young Inness was conscious of this, but it did not swerve him from his inclinations. In his secret heart he resented the attitude of his family, especially the attitude of his brother Joe, and he made up his mind to get even with him at the first opportunity.

He told the following anecdote in after life with considerable satisfaction. His brother Joe was a cash boy in a drygoods store at the time, and a most important person in his own eyes. One day he met young Inness on the street, and assumed his usual superior attitude towards him.

"Hello, George," he said, rattling his coins in his pocket. "Made any money painting pictures? Why don't you go to work and do something — make a living like I'm doing, instead of wasting your time painting pictures? Who wants pictures?"

In a moment his younger brother George was upon him, seized him by the scruff of his neck, and when he got through with him there was not enough left of Joe to listen to his answer. Though Inness was a so-called delicate boy, he had the spirit of a tiger in him when his anger was aroused, and it was aroused this time, so in the future brother Joe kept clear of him.

George's father held a faint hope in his breast that he might find a way of turning his son's attention to the advantages of a commercial career, so at the age of fourteen he made him sole proprietor and owner of a little grocery store on the corner of Washington Street and Newark Street, thinking that if it were his own, he would naturally become ambitious to make a success of it. But the following anecdote which George enjoyed telling about those days shows how futile it is to try to force a square peg into a round hole.

It appears that he concealed a canvas and paints behind the counter of his little store, and he would sit and paint by the hour "in the midst of the odor of onions, soap, sulphur matches and kindling wood." When customers came in he would duck behind the counter and stay there until they left in disgust at finding no one to wait on them. It goes without saying that business dwindled away to nothing, but a final episode brought it to a close. One day a little girl entered the store, and as usual Inness hid beneath the counter. Evidently she suspected he was there, for standing up on tiptoe she leaned across the counter and rattled her pennies against the glass so persistently that the young painter's nerves gave way, and he sprang from his lair like a jack-in-the-box and yelled:

"What in the name of all the devils do you want?"

Terrified, the little girl rushed from the store and down the street crying, "Candles! Candles! Candles!"

Exasperated at having been interrupted in his painting, the would-be artist seized the shutters and put them over the windows, locked the door, and left the building, never to return. He had been in the grocery business just one month.

His long-suffering father now saw that there was no use in trying to make a businessman of him, and Nature must be allowed to have its way, so he sent his boy to study art under a man named Barker. After a short period of instruction this artist notified the anxious parent that he could not continue to teach his son because the latter knew just as much about art as he himself did. This was somewhat disconcerting, but hope again rose in the paternal breast and it was suggested to the boy to try engraving to start with, but that also failed. His son did not like engraving, but when it was heard that a French landscapist named Régis Gignoux was making a good name for himself in New York, he was put under his tuition. Inness learned from him the handling of colors as well as some theories of composition, but that was all. He claimed that Gignoux was painting by the same methods that all the contemporary artists were using, and he did not want those methods; he wanted to paint as he felt inclined, and not to feel hampered by rules and theories. He explained his views thus: "Every artist who, without reference to external circumstances, aims truly to represent the ideas and emotions that come to him in the presence of nature, is in process of his own spiritual development, and is a benefactor to his race. His environment affects him, but the true artistic impulse is divine."

His family could not follow him into such heights of thought so from then on they let him go his own way.

Now, Inness was born in a period of the world when religious thought was uppermost in the minds of thinking people, and he was practically brought up on religious discussion. "His mother was a devout Methodist," so says his biographer. "His aunt, who later became his stepmother, was an equally devout Baptist. His uncle was a staunch Universalist, therefore religious discussion, even argument, became the principal topic of conversation in the home circle." Extremely emotional by nature, this condition of affairs drove him into a habit of self-investigation. The search for truth became a passion in the life of the young thinker.

All this seemed in direct contrast to the nervous, dissatisfied boy who in earlier days could find nothing to his liking, but it was the Inness in later years from first to last. He lived half of his life searching for a spirituality that satisfied him. He wanted that which would put God into his everyday life, so he went from church to church hunting for it. He failed to see that the trouble was in himself. He rebelled against all thought that did not agree with his thought, instead of studying the subject with an open mind. This peculiarity cropped out on many occasions during his life in regard to his art, his religion, and his intercourse with people. It brought much unnecessary suffering, for it was not understood by his friends, who thought everything of him, nor by the public at large. It is rather interesting to learn that back in his school days even, his teachers reported to his family that the boy, George Inness, "would not take education." And yet at heart he was eager to learn. The trouble was that, to his way of thinking, teachers usually taught by rote and not by conviction. So his instruction from Gignoux came to an end. It was really the only technical training he ever had.

About 1845 he opened a studio for himself, determined to put his views concerning art on canvas, and find out what the public thought of them. He boarded at the Astor House, and having little money to pay for his venture he paid for his board in pictures.

His first picture, called "Afternoon," was exhibited at the Art Union. It was considered rather crude, but it had an air of authenticity about it that was unmistakable. After that more were exhibited. Ogden Haggerty, a well-known auctioneer and a connoisseur of art, saw from the first that here was a genius in the making. He bought several of his paintings, and, eager to promote him, he suggested his going to Europe to complete his studies, and offered to finance his trip. So in 1847 Inness sailed for Italy, and like all the rest of the artists, he went to Rome, where he studied for a year, meanwhile living in the suburbs of that great city.

Soon after his return he met a young girl named Delia Miller. She lived in Newark, and they met frequently, and it ended in marriage. She, poor girl, had a short life with him, for she died about six months later.

His biographer states that this marriage and the loss of his young wife seemed to be only an episode in his life, for a great love was awaiting him. It was given to a very beautiful girl named Elizabeth Hart. He was so completely taken with her the very first time he saw her that he vowed then that he would win her and make her his wife, proceeding to go about it in a wholly characteristic way. The courtship started while he was attending the Baptist Church in New York, on Sixteenth Street. He caught sight of her sitting in a pew across the aisle, and he could not take his eyes off her. He was like one spellbound. When church was over he had the audacity to follow her to her home which was on Varick Street.

In telling of her feelings afterwards. she declared that she was frightened at first, on realizing he was following her, and hastened as fast as she could to her home. But when she got inside the house, with true feminine curiosity she peered through a slit in the window curtain to see what the young stranger was like. He proved to be quite a dashing young man with long hair and a flowing coat. He was pacing back and forth on the sidewalk in front of the house. Being inside the house she felt quite secure, though she was alone there, but when in a few moments the doorbell rang, she was taken aback and did not know what to do. However, she thought she would take a chance, and went to the door.

When she opened it and Inness saw the young girl face to face, she appeared even more beautiful to him than in the church. But he kept his wits about him. He bowed low, and with a solemn face inquired if Miss Mary Inness lived there, knowing perfectly well that he had left his sister at his home on Broome Street when he went to church. The young lady answered "No" very demurely, and with that he bowed low again and went his way.

In both cases the die had been cast. She was seventeen and he was twenty-five. An introduction was soon obtained, and in 1850 they were married. For forty-odd years their love for each other remained staunch and beautiful through all the ups and downs and vicissitudes of an artist's career.

In 1851 Mr. Haggerty came to the fore again. Inness had more than ever thrown himself headlong into his work, now that he had a wife to care for, and his health began to show it. His generous patron urged him to consult a doctor. The latter declared that a sea voyage was what was needed, and a long one at that, so Inness and his wife boarded a sailing vessel bound for Italy.

They remained there for two years. Once there, Inness plunged into work again regardless of consequences. He searched out the methods of the great masters with an eagerness and intensity that almost consumed him. Not that he wished to copy them; he wished to see for himself the technique and methods by which they had attained such great heights in art.

From Rome they went to Florence, and there their first child was born. During this time Inness became very much imbued with the romantic historic events of ancient history, and did some work in painting along that line, but these pictures were few and far between, though they were greatly approved of. Once away from Italy, however, he found nature calling him as before and he became restless for the scenery of his home, so in 1852 they returned to America and settled in Brooklyn. After a time Inness became uneasy, and anxious to study more of European art, so in 1854 they again set sail, this time going to France, where they got lodgings in the Latin Quarter of Paris, and there another child was born to them. He was named George, after his father.

These trips to the art centers of the world made a tremendous impression on Inness. It was at this time that the Barbizon School was making itself felt in France, and Inness felt the influence of it; not that he was directly influenced, but he was unconsciously so. It opened new avenues of thought in him. He believed so thoroughly in his own destiny and in his own views on art that he had grown to feel he could surpass any artist that ever lived, but for all that, the French school made a great appeal to him. He could have stayed on indefinitely in the atmosphere of the French capital, but as his family was growing apace, it became necessary for him to be where he could attend to the selling of his pictures, so they came back again to Brooklyn, and Inness opened a studio in New York.

During his boyhood Inness knew nothing of financial difficulties, but now all was different. He had to make his way alone without the aid of his family. So far, though he had a firm position in the art world, he had no gift at all in regard to selling his pictures. At that very time he was producing pictures that in later years were sold for many thousands of dollars in New York, but which then brought in only small amounts. He would have been glad to sell the whole lot of them for one hundred dollars at that time.

For several years this condition continued. He launched many paintings in current exhibitions, but the innovations that were visible in his style and technique were not approved of. The public resented the change they saw in him, and they made him feel it, so much so that he and his family moved to Boston, and an arrangement was made with the picture dealers, Williams & Everett, to take over the management of his pictures. This seemed to work well. His pictures began to sell better, and everything looked brighter. During these years a third daughter was born, and two years later still another, who eventually became the wife of J. Scott Hartley, the sculptor. Then a sixth child, a boy, was born but he died in infancy.

With this rapidly growing family they decided to go into the country to live, where open air and sunshine would make strong bones and muscles, and they chose Medfield, a lovely New England countryside near Boston, living there for five years.

For the first time Inness found himself in truly sympathetic surroundings. Here he could give himself to his family as he had never done before. Time was his own. He could do what he liked without the perpetual interruptions that made him nervous and constrained. His biographer says of him at this period: "His tenderness and love for his family were beautiful. He sought to understand his children, and entered into their games and pleasures, and even spent hours making kites and jackstraws for them."

The River Charles flowed near their home, and if there was a sport that Inness enjoyed, it was skating on it of a winter's afternoon. They all took to it like ducks to water and on a bright winter's day the Inness family could be seen twirling and circling on the ice.

When Inness skated, he wore a shawl. Most men wore shawls in those days, with one end thrown artistically over the left shoulder, and Inness, with his long hair and plaid shawl floating in the breeze, made a picture worth looking at, though he was quite unconscious of the effect he was producing.

On the place at Medfield there was an old barn. He transformed it into a studio, and in that dilapidated old building some of his most celebrated pictures were painted. The original sketch of one of the finest examples of his work was done there. It was called "Medfield Meadows." The finished result was a most beautiful painting — one of his best. His biographer describes him in the act of painting, which is worth recording: "When he painted he put all the force of his nature into it. Full of vim and vigor he was like a dynamo. It was a punch here and a dab there. He was truly indefatigable. He was a totally different man in his studio from what he was out of doors. Out of doors he was quiet, rational and absorbed. But in his studio he was like a madman."

The years in Medfield were happy ones, but they were lean ones when it came to getting large prices for his pictures. He fared better in Boston than in New York, but at times his purse was very low. If it was hard on him, it was doubly hard on his wife whom he adored, but she made the best of it and always kept a smiling face, for to her he seemed like a wonderful being and a great genius. She was proud of him, and that was enough.

Among the frequent visitors who came to see them and wanted to see what Inness was painting were Mark Fisher, George N. Cass, and J. A. S. Monks. These men were ardent admirers of Inness, and lovers of art.

It is stated by his biographers that in middle life "Inness at last found a branch of religious thought that satisfied his soul." The writings of Swedenborg made a tremendous impression on him, and he ordered his life by them. Symbolism then appeared to him as they might to a mystic or an idealist. His attitude towards painting was noticeably changing. Suggestion was taking the place of form. He sought as subjects the light, air, and color of nature instead of the forms. He became absorbed in speculation and metaphysics. He literally lived in a world of deep thought, and half the time was so absent-minded that he forgot the simplest things of daily living. All through this time his wife shielded him lovingly from the results of some of the perfectly impossible things he did. She could not follow his thoughts — they were far too deep for anyone except an adept to follow — but she never let him know this.

It was the portrait painter, William Page, who was at one time president of the Academy of Design, who brought to Inness the teachings of Emanuel Swedenborg. "The latter threw himself into those teachings with all the fire and enthusiasm of his nature. He became full of theories on art, religion and ethics, and would talk theory to all who would listen to him. It made no difference to him whether they agreed with him or understood, he kept right on talking theory. I have seen him pin a man to a chair and pound his ideas into him for hours at a time, until he and his listener were both exhausted."

All this had a more or less detrimental effect on his ability to make the two ends meet in daily life. In the midst of the period when their financial status was low, he went to Boston one day in the exhilaration of having sold a picture, and immediately sought out a jewelry shop and brought home to his beautiful wife a gorgeous diamond necklace which she clasped around her neck. Fortunately she knew perfectly how to meet the situation.

"O George," she exclaimed, "how beautiful! O my dear, the wish of my life has been to possess a diamond necklace!" Everything was happy that evening; even the children entered into the general joy of this present to their mother.

A few days after this Inness said: "Lizzie, why don't you wear your necklace? I haven't seen it round your neck since the night I brought it to you."

His wife replied: "Why, how would I look with a diamond necklace on this calico gown? Some day before long, when our ship comes in, you will get me a velvet gown, and we will go to New York and to the reception of the Academy of Design, and I can wear the necklace, and show people how proud I can be as the wife of the great genius."

But Inness was not satisfied. He insisted that she was the most beautiful woman God had ever made, and he wanted to see how her beautiful neck would show off the diamond necklace.

Then his wife put her arms around his neck and said: "Dear husband, I have not got the necklace."

"Not got the necklace! What in the world has become of it?"

"You see, my dear, I went to Boston the next day, and the jeweler gave me the money you paid for it, and I put it in the bank."

Inness then clasped her in his arms and sobbed: "You are the best little wife a man ever had."

George Inness was the most lovable and sympathetic man in the world, but one of his great troubles was that he could not keep his thoughts to himself. His son George writes on this subject (*Life and Letters of George Inness*): "Father could never learn to be politic. Once when a prospective purchaser criticized something in a picture he was considering, Father told him not to make an idiot of himself by talking of something he was absolutely ignorant of. Needless to say the sale was not made, and the rent still was due."

Again his son says: "If anyone criticized my father's work, even though he did not know where the next meal or house rent was coming from, he would blow out in a passion of abuse and lose a sale."

Fortunately his son saw the humorous side of those peculiarities. Long afterwards when he was recalling them, he wrote:

> As I sit and write of those days, a flood of memories come back to me. I can see my father so plainly in all the phases of his life. Many-sided versatile Pop! Truly a contradiction. As gentle as a lamb, and as ferocious as a lion. Sensitive, introspective, absent-minded, light-hearted and fun-loving, and under all conditions consumed with a passionate belief in his own destiny, and intense desire for its fulfilment. No matter what the mood, the desire for self-expression surmounted everything.

But it was costly sometimes to those sitting by.

To show how soft his heart was when his sympathy was called upon, this anecdote is told of him:

> George Inness was generous to a fault, and no man in the world was so easily imposed upon. When he had a studio in New York there was a man who frequented the various art centers and made his living by his wits, turning his hand to anything that would bring him a penny, honest or otherwise — usually otherwise. One day he rushed into my father's studio, his face a picture of despair. Throwing himself into a chair he cried: "O my God! my wife, my poor wife — the mother of my little children! God help them! I cannot! O George, what shall I do? I fear I will kill myself!" and he buried his face in his hands and cried like a child.
>
> Father, wild with anguish, sprang up and grasped him by the shoulders. "What is it?" he cried. "Your wife, you said — tell me, is she, is she dead?"

"No, George, not dead, not yet, but she soon will be, I'm afraid. I left her with two doctors, and I have no money to pay for medicine or food. O God, what shall I do! Where can I find a friend in this hour of need!"

Father felt in his pockets and found nothing. "I have no money," he cried; "but wait, old man — be calm, wait here."

With tears streaming down his face he dashed out of the studio and to the art rooms of John Snedecor, on Broadway.

"John," he cried frantically; "I must have money; give me money, quick! It's a case of life and death. I must have it now — not a minute to lose. I'll pay you back — haven't time to explain!"

Snedecor thrust twenty dollars into his hand, and he rushed back to the studio. "Here, man," he shouted; "take this, and God be with you. Hurry, for God's sake!"

When he left, Pop collapsed. He was completely unnerved with the agony of seeing one go through that thing which he most dreaded in his own life. He was so weakened by the experience that he went home, and was not able to leave his bed for two days. On the third day, when he returned to the studio, spent and worn, his friend came in whistling, and Pop grasped him by the hand. "Your wife," he asked. "Tell me, how is she?"

"Oh," the other one replied nonchalantly, "she's all right, I left her at the wash tubs."

"But the other day she was ill, man, dying — "

"Oh, pshaw," he replied, "that was because I wanted twenty dollars. Never mind, old man; I'll pay it back some day."

But he didn't pay it back, nor did he ever come to the studio again.

The country in Medfield was quiet and pastoral, and the lack of the excitement of city life, with competition always confronting an artist, kept him more serene and tractable. They remained there five years, and during that time three more children were born, making three more mouths to feed.

It became necessary for his wife to take over the management of his property and to become the banker of the family. The time had come when he was so steeped in metaphysical thought that his family felt it almost unsafe for him to go out alone. His wife never knew from one hour to another where he might turn up next.

She thought perhaps he needed a change of scene, so they decided to try Englewood. It was a place where many artists gathered, and they crowded around Inness when he appeared. He found it very stimulating, and some of them persuaded him to take them on as pupils, and altogether their move to that place was a success. It lasted until 1867, when they picked up stakes again and moved to Brooklyn. He began to long for a broader field. At Brooklyn he could feel the rush of human life surrounding him. While it had irritated him before, now he craved it, and the year after his arrival he was elected an associate of the Academy of Design. The public was feeling more and more that a real genius was among them, and his pictures were being sought. He was giving them something new to look at, which made an appeal in itself, and it was very gratifying to him, but to rear and feed a family of the size that his had grown to be meant the sale of many pictures, and he painted so continuously and without giving himself a chance to rest, that Williams and Everett, the dealers who had charge of his works, induced him to go to Europe again. In 1870 they all set sail for the other side, stopping in London and Paris but ending up in Rome.

It was in 1872 that news came of the disastrous fire in Boston. Inness thought of his paintings there, and distraught with anxiety he left his family and hurried back to the United States to make sure of their safety. His faithful wife went with her children to Paris to await his return. She was nervous at the thought of his going alone, but with her family to care for there was nothing else she could do.

"If I am not there to look after you," she told him, "I don't know what will happen." But she had to let him go.

He was so used to having her remind him of his engagements and so on that he was quite bewildered when he arrived in Boston, especially as, now that he was fully recognized as a great artist and a genius, many of his friends and those also with whom he was little acquainted, laid themselves out to do him honor by giving entertainments to meet him. A Mr. Maynard of Boston gave a description to Inness' son of the experience he had in giving a large dinner to which he asked the élite of Boston to meet the famed artist, George Inness.

George Inness, Jr., relates what this gentleman told him as follows:

The dinner was a large and brilliant one. The guests arrived on time eager to meet this celebrity. Dinner was announced but the guest of honor had not come. I became very nervous. The steward was growing impatient — the dinner was getting cold, and I was almost beside myself. Finally I had to take my guests to the dining room. We all sat rather glum; occasionally one would tell a story of some eccentric fellow he had known, and as the soup and then the fish were served we told some more, and after the entrée and the roast had gone, tales of accident and death were cited — when suddenly the door flew open, and there stood our guest George Inness. He was quite out of breath, and exclaimed:

"I beg your pardon, Maynard. I am late, I fear; but the fact is I forgot all about the dinner. But never mind, I'll join you right here. No, thank you, nothing, please. I got my dinner at a little restaurant before I remembered. I'll just have some dessert."

His hair was dishevelled, and the little pea jacket that he was wearing was stained with spots of paint; but he began to talk, and he talked and talked as never man talked before: of color, God, tone, the triumph of the mind, and of Swedenborg — and when the party finally broke up, every guest was in a state of delight. No matter whether we followed him or not, he was most entertaining. His gestures, which at times threatened to play havoc with the china, were eloquent.

The dinner was a great success, and I would not have missed it, or had it different for the greatest picture he could paint.

The family which had remained in Paris soon came back to America and joined him in Boston. But Inness decided to try New York again, having had some difficulty over his pictures in the former city. His son, who had been named after him, had by this time grown up, and had also become an artist, and he and his father now had a studio together in the old Booth Theater at Broadway and Sixth Avenue. It was with never-ceasing astonishment that the son watched the father paint. He said of him:

Pop was growing richer and broader in expression with his maturer years. When he painted he painted at white heat. Passionate, dynamic in his force, I have seen him sometimes like a madman, stripped to the

waist, perspiration rolling like a mill-race from his face, with some idea
struggling for expression. . . . What was his masterpiece one day would
be "dish water" and "twaddle" in the next. He would take a canvas before it was really dry, and being seized with another inspiration, would
paint over it. I have known him to paint as many as half a dozen or
more pictures on one canvas, in fact as many as the canvas would hold.

Nothing ever cured him of this habit, and it became more and
more of a passion with him. By now he had become a true impressionist, and pointing out one of his pictures to his son he explained
it thus to him: "The only charm in this picture is in deceiving
you into the belief that it is a real barn door that you see. Now in
art — true art — we are not seeking to deceive. We do not pretend
that this is a real tree, a real river, but we use the tree or the river as
a means to giving you the feeling or impression that through them
a certain effect is produced upon us."

Nothing warmed him up to a pitch of inspiration so much as to ex-
pound his theories. After he had finished speaking, his eyes were beginning to flash; he was becoming tense, and as he turned, with a swift
movement, towards the easel one could see the picture on it was doomed.
He seized his palette, squeezed out a great quantity of black, and pounced
upon the canvas like a lion. He dashed at a tree in the corner with a
glaze of black which he carried through the foreground. He sprang back
several paces, held his hand over his eyes, and looked at the canvas
through half-closed lids.

"Confound it, George! It's got too much tone! We don't know just
what it's going to be, but it's coming. We don't care what it is so it
expresses beauty."

With a wild rush he swiftly painted out two sheep in the foreground.
"Too much detail, I tell you." His hair was dishevelled, his eyes burned
with the fire of creative intensity, and the tail of his shirt, responding
to the emotional stress of its owner, had been jerked from its usual abid-
ing place. "Now," he continued, waving his palette in the air, "we are
getting some kind of effect. Don't know what the deuce it's going to be,
but we are getting a start."

Now he stood off again, held his palette to his eyes, and with another
dash obliterated the tops of the trees with a patch of blue sky. The

atmosphere was electrified. Pop was quivering with emotion, and I too caught the tenseness of the situation. He dabbed and smeared, and for a quarter of an hour the silence was broken only by his quick breathing, and the jabs of his brush on the canvas. He was bringing a composition out of chaos.

I have known him to stay in bed as long as two or three days at a time, writing and thinking, and in answer to my solicitations in regard to his health he would reply:

"Oh, no, not ill; only resting and having a good time. Don't have to dress, and I believe your mother has a new suit for me."

Pop hated new clothes as he hated the barber and the dentist, and mother, who had given his measure to the tailor, would order two or three suits at a time, and when she thought it necessary, would remove the old ones after Pop had retired, and put new ones in their place. But try as she might, Pop was extremely careless. He never knew or cared what he looked like. He lived too much in the abstract for that.

Let it be said here: "Mr. Inness was most happily fortunate in his marriage. To one of his impetuous, easily ruffled nature, the lack of sympathy in his wife would have been a constant irritation and impediment to his progress; but his wife was sensitive to his every mood, careful of his needs, keenly alive to his hopes in his works, and to the last hour of his life his comfort and his friend." Thus his son wrote of him and his mother — and here is another thing that he wrote of them:

Throughout his whole life he was plastic as clay in my mother's hands He loved her with an overwhelming love, and had she been less wise in her gentle guidance, the world might never have known George Inness. Throughout their struggles and trials she was his counselor, watching him and guarding him with the tenderest love. He depended on her for everything, from the arranging of his necktie to the solving of his deep metaphysical problems. He was perfect in her eyes, and their life was beautiful. Often right up to the close of their lives I have seen them go off hand in hand like lovers. He talked to her of his theories and ideals which were often very involved, and whether she understood all of them or not, she made him feel that she did.

It was in the year 1878, when Inness was past middle life, that fortune and fame came to him. The public had been growing in sympathy for some time with his views on art and painting, and when the great Niagara was painted it raised a tumult of applause. The painting of it was characteristic of him in the extreme. Inness went out to see the Falls, and he became so inspired by an inspiration to paint them that he rushed to the studio of his old friend Selsted, in Buffalo, and rousing him from his bed at an unholy hour, demanded studio, canvas, and brushes — in fact everything that he needed.

"I must paint, Selsted" [he said]. "Quick! I can't wait a minute! I must get my impression of the falls down right away." And poor Selsted, like all the rest of us, gave up everything, and was not allowed to use his studio or anything in it until the sketch was made, which I might add was taken from an imaginary point in the middle of the rapids. The finished canvas was later painted in the old University building on East Washington Square.

In the various times that Inness went to Europe and stayed a number of years, especially in France where he became friends with the artists of the Barbizon School, he sent many paintings back to this country, and little by little his new views on art began to be absorbed by some of the younger men in the profession. Being used to our own Hudson River School of art, the public did not understand these new and utterly different standards, but the public is apt to be volatile, and follows whatever is the fashion, especially if it sells. So Inness, with his impressionist paintings, finally won his claim to fame.

Soon after his return to this country the French portrait painter, Benjamin Constant, came to America, and seeing all the work that Inness had done, he became very enthusiastic over it, and incidentally was an important factor in the establishment in Europe of Inness' reputation as a man of genius. He went frequently to see him at work in his studio, and it is said to have been a wonderful sight to see these two great artists exclaiming and gesticulating over some picture they were considering. Neither could understand the language of the other, but they managed to convey a certain amount of meaning by their gestures. On one occasion they were seen sitting on the floor, sketches strewn all about, hands waving in every direction, punctuated with exclamations such as "Tres bien!" "Magnifique!" "Chef-d'œuvre!" and the like.

The upshot of it was that Constant took back a number of sketches by Inness to Paris, in order to show the type of paintings that were appearing for sale in America. He went further than that — he advised collectors to buy up all the Inness paintings they came across, as it would certainly be to their advantage to do so, and he called the attention of Bouissart-Vallidon and Company to them, which proved of great value in results.

In the meantime Mr. Thomas B. Clarke, a prominent collector, bought twenty-five Inness paintings, and that set the ball rolling. Others followed suit, and soon every exhibition and collection had a number of examples of his work. As a result his days of poverty were ended, especially as Mr. Clarke, seeing the necessity of it, took over the care of his property, as well as the management of the sale of his pictures, so for sixteen years until his death Inness' financial difficulties were over. His son wrote of him at this time as follows: "Wherever he went now he was treated royally; but he remained to the day of his death the plain, simple-hearted great man that he was. He lived for his art, and was affected neither by praise nor criticism. To be made a lion of embarrassed him; in fact, he saw no reason in it, and he did not like it. The joy of self-expression brought its own reward."

Now that his property was well cared for, he settled in Montclair, New Jersey, and there in the old Mapes homestead on Grove Street he built himself a studio where he continued to paint, without the sense of hurry and necessity dogging his footsteps. The newspapers were excessive in their praise of him as an artist, and whatever he put on the market was sold as soon as it appeared.

All this was like a happy dream, but in 1894 it became evident that his health was beginning to falter. In order to get a complete change away from his work he and his wife took another ocean voyage, and this time went to Scotland, to the little town of Bridge-of-Allan. Here

he could rest satisfactorily, and for a time his health seemed to improve. His old vigor was asserting itself. So, late one afternoon,
they decided to take a drive. While his wife was dressing to go out
Inness took a stroll to a spot near-by where he could watch the sun
go down. The sunset was unusually beautiful that evening, and
Inness, whose capacity for absorbing the beauties of nature was almost supernormal, felt on this occasion "an ecstasy too profound —
a pain too exquisite for the frail human body." Just as the golden
ball sank below the horizon he threw his hands up into the air and
exclaimed, "My God! Oh, how beautiful!" and fell stricken to the
ground.

He was carried to the house and upstairs to his wife, and in a few
moments "died in the arms of the woman he loved better than anyone else in the world."

They brought his body back from Scotland, and it lay in state in
the Academy of Design where the funeral was held. This was a
special honor bestowed on only a few among the elect in art. Inness'
biographer says: "It is true that the Academy was slow to acknowledge George Inness, fifteen years elapsing between his election as
Associate and his election as a full Academician, the latter occurring
in 1868. But when at last he was recognized, it was with full and
complete recognition."

His paintings are in the museums of Chicago, New York, Boston,
Philadelphia, Washington, Pittsburgh, Buffalo, Worcester, and many
other cities.

A great sale of his paintings was held after his death. The total
sum brought in was one hundred and eight thousand dollars.

CHAPTER 19

Alexander Helwig Wyant
(1836–1892)

THE NAMES OF George Inness and Alexander Helwig Wyant fall naturally together. Wyant owed his reputation to the counsel given him by Inness, whose theories on art, the meaning of that great profession, and the real goal of it sank deeply into the groundwork of the soul of the younger man.

Wyant was born in Ohio, in Evans Creek, Tuscarawas County. He was an imaginative, temperamental, somewhat oversensitive boy, craving an outlet through which he could express himself. As a matter of course in those days, his family tried to smother these materially unprofitable aspirations, but fate is stronger than they, when desire is born of a vital source, and Wyant followed the path it laid out for him with a firm tenacity. He had been apprenticed to a harness maker, and through the restlessness of one possessed by an inner longing which seemed beyond his reach, something happened.

One day he came across the illustrations of some paintings by George Inness, and they fired his imagination. He studied them until a great plan grew and expanded in his mind. He was then twenty-one years of age and during his years of apprenticeship had managed to put aside some of the money he had earned, which now came to his aid, and when the time seemed ripe for his adventure he gathered up his savings and set his face towards the big world beyond him with the determination to seek out the artist Inness, and find out from him the right road to follow, for every mile that brought him nearer to the great city of New York made that road look tortuous and misleading. In the end, however, he found the artist sitting at work in his studio, and with the wholly unconscious audacity of a boy he sent in his name — Alexander Helwig Wyant.

Strange to relate, Inness was willing to see him. Perhaps there was something definite and unusual in the manner of announcement, for as a rule Inness refused to allow interviews with young and unknown artists or those wishing to become artists, who might or might not amount to anything, but in this case, whatever the reason, Inness gave in. Evidently the latter talked at length to the eager young man about art and his views concerning it, and the fact that Wyant seemed able to follow him in his somewhat complicated discourse must have made an impression on Inness, for as a result of the interview he went to the trouble of interesting the noted collector, Nicholas Longworth, of Cincinnati, in the young man's career, and made it possible for him definitely to study in the profession he had longed to adopt.

The results were more than gratifying to this generous encourager of art. Seven years later, in 1864, a painting which Wyant sent to an exhibition of the Academy of Design met with a real appreciation of its worth. That it was well received was a great encouragement, and under the same kind patronage he sailed for Europe the following year in order to study the Düsseldorf method of painting under Hans Gude, at Karlsruhe.

Like many of the other young American artists who studied the Düsseldorf method, he found himself rebelling against the many restrictions that seemed to curb the freedom of his individual talent, and he decided to return to his own country; but before returning he traveled in England and Ireland, and this brought him in contact with the paintings of Turner and Constable in London. These impressed him deeply. In them he saw something to which his soul was akin, and this influence, added to the indelible impression made on him by the paintings of Inness, created a style and method of his own which rewarded him with a reputation that no one could belittle. But his technique changed somewhat with the passing of years. He started as a firm adherent of the Hudson River School of painting, but the influence of the French School, just coming into vogue, caught him, and proved too much for him. He became more and more of an impressionist, and the objective gave way to the imaginative.

On his return to New York some of the longings for adventure that had assailed Thomas Cole and Bierstadt caught hold of him. He too was filled with a desire to see more of his country and to reveal its beauty, as they had. But he had another reason which was a personal one. He had been working very hard and it left him with a curious sense of fatigue which he thought a change of scene and air might rectify. So when he heard that the government was about to send an exploring expedition into the wilds of Arizona and New Mexico he eagerly joined. He felt in the mood for travel of that kind. Things had been going well with him; in 1869 he had been elected a full member of the National Academy of Design, largely on account of his painting, "The Upper Susquehanna," which was a decided success, having captured the imagination of the public. He thought he owed himself a vacation like the expedition which he had joined, so he started off with hopes of accomplishing something unusual, that would greatly add to his already gained reputation. But the results were disastrous. He had never been in what might be called rugged health, and was too delicately organized for the rough-and-tumble of pioneer life with its privations, lack of food, and climbing of high mountains across which no paths had yet been made. More than that, he evidently did not meet with sympathy from the conductor of the expedition, who must have been a hard-fisted sort of man to have undertaken such a trip and who had no patience with anyone who could not stand the strain, and this added to Wyant's physical and mental discomfort. After struggling to keep up with the expedition he was one day stricken with paralysis of his right side. His arm fell useless from his shoulder — that arm on which he counted to do his bidding, and to accomplish all he had planned to do.

It was a terrible and overwhelming blow to his future, his ambition, and all that he could do in the realms of art. History does not tell how they managed to return him to civilization, but it is recorded that the attack was followed by a long and suffering illness, during which it was thought that he would never work again. This seemingly cruel fate made inroads upon his disposition. He became morose and morbidly sensitive to any reference to his ill health, which made it difficult for those who had to take care of him. After a time he rebelled at the restrictions put upon him, and with grim determination he forced himself to learn to paint with his left hand. Little by little he found himself succeeding, and by this great effort he was putting upon himself he discovered that at least his talent had remained unimpaired, but his methods of applying it differed more decisively from his early paintings, which followed the ideals and technique of the Hudson River School — the impression made on him of the Impressionists became more and more in evidence — his left hand obeyed the theories of the Barbizon School instead of those of his homeland.

Now it probably was sympathy with him, and pity for his terrible affliction, that a young girl, Arabella Locke by name, a daughter of John Bell Locke, fell in love with him. In 1880 he married her, and later a son was born to them.

But in spite of this piece of good fortune, Wyant's physical condition grew worse as time went on. Still he would not loosen his hold upon his palette and brush. His soul seemed to express itself in his paintings as though that were its only means of escape from the physical bondage that threatened to shackle it. Outwardly he became introspective and more or less of a recluse. At the same time, instead of his reputation as an artist lessening it increased, and some of his most noted pictures were painted at this time. And so it went — a fight for mastery all the way along.

It must have been pitiful to have to sit by and watch the struggle he made day in and day out, but his wife bore it with courage and did all she could to make his life easier, in 1889 securing a studio for him in Arkville, deep in the Catskill Mountains. From this studio he had a wonderful view of the long stretches of the Delaware Valley below him, which gave him an opportunity to study the lights and shades passing over the hilltops, and the ever changing aspects of the sky which always formed the center point and nucleus of his pictures. So, probably unconsciously, he had picked out the surroundings so dear to the other artists of the Hudson River School in which to live as he felt his life waning.

The time came when all he could safely do was to take an occasional drive. Other than that he did not venture outside of his small domain. His work was over.

He had gone to New York when the end came, and was in his studio on Fifty-Second Street, which he had kept all along, hoping against hope that some day he would be able to return there.

He died on November 29, 1892.

All the prominent museums in the country have one or more examples of his work.

Samuel Isham says in his volume, *American Paintings*: "With these three men — Inness, Wyant and Martin [*author's note*: a specimen of the latter's work I have not yet acquired] — the early American Landscape School culminates." There were younger men who followed them and still painted in the Hudson River style, but they did not belong to the original group.

In speaking of Wyant's art, the *Dictionary of American Biography* makes this statement:

> A poetic tonalist, Wyant remains one of the outstanding masters of American Landscape painting during the latter half of the nineteenth century. . . . Not so emotional as Inness, he does not attain the same dramatic effect. His work is more limited and his expression more reserved, but in consequence his pictures are more even. As a pure naturalist he is unsurpassed. He had not the austere solidarity, the fullness of form, or the perfect relation of method to style which characterizes his prototype Theodore Rousseau, but he had a more subtle sense of tonal relation and atmospheric envelopment. This brought to his technique a greater freedom of brushwork, and the suggestion rather than the precise definition of form. In this respect he is more truly related to Corot, and his art is a transition from the earlier school to the later impressionists.

The Art Journal, December, 1876, says: "As a painter of the wild and rugged scenery of the northern wilderness of New York, Wyant has but few equals in the Academic ranks."

CHAPTER 20

Thomas Hill
(1829–1908)

THOMAS HILL had the gift of taking one right into the heart of the Yosemite Valley by his paintings. It was with the Yosemite Valley that he was largely associated. He was English by birth and was born in Birmingham, September 11, 1829, and while still very young, his parents (Thomas and Maria Hill) left England and emigrated to the United States where they settled in Taunton, Massachusetts. He was never a strong child but he managed to get a common school education. As was so apt to be the case with all these young artists, he was apprenticed to a coach painter and showed great aptitude. His family moved to Gardner, Massachusetts, where he was employed by the Heyward-Wakefield Company as a decorator. A set of furniture which was "very beautiful with its fruit, flowers and gold stripings made testimony of the work he did in those early days and it is now in the possession of the Historical Society of Concord, New Hampshire. It has been honored and preserved through all these years by the Heyward family." (From a letter written by his daughter, Adeline M. Hill, in 1927.)

It is said that "in private life he was essentially a family man, and lacked to a marked degree the Bohemian habits which are wont to characterize his brethren in the art. But his home life was a happy one and he had a large family of sons and daughters — the exact number of which is not recorded."

Feeling that his environment was too limited, he went to Philadelphia. During this time he devoted his attention to painting in oils and worked at the Pennsylvania Academy of Fine Arts where he showed great promise as a pupil. In 1853 the Maryland Institute at Baltimore held an exhibition at which one of his pictures took the first prize.

But during all this time his health was causing him great trouble. He showed distinct weakness of the lungs, which he could not overcome, and so in 1861 he went to San Francisco and opened a studio there. His great desire was landscape painting, but because of the peculiar advantages of portrait painting he devoted himself more or less to that for the time being. Besides landscape painting, he was drawn very much towards the painting of historical and literary subjects which was very much in vogue at that time. And when the San Francisco Art Union held a big exhibition in 1855, his picture, "The Merchant of Venice," won the first prize. He was very much encouraged by this and it stirred his ambition, so in 1866 he went to Paris, determined to acquire more knowledge than he could have got in his own country. He became a pupil of the artist, Paul Meyerheim, which was the only instruction in oils he ever received. When the latter saw some of the sketches he had made of the Forest at Fontainebleau, where he stopped for a day or two, he advised him very distinctly to devote himself to landscape painting. Two years later Hill returned home and settled in Cambridge, Massachusetts, with a studio in Boston. That was in 1867. Here he painted a number of pictures of the White Mountains, and it was here that he painted his great panoramic canvas, called "Yosemite Valley," measuring ten by fifteen feet in size. The newspapers were full of the praises of this work and brought it into great prominence. It was exhibited at Child's Gallery, Tremont Street, to which the public flocked to view it. It was so much admired that in 1870, L. Prang & Company reproduced it by the process of chromo-lithography which at that period was in great demand. It was also engraved as a frontispiece to a book called *Scenes of Wonder and Curiosity in California* by J. M. Hutchings in 1870. Later the original picture was in the possession of Charles Crocker in San Francisco. Still later it hung in the E. B. Crocker Gallery in Sacramento.

Thomas Hill seemed destined to have ill health dog his footsteps. He was continually overdoing in his work and was finally advised to return to California where he could live more in the open air. On his return there the Yosemite Valley drew him to its heart even more than before. He opened a studio where he could get the full view of it. In a letter to Mr. Levi Greenwood, in 1927, Adeline M. Hill, the daughter of Thomas Hill, writes: "His daughter, Mrs. John Washburn, was one of the owners of the Wawona Hotel in Yosemite Valley, and father made his home there from early spring until snow began to fall. My sister's late husband with his two brothers were the first to settle in the Yosemite Valley, opening a small hotel which has now grown to be one of the finest in the Valley. All three brothers were from New Hampshire."

Life in those days was rough in the extreme but he found the air just what his physical being needed and, as far as his physical strength would allow, he became a tireless worker. He felt that the grandeur of the Yosemite Valley could be shown only on a large canvas and these paintings he brought to a high finish. By this time his name was well known among the artists and the public as well. It was a pathetic point in his life that living in the wilds of California (as it was then) debarred him from intimate association with the Hudson River artists, but he was essentially of that group in spite of the great distances that lay between them. He had the same desire as Cole and Bierstadt to reveal the beauty of scenery to be found on our continent. When the great Centennial was held in Philadelphia in 1876 he was awarded the first prize for his paintings "Donner Lake" and the "Yosemite Valley." Both pictures were purchased by Leland Stanford for $11,000. He painted another very large picture called "The Great Canyon of the Sierras," which won the medal of the New York Palette Club and was sold for $5000, and his other great picture, "Heart of the Sierras," was bought by E. J. Baldwin of San Francisco for $10,000.

He painted the Valley from all corners. The reproduction in this book is a very beautiful example of the cliffs with El Capitan on the left and the Falls of the Bridal Veil on the right. This pouring out of his soul into the pictures he painted, revealing beauty almost unknown to the general public of the rest of the country, comprised the whole of Thomas Hill's life.

At the time of his death, which occurred in 1908 in Raymond, California, he possessed thirty-one medals from various art societies.

He was the founder of: the Bohemian Club, the San Francisco Art Association, and later, the San Francisco School of Design.

CHAPTER 21

William M. Hart
(1823–1894)

THERE WERE TWO Hart brothers, William M. and James M., both painters. William was born in Paisley, Scotland, in 1823; and James, the younger, in 1828 in Kilmarnock, Scotland. However, it is William whose career we shall follow. When his family came to this country they settled at Albany and almost immediately bound William to a carriage maker who set him to painting carriages, and after a certain amount of training he was assigned the decorating of panels for the coaches. In those days there was a great deal of rivalry over these panels among the coach makers, and artists were eagerly looked for who could make them striking and ornamental. Young William proved himself able to vie with any of these competitors. So much was said about the excellence of his work that, although he was only eighteen years of age, he decided to make an attempt at painting portraits. He had his sitters pose for them in his father's woodshed and charged five dollars for his work. Full of ambition, he tried his hand at landscapes, but this was a more difficult problem, so he went on with his portraits. He had pretty well exhausted the field where he was, so he started out for Michigan. He was now charging twenty-five dollars, suspecting that five dollars was undervaluing his work; but it so happened that at the time he went there money was scarce; so in order to make the best of a bad bargain he often took his payment in board and lodging and sometimes barter. His boyhood home had been a very comfortable one and his encounter with the world, though limited, wore upon his strength and he was kept in a state of depression by malaria, so much so that he finally decided to go home and get a good rest. His condition worried the family not a little and a friend came forward and offered to assist him to make a trip to Scotland. The change of scene did him good but he roamed about rather restlessly, finally deciding to return to America. His ambition, however, had not diminished and he decided to open a studio in New York City. He belonged to the type that loves detail and some of his small pictures were almost like miniatures, but the public liked them and he built up a good standing for himself in the art world.

In the meantime, his brother James was following the same profession. It is said that "he garnished his landscapes with barnyard animals, chiefly cows, and painted them with such fidelity that his customers thought they could distinguish the Alderneys from the Guernseys." (*Dictionary of American Biography.*) William painted cows, too, but he surrounded them by such beautiful trees and streams and mossy banks that the animals were merely a part of the whole scene. There was something very restful in his pictures; they suggested the rural scenes familiar to every landholder of that time and they did not lose their popularity. However, when he heard his brother's cows spoken of with so much praise a twinge of jealousy swept through him, and on one occasion he was heard to say, in his broad Scotch accent which he had never discarded, "Jeams, he's a fair mon but he cannot paint a coo," and this with much decision. Still James went on painting cows and the public went on admiring them. Of the two brothers, William acquired the most lasting reputation and his pictures are among the collections at the Metropolitan Museum, New York. He was elected to the National Academy in 1858. The two illustrations of his paintings reproduced herewith are a part of this collection. He died at Mt. Vernon, New York, in 1894.

Author's note: James's paintings may be found in the Corcoran Gallery, Washington, but there are none of his in this collection.

CHAPTER 22

George L. Brown
(1814–1889)

GEORGE L. BROWN was a very popular artist among the group of the Hudson River painters. He had a gay, laughing way with him that was exceptionally cheerful. He was a native of Massachusetts, having been born in Boston in 1814. In his early life there is little told about him. He was very successful then at wood-carving and was more or less of an illustrator for some juvenile publications that were then in vogue in Boston. Luck always went with George L. Brown and he certainly experienced it when one day a wealthy Boston merchant, who was also a great art lover, noticed some of the work he was doing, and, feeling sure that he saw a young man with unusual talent before him, made it possible for him to go to Europe and see for himself what art was like in the countries there. Brown went to Europe in 1853, going to Paris first; and as he wandered through the galleries of the Louvre, he felt there could be no better place for him to learn the art methods of the various great cities of the world. The result was that he stayed there and became a pupil of the noted artist Isabey. Then of course, he was no different from any of the other artists, for his real goal was Rome. There he joined the group of American artists and dined with them at the Café Greco, enjoying all that wonderful interchange of social comradeship in the off hours from work. In the lists of the artists in Rome at that time the name of George L. Brown appears, and as a result of the conscientious work he did there, his name became known in the art world. After spending some time in Rome, he went to Florence and spent several years there, with the result that he painted sixty landscapes which he sent back to America. There they met a ready sale.

He returned to America in 1860 "with a high reputation as a landscape painter." (Mantle Fielding.) He took up his residence in South Boston, and here he painted very assiduously. One painting of his which was greatly thought of was called "Crown of New England," and it is an interesting fact to record that the Prince of Wales (later Edward VII) then visiting this country purchased it, as a typical New England scene. Also, his "Bay of New York" was chosen by a few New York merchants to present to the Prince of Wales as a memento of their state. He exhibited several paintings at the Centennial Exposition in Philadelphia in 1876. While he painted some of our New England scenery and places further afield, such as "The Niagara by Moonlight," the greater number of his works were from sketches taken in Italy, such as a large picture of Capri, and also one of Amalfi; the latter is in the Metropolitan Museum in New York. During this time he moved his residence to Malden, Massachusetts, which was where he died in 1889. The *Art Journal* of May, 1875, said of his "Sunset at Genoa" that it was "one of those gorgeous, idealized hazy Italian scenes for which this artist is so much noted, in the vein of Turner."

Author's note: The painting by W. R. Miller is included in this book because he was a well-known artist of his time. However, no facts of his life have yet been found.

THE END

Afterword

THE GLORIOUS DAYS of The Hudson River School faded into the past. The men who created it, one by one, went the way of all flesh. The Barbizon School came in and was greeted with enthusiasm and it too, faded away. Then came the Impressionists, and then the Cubists, and after them the Futurists; all these had their ardent adherents, and passed away. Now, we are in the throes of Modern Art. How long its life will last, we cannot tell. One thing is sure, beauty does not die. It returns and returns, and now after a century comes the Renaissance of the Hudson River School of painting, and every gallery is seeking the results left by it, and the spirit that evolved from those earnest artists will take hold on others. Change is the very part of life. Tastes change. Fashions change. Standards change — all in accordance with the prevailing ideas of men, but as Keats says, "A thing of *beauty* is a joy forever."

CLARA ENDICOTT SEARS

Bibliography

Appleton's Cyclopaedia of American Biography.
BALDWIN, C. C. *The Baldwin Genealogy.*
BAUER, JOHN I. H., editor. *Autobiography of Worthington Whittredge.*
BOLTON, THEODORE. *Early American Portrait Draughtsmen in Crayon.*
BROWN, ROSSITER. *Little Classics.*
Bulletin of the American Council of Learned Societies.
Catalogue of the David Hewes Collection of the late Thomas Hill. San Francisco, 1916.
CLARK, ELLIOT. *Alexander Wyant.* 1916.
————. *Sixty Paintings by Alexander Wyant.*
CLEMENT, CLARA ERSKINE, and LAURENCE HUTTON. *Artists of the Nineteenth Century.*
Cyclopaedia of Paintings and Painters.
Dictionary of American Biography.
Doughty manuscripts (unpublished).
DUNLAP, WILLIAM. *History of the Rise and Progress of the Arts of Design in the United States.*
FIELDING, MANTLE. *Dictionary of American Painters, Sculptors, and Engravers.*
Fisher Family Records.
FRENCH, H. W. *Art and Artists in Connecticut.*
GILLESPIE. *Rome as Seen by a New Yorker.*
History of Milton.
History of Staten Island.
INNESS, GEORGE, JR., editor. *Life, Art, and Letters of George Inness.*
ISHAM, SAMUEL. *Growth of a Landscape School.* 1905.
————. *History of American Painting.*
JARVIS, J. J. *The Art Ideal.* 1864.
Lamb's Dictionary of the United States.
Letters of Adeline M. Hill to Levi Greenwood. 1927.
Life and Letters of Christopher Pearse Cranch.
National Cyclopaedia.

NOBLE, LOUIS L. *The Heart of the Andes.*

———. *Life and Works of Thomas Cole.*

SCOTT, LEONORA CRANCH, editor. *Diary of Christopher Pearse Cranch.*

SHELDON, G. W. *American Painters.* 1895.

TRIMBLE, ALFRED. *A Memorial. Student, Artist and Man.*

TUCKERMAN, HENRY T. *Book of the Artists.*

Tuttle Genealogy.

WARNER, CHARLES DUDLEY. *Catalogue of Memorial Exhibition.* New York: Metropolitan Museum, 1900.

Wyant Obituary. *New York Tribune.* November 30, 1892.

Index of Hudson River Artists

ILLUSTRATIONS

1.
Beacon-on-the-Hudson
Leavitt House on the Left
Artist unknown

2.
PALISADES

Artist unknown

Size 25 × 18½

3. LAND-LOCKED LAKE

Artist unknown

Size 35 × 27

4.
Landscape

O.E.S. *Frinck* (1845)
Signed   Size 27 × 21

5.
SILVER LAKE,
NEW HAMPSHIRE

Artist unknown (*c.* 1830)

Size 30 × 25

6. In the Heart of New
Hampshire

Artist unknown

Size 36 × 27½

7.
SUMMER
Artist unknown

Size 24¼ × 18

8. THE COMING STORM

Artist unknown

Size 32 × 24½

9.
VIEW OF THE PALISADES
Suggestive of the music of
Richard Wagner
Artist unknown

Size 27½ × 22¼

10.
Horses in a Stream

Artist unknown (c. 1830)

Size 24 × 18¼

12.
Sunset by the River

Artist unknown
Signed: F. P.   Size 25 × 19

13.
THE OLD COVERED WAGON

John W. A. Scott (1815–1907)
Signed — Size 17 × 14

Faneuil Hall, from the Water

14.
FANEUIL HALL, FROM THE
WATER

William H. Bartlett
Water-color sketch made
ready for engraving

Size **22** × 14½

15.
VIEW OF THE HUDSON
RIVER

Artist in doubt
Copied from a drawing by
William H. Bartlett

Size 25¼ × 21¼

16.
View of Niagara Falls

Victor De Grailly
After a drawing by William
H. Bartlett

Size 23¼ × 17

17.
WASHINGTON'S HEADQUAR-
TERS
NEWBURGH-ON-THE-HUD-
SON

Victor De Grailly
After a drawing by Wil-
liam H. Bartlett

Size 16 × 12¼

18.
VIEW FROM WEST POINT

Victor De Grailly

Size 21¼ × 28½

19.
Washington's Tomb at
Mt. Vernon

Victor De Grailly
After a drawing by William
H. Bartlett

Size 21¼ × 11

20.
A HOME ON THE HUDSON

Thomas Doughty
(1795–1856)
Signed   Size 21 × 30

21.
SUMMER IN THE CATSKILLS

Thomas Doughty
(1795–1856)
Signed   Size 27 × 34

22.
A Castle in England or
Ireland

Thomas Doughty
(1795–1856)
Signed   Size 15½ × 11½

23.
The Fishing Pool (1850)

Thomas Doughty
(1795–1856)
Signed   Size 20 × 16

24.
MOUNTAIN TORRENT

Thomas Doughty
(1795–1856)
Signed   Size 17½ × 21

25.
SKETCH
(ENGLAND OR IRELAND)

*Attributed to Thomas
Doughty* (1795–1856)
Unsigned   Size 17½ × 21

26.
Landscape

Walter M. S. Bayne
(Painted in the style of
Doughty)
Signed: Boston 1853
Size 30 × 40

27.
OFF THE MAINE COAST
(1835)

Thomas Birch (1779–1851)
Signed   Size 39½ × 59½

28.
SEASCAPE

Thomas Birch (1779–1851)
Signed   Size 17¼ × 25¼

29.
UPPER HUDSON

Thomas Birch (1779–1851)
Signed   Size 12½ × 10

30.
THE WATERING PLACE

Alvan Fisher (1792–1863)
Signed   Size 7¼ × 5

31.
THE HIDDEN POOL
From the Estate of the
Hon. David Sears

Alvan Fisher (1792–1863)
Signed   Size 30 × 24¼

32.
THE WHITE MOUNTAINS

Alvan Fisher (1792–1863)
Signed   Size 24 × 36

33.
NORTH MOUNTAIN RESER-
VATION, SOUTH ORANGE,
NEW JERSEY

Asher B. Durand (1796–
1886)
From the Durand Sale,
1887 (Sale Stamps on Back)

Signed   Size 16¾ × 23¾

34.
MOUNTAIN VALLEY

Asher B. Durand, P. N. A.

Size 30¼ × 41½

35.
VIEW NEAR PORTLAND,
MAINE

Charles Codman
(1800–1842)

Panel 25⅞ × 19⅛

Exhibited:
    Chicago Institute of
        Art, 1945
    Whitney Museum of
        Art, New York, 1945

36.
THE WOUNDED DEER

Charles Codman
(1800–1842)
Signed   Size 25 × 22½

37.
THE HAYFIELD

Charles Codman
(1800–1842)

Signed   Size 36½ × 24

38.
THE MOUNTAIN FORD

Thomas Cole (1801–1848)
Signed   Size 22 × 30

39.
Tropical Sunset

Frederick E. Church
(1826–1900)
Signed   Size 21½ × 36

40.
A REMINISCENCE OF THE
GENESEE RIVER

John William Casilaer
(1811–1893)

Signed   Size 30 × 4?

Exhibited:
    Chicago Institute of
        Art, 1945
    The Whitney Museum
        of Art, New York,
        1945

41.
Moonlight

John William Casilaer
(1811–1893)
Signed   Size 13 × 10

42.
IN THE CATSKILLS

THE HUDSON RIVER
SCHOOL OF PAINTING

John Frederick Kensett
(1818–1872)
Signed   Size 23 × 18

43.
GLIMPSE OF LAKE GEORGE

THE HUDSON RIVER
SCHOOL OF PAINTING

John Frederick Kensett
(1818–1872)
Signed   Size 20 × 16

44.
A VIEW OF THE HUDSON
FROM WEST POINT

Robert W. Weir
(1803–1889)
Signed and dated: 1869
Size 35 × 61

Exhibited:
Museum of Modern
Art, New York, 1945
National Gallery of
Art, Washington, 1945
Chicago Institute of
Art, 1945
Whitney Museum of
Art, New York, 1945

45.
MORNING IN THE BLUE
RIDGE MOUNTAINS

William Louis Sonntag
(1822–1900)

Signed   Size 24 × 36

46.
San Rafael, California

Albert Bierstadt
(1830–1902)
Signed   Size 31⅛ × 48

47.
Ascutney Mountain
from Claremont, New
Hampshire

Albert Bierstadt
(1830–1902)
Dated: 1862

Size 71 × 41½

48.
DRACHENFELS

T. Worthington Whittredge
(1820–1910)
Signed and dated: 1850
Size 12¼ × 18½

49.

UPPER HUDSON

Jasper F. Cropsey
(1825–1900)
Signed   Size 20 × 35

50.
COWS AND SHEEP
IN PASTURE

Thomas Hewes Hinckley
(1813–1896)
Signed   Size 14¾ × 10¾

51.
NOON

Thomas Hewes Hinckley
(1813–1896)   Size 21 × 14
Signed

52.
GREAT BLUE HILL AND
NEPONSET RIVER

Thomas Hewes Hinckley
(1813–1896)
Signed   Size 20½ × 14½

53.
A MOUNTAIN VALLEY
François Régis Gignoux
(1816–1882)

Size 40½ × 62½

54.
WINTER LANDSCAPE WITH
SKATERS

*Attributed to François Régis
Gignoux* (1816–1882)
Unsigned   Size 24 × 36

55.
MARCH OF THE CRUSADERS

George Inness, N.A.
(1825–1894)
Signed Size 36 × 48

56.
LAKE GEORGE

Alexander Helwig Wyant
(1836–1892)
Signed   Size 7¼ × 4½

57.
On the Upper Hudson

Alexander Helwig Wyant
(1836–1892)
Signed   Size 9 × 14

58.
BRIDAL VEIL
AND EL CAPITAN   YOSEMITE VALLEY

Thomas Hill (1829–1908)

Size 53 × 35¼

59.
AUTUMN IN THE CATSKILLS

William M. Hart
(1823–1894)
Signed   Size 12 × 10

60.
Cattle in a Stream

William M. Hart
(1823–1894)
Signed   Size 12¾ × 10½

61.
EVENING IN THE KEENE
VALLEY, ADIRONDACKS

William M. Hart
(1823–1894)
Signed and dated: 1872
Size 16¼ × 26¼

62.
OLNEYVILLE, RHODE IS-
LAND

George L. Brown
(1814–1889)
Signed   Size 20½ × 12½